Anyone can still make a Million

Anyone can still make a Million

MORTON SHULMAN

STEIN AND DAY/*Publishers*/New York

Copyright © McGraw-Hill Ryerson Limited, 1972
First published in the United States
by Stein and Day/*Publishers*/1973
Library of Congress Card No. 73-77963
All rights reserved
Printed in the United States of America
Stein and Day/*Publishers*/ 7 East 48 Street, New York,
N.Y. 10017
ISBN 0-8128-1598-X

THIRD PRINTING, 1973

CONTENTS

PREFACE

"Anyone Can Make A Million" was written in 1966 as a primer of what to do in the market so as to substantially increase one's income. Proof of its success has come both from its incredible sales and from the thousands of fan letters which have followed successful application of its ideas.

Unfortunately a lot of changes have taken place over the past seven years and many of the thoughts that were valid in 1966 are outdated today. For example in the original book I recommended the purchase of gold options because of my certainty that the price of gold was sure to rise. Despite the fact that gold's price has now soared, new readers keep writing to ask where they can purchase the now extinct gold options.

Although the basic ideas are still correct, the entire book has been revised for this edition with considerable new material and several new chapters. The original edition succeeded in enraging stock brokers, financial experts and life insurance executives. If I succeed in annoying this group again it will be proof to me that my ideas are of value to Mr. Joe Public.

Toronto, 1972   *Morton Shulman*

INTRODUCTION

"I was at the club yesterday, and George McKeown played in our foursome. He's the Chicago manager of Park Reid and Co. Over the nineteenth hole he told me in strictest confidence that Park Reid's earnings are 'way up this year and that they may split the stock. I bought 1,000 shares this morning."

"You know how many good things my New York broker has let me in on recently. Well, this morning he phoned with some really hot news! A small mining prospect called Jenny Metals just took over a property connecting with the fabulous Pyramid mine — that's the company that drilled and rose from 25¢ to $20 in six weeks. Jenny Metals is going to begin drilling immediately. I paid 78¢ and it closed at 85¢. I'm selling my I.B.M. tomorrow to buy more Jenny!"

Familiar? Of course. Everyone has heard variations of these two stories. And year after year supposedly intelligent business people similarly lose their heads and throw away their money in search of the easy dollar. After each bitter experience they say, "Next time I'll be smarter," but strangely, they never are.

The interesting thing is that there *is* an easy dollar to be made in our stock markets, but those who make it are almost exclusively promoters and stockbrokers. There is a story of a promoter who, when asked by a close friend what stock to buy, replied with the classic comment, "Buy?! The only way to make money in the market is to print the stuff and sell it!"

He is dead wrong. There are good stocks to buy in the market, but *never, never* on tips.

There are simple ways to make a great deal of money, and some of them don't even involve any investment! Sound unbelievable? It's done every day by a few knowing traders. This book explains the secrets of the market and shows how any speculator can do the same thing.

There are really two stock markets. One is the world of high-grade bonds — of A.T.&T., General Motors, and R.C.A. This is the "Widow and Orphan" market. These securities are purchased for safety, yield, and growth by insurance and trust companies and other institutions, by mutual funds, and by individuals building an estate or seeking a secure income. The other stock market is the one for the speculators. But it is hidden beside and inside the first market, and a person who is speculating often thinks he is investing. The speculative market is the exciting one. It is vibrant and changing and challenging, and it offers to the intelligent and to the nimble unlimited profits and opportunities. Unfortunately, many who challenge it are neither intelligent enough nor nimble enough, and to them it brings heartache and financial loss. This book is an effort to help make the public a little more intelligent and a great deal more nimble. Once the secrets of this speculative market are known, it is immeasurably easier to play its game.

It has always appeared strange that no stockbroker has written a book explaining these relatively simple matters, and the reason apparently is fear of associates' disapproval. For the simple fact is that brokers as a group do not want the public to know. Each individual broker wants *his* clients to make money, for then there are more and higher commissions, but as a group it is to the brokers' advantage if the public continues to buy and trade Park Reid and Jenny Metals. Individuals try to educate their clientele as best they can, but sadly the majority of customer's men do not have a good knowledge of the market themselves; all too often they advise their clients on a basis of limited knowledge and "hot tips." A few leading firms are very thorough in researching individual companies and go to great lengths to educate their customer's men; Merrill Lynch is an outstanding example. Alas, their advice and training is directed largely to the "Widow and Orphan" market and rarely reaches the speculator, who would spurn their advice if offered.

So this book is dedicated to the speculator, that much-maligned creature. After reading it, I hope he will speculate more successfully.

Morton Shulman

Anyone can still make a Million

1
FOR WIDOWS
AND ORPHANS

This chapter deals with investments suitable for those who cannot afford to take the chance of loss. These include not only the widow and orphan, but also the wage earner with limited savings and the businessman who may need his cash on short notice for opportunities in his own business. The sought-after qualities of investments of this type are various combinations of safety, yield, and growth associated with easy liquidity. There are several subdivisions:

1. government bonds
2. municipal bonds
3. state bonds
4. high-grade corporate bonds and debentures
5. blue chip stocks
6. mutual funds

1. UNITED STATES AND CANADIAN GOVERNMENT BONDS give very good yields, anywhere from 5 to 7% — excellent rates compared with bank interest. There is, of course, no possibility of capital gain, but the factor of safety is the important one in these securities because they are direct obligations of the government.

One would think that the government bonds are the ultimate in safety, with absolutely no chance of loss if they are held to maturity. They do, however, fluctuate greatly in value during the years before maturity, the amount of fluctuation increasing with the duration of the bond and the size of fluctuation depending on the general trend of national and worldwide interest rates. As interest rates rise, the market value of outstanding bonds falls. This can be disastrous for the individual with limited means who is forced to sell his government bonds at a time of high interest rates.

Far more serious is the danger of a massive devaluation of the U.S. dollar. During the 1960s there was a persistent run against the American dollar which the government fought by many marginal measures, including taxes on overseas purchases by American tourists and restrictions on the investment of U.S. dollars abroad. Throughout these years, despite the obvious failure of these weak efforts by the treasury, various U.S. presidents continued to voice their faith in the value of the U.S. dollar and their determination "never" to devalue. Unfortunately they convinced no one, and by late 1971 corporations and governments everywhere were rushing to get rid of their American paper money and to purchase in its place either gold or foreign currency.

In January 1972 Richard Nixon finally threw in the towel and devalued the U.S. dollar by about 12% in relation to other currencies. Simultaneously he raised the price of gold by 10% to $38.50 but — and this is most significant — he said that the U.S. government would not be willing to sell gold in exchange for paper money at that price (or at any price, for that matter).

When this initial step did not reduce the flight from the dollar, President Nixon ordered a further 10% devaluation in February 1973. It is obvious that if a 12% devaluation did not work in 1972 a 10% devaluation will not work one year later.

The significance of this disastrous economic move has not been lost on U.S. or foreign economists, for if the president of the U.S.A. has no faith in the present value of the U.S. dollar and prefers to hoard gold instead, what should everyone else do? At the time of writing, the rush has begun to get rid of U.S. paper money and this must end with a massive raising of the price of gold ($100 perhaps) and an equivalent devaluation of the dollar. The step is inevitable, and the subsequent rise in the cost of living will cut the true value of government bonds and of all other fixed-income securities by very drastic percentages.

While it is true that when the government bonds become due they will unquestionably be paid off dollar for dollar, the sad fact is that the bond owners will pay today's relatively solid money to the government when buying their bonds, but will be given back a devalued dollar as the result of inflation. To make this clearer, let us consider an example. Mrs. Mary Smith has been left an estate of $20,000 by her late husband, and because she feels she can't take the chance of loss, invests all of the inheritance today in U.S. government bonds. When the government is forced to raise the price of gold, other prices will rapidly fall in line, because dollar holders will wish to get rid of this paper money by buying "wealth in the ground" stocks — gold, other metals, oil, coal, and so forth – or physical things like real estate, automobiles, and diamonds. Thus when the government repays poor Mary Smith her $20,000 ten years from now, she will find to her dismay that the money which would buy a Rolls Royce today will probably not buy a Cadillac then, perhaps not even a Buick. In other words the government will have stolen one-half or more of Mrs. Smith's capital, and she will have no hope of recourse.

This is the long-term effect, but the short-term results can be even more disastrous. Because many government bondholders will panic (and justifiably so) when gold is raised in price, millions of dollars' worth of long-term bonds will be sold for whatever they will bring, thus driving down the market value and producing an unbearable situation for those forced to sell. Thus a long-term government bond with a face value of $1,000 may bring in only $700 or less if it is necessary that it be sold. When Roosevelt raised the price of gold in 1933, the overnight fall in the value of bonds produced bankruptcy for many individuals and bond firms.

What about outstanding government bonds that were issued in the late 60s at high interest rates and now sell at a premium because interest rates have fallen? A list of these is published daily in the Wall Street Journal.

This strange situation is a temporary quirk brought about by the U.S. elections of November 1972. In preparation for these elections, and as their major effort to be re-elected, the Republican administration worked overtime printing money, increasing the currency available and driving down interest rates. The Canadian government was delighted to follow suit because they too had a 1972 election to fight.

New high for supply of money

OTTAWA (CP) — Canada's money supply continued its record-breaking climb last week, reaching $38.52 billion on Jan. 5, the Bank of Canada reported yesterday.

Currency in circulation and deposits in chartered banks totalled $36.02 billion, up $186 million from a week earlier.

The government, its moneybags still bulging from last November's unusually-successful sale of Canada Savings Bonds, had $2.5 billion deposited with chartered banks, up $42 million from a week earlier.

Treasury Bonds

				Bid	Asked	Bid Chg.	Yld.
4s,	1972	Feb	....	100.8	100.10	.....	0.03
2½s,	1967-72	Jun	....	99.22	99.26	.....	2.96
4s,	1972	Aug	....	100.5	100.9	+ .1	3.51
2½s,	1967-72	Sep	.-+........	99.5	99.9	+ .1	3.61
2½s,	1967-72	Dec	....	98.24	99.0	+ .2	3.63
4s,	1973	Aug	....	99.12	99.20	+ .3	4.25
4⅛s,	1973	Nov	....	99.12	99.20	+ .3	4.34
4⅛s,	1974	Feb	....	99.3	99.11	+ .4	4.46
4¼s,	1974	May	....	99.3	99.11	+ .4	4.55
3⅞s,	1974	Nov	....	97.16	97.24	+ .8	4.73
4s,	1980	Feb	....	87.28	88.12	+ .8	5.82
3½s,	1980	Nov	....	84.10	84.26	+ .4	5.71
7s,	1981	Aug	....	108.16	109.9	+ .4	5.76
3¼s,	1978-83	Jun	....	78.6	79.6	+ .2	5.76
3¼s,	1985	May	....	77.16	78.16	+ .2	5.55
4¼s,	1975-85	May	....	82.14	83.14	+ .2	6.08
6⅛s,	1986	Nov	....	99.22	99.30	+ .8	6.14
3½s,	1990	Feb	....	77.26	78.26	+ .6	5.34
4¼s,	1987-92	Aug	....	79.24	80.24	+ .4	5.87
4s,	1988-93	Feb	....	77.28	78.28	+ .2	5.74
4⅛s,	1989-94	May	....	78.12	79.12	+ .4	5.78
3s,	1995	Feb	....	77.16	78.16	+ .4	4.51
3½s,	1998	Nov	....	78.6	79.6	+ .4	4.90

U.S. Treas. Notes

Rate	Mat	Bid	Asked	Yld
4¾	2-72	100.10	100.12	...
7½	2-72	100.18	100.20	...
4¾	5-72	100.13	100.17	3.08
6¾	5-72	101.4	101.8	2.86
5	8-72	100.23	100.27	3.52
6	11-72	101.23	101.27	3.72
4⅞	2-73	100.24	100.26	4.10
6½	2-73	102.14	102.18	4.05
7¾	5-73	104.14	104.22	4.09
8⅛	8-73	105.18	105.26	4.28
7¾	2-74	106.3	106.11	4.52
7¼	5-74	105.13	105.21	4.66
5⅝	8-74	101.30	102.6	4.71
5¾	11-74	102.5	102.13	4.83
5¾	2-75	102.4	102.11	4.92
5⅞	2-75	102.10	102.16	4.99
6	5-75	103.2	103.10	4.91
5⅞	8-75	102.10	102.18	5.08
7	11-75	106.8	106.16	5.11
6¼	2-76	103.30	104.6	5.10
6½	5-76	104.26	105.2	5.19
7½	8-76	108.26	109.2	5.25
6¼	11-76	103.23	103.31	5.31

U.S. Treas. Bills

Mat	Bid Discount	Ask	Mat	Bid Discount	Ask
1-20	3.15	2.55	5- 4	3.39	3.05
1-27	3.09	2.49	5-11	3.29	3.05
1-31	3.09	2.49	5-18	3.31	3.05
2- 3	3.08	2.62	5-25	3.31	3.05
2-10	3.08	2.62	5-31	3.31	3.05
2-17	3.04	2.56	6- 1	3.40	3.22
2-24	3.06	2.56	6- 8	3.40	3.26
2-29	3.07	2.59	6-15	3.43	3.29
3- 2	3.14	2.84	6-21	3.42	3.32
3- 9	3.15	2.89	6-22	3.45	3.31
3-16	3.16	2.92	6-29	3.45	3.31
3-23	3.17	2.93	6-30	3.43	3.20
3-30	3.17	2.97	7- 6	3.44	3.32
3-31	3.17	2.95	7-13	3.43	3.36
4- 6	.3.21	3.07	7-31	3.52	3.36
4-13	3.20	3.10	8-31	3.62	3.48
4-20	3.22	3.02	9-30	3.62	3.52
4-21	3.29	3.19	10-31	3.65	3.51
4-27	3.27	3.05	11-30	3.66	3.52
4-30	3.26	3.06	12-31	3.61	3.51

The short-term effect of this madness has been delightful; money is freely available, interest rates have fallen, bond prices have risen, companies have expanded and unemployment has shrunk somewhat — in short, everyone is happy. Unfortunately now that the elections are over we are going to have to pay the bill for this party, and the price is high. With so much currency in circulation, prices and wages will begin to rise at an even higher rate than in the 60s and as inflation takes over people will prefer to buy things (whose price is rising) rather than hold money (whose buying value is falling). The government will be unable to continue overworking the currency printing presses because the opposition political pundits who so resented government's efforts to control inflation will scream even louder at the results of inflation.

As the buying power of the dollar decreases, lenders will be reluctant to purchase bonds whose interest rates don't even cover the losses produced by inflation, and the interest rates on bonds will have to increase to two or three times the current rates so as to attract purchases. When this happens (probably 1974) bond prices will plunge—so if you have any government bonds at the present time they should be sold immediately.

The one thing bonds should guarantee, safety, is completely lacking. In fact government bonds represent a rank speculation without giving the advantage a speculation should give — the possibility of capital gain.

Don't buy them.

Government savings bonds come in an entirely different category. By law these may be purchased only in limited quantities by any individual, and they are redeemable at any time at their face value. Saving bonds are comparable to cash in the bank but are preferable to cash in that they receive much higher interest (from 5½% to 6½%). They are a perfectly adequate, safe investment but give no protection against the inflation which has afflicted our economy since 1945. A small proportion of funds in such bonds is a reasonable investment to use in place of a cash reserve.

2. MUNICIPAL BONDS are direct obligations of the municipality borrowing the money, just as federal bonds are obligations of the federal government. United States municipal bonds have the unique advantage that their income is tax exempt to American citizens, and so they can be issued with a relatively low yield because of their attraction to those in high tax brackets. Canadian municipal bonds are not tax exempt and so give much higher yields, at present around 6% to 6½%. The safety of the capital invested is considerably less than with government bonds, for unfortunately in bad times many a municipality has been unable to repay its bondholders. There is, of course, no possibility of capital gain.

The likelihood of a rise in the price of gold and thus a devaluation of the dollar must be considered in reference to municipal bonds also, and the same painful facts once again apply.

Thus it is obvious that the average investor should not give any consideration to the purchase of such bonds. They give poor yield, no safety of buying power, and no chance of capital gain. Even the individual with a very high income, who buys such bonds in order to cut down his income tax, is making a very serious error; for when the game is over he may very well find that he has gained ten per cent in income and lost fifty per cent in purchasing power.

Don't buy them.

3. STATE AND PROVINCIAL BONDS are obligations of the state or province borrowing the money. The remarks made in reference to government bonds all apply here, with the exception that yields are somewhat higher. Once again there is no protection against inflation, and the potential loss in purchasing power is not offset by any other advantage.

Don't buy them.

4. CORPORATE BONDS AND DEBENTURES (exclusive of convertible bonds, which are discussed in Chapter 6) differ from government, state, and municipal bonds in having a higher yield and a somewhat lower safety factor. The vast majority of these bonds and debentures are straight loans from the purchaser to the corporation and present no more protection against inflation than do government bonds. They should not be purchased for the reasons previously outlined. The prices

—1972— High	Low	Bonds	Sales In $1,000	High	Low	Close	Net Chg.
104	98	Con Edis 7.90s2001	75	100¾	100¼	100½	+ ½
78	73½	Cons Edis 5s87	35	74½	74¼	74½	+ ⅛
78	70	Cons Edis 5s90	10	71	70½	70½	+ ½
69½	65	Cons Edis 4⅝s93	4	65¼	65¼	65¼	.....
71	67¾	Cons Edis 4¼s86	20	69⅜	68⅞	69⅜	+1
66¾	62¼	Cons Edis 4s88	6	63	63	63	.....
64⅛	61⅜	Cons Edis 3⅜s85	15	64⅛	64⅛	64⅛	.....
72	70	Cons Edis 3¼s81	8	70½	70½	70½	+ ¼
67	65	Cons Edis 2¾s82	20	65½	65½	65½	.....
83½	80	Cons Edis 2⅝s77	40	82½	82½	82½	.....
107	105½	ConsNatGs 8⅜s96	5	106½	106½	106½	+ ½
104⅝	99	ConsNatGs 7¾s94	19	100⅝	100	100	− ¾
80	76	ConsNatGs 4⅜s83	20	76½	76½	76½	− ¼
78	73⅝	ConsNatGs 4⅜s86	25	74¾	74¾	74¾	.....
89	86⅜	ConsNatGs 3¼s76	2	88⅜	88⅜	88⅜	− ⅝
111	107	ConsumP 8⅝s2000	5	106	106	106	−1
104¼	100	Consum Pw 7⅝s99	1	101	101	101	− ¼
99	92¾	Consum Pw 6⅞s98	7	92¾	92¾	92¾	.....
87⅛	81½	Consum Pw 5⅞s96	3	82	81¾	81¾	− ¼
90½	88	Consum Pw 2⅞s75	15	90	88⅝	90	+2
91	68½	ContAirL cv3½s92	67	85⅝	84½	85	− ⅜
110	105¾	Cont Can 8½s90	5	107	107	107	− ¼
89	82	Cont Mtg cv6¼s90	85	86¼	86	86	.....
74¼	72⅛	Cont Oil 4½s91	5	73	73	73	.....
108¾	106	Cont Telep 9⅝s75	1	106½	106½	106½	−1
105	85	CoppwldStl cv5s79	7	99½	99⅜	99½	− ½
89	85	CornProd 5¾s92	12	84¾	84¾	84¾	− ⅜
81⅜	77	CornProd 4⅝s83	27	78¾	77⅛	78¾	+1¼
86	82	Crane Co 7s93	5	84⅝	84⅝	84⅝	− ⅜
85	81	Crane Co 7s94	13	82¼	82¼	82¼	.....
109⅛	90¼	Crane Co cv5s93	2	100½	100½	100½	−1½
72	65	Crescent cv5½s80	1	68½	68½	68½	−1
100¼	98	CrockNat cv5¾s96	31	99½	98¾	98¾	− ¼
73¾	65	Crow Coll cv4s92	6	69	69	69	− ⅞
107	95	DaycoCp cv6¼96	114	98½	98¼	98¼	− ¾
93⅛	79½	Dayco Cp cv6s94	12	81½	81½	81½	− ¼
114¾	110½	Daytn Hud 9¾s95	12	113½	113½	113½	+1½
106¾	104¾	Deere Cred 8¾s75	10	104¾	104¾	104¾	.....
34⅞	29½	DelLkW 4s-6s2042	5	32	32	32	+1¼
90	84½	DelMont cv5¼s94	20	84½	84½	84½	.....
107½	105	Det Edis 8.15s2000	5	104½	104½	104½	−1
101⅛	98	Det Edis 7⅜s2001	5	100⅛	100⅛	100⅛	.....
103½	100⅝	Det Edis 7s76	14	101½	101	101	− ⅜
93	85¾	Det Edis 6.40s98	5	86	86	86	+ ¼
77	75	Det Edis 3¼s80	2	75	75	75	− ⅝
105	100	Dial Finan 8¼s89	3	102	102	102	+2
77	64	Dillnghm cv5½s94	40	73½	72½	72½	− ½
96	76½	Divers Ind 9⅞s91	67	81¼	80¾	81¼	− ¼
88½	81¼	Douglas Airc 5s78	17	88½	87⅞	87⅞	.....
112½	109½	DowChm 8.90s2000	5	109½	109½	109½	− ⅞
106	101½	DowChm 7.75s99	1	101¾	101¾	101¾	+ ¼
98	90	DowChm 6.70s98	3	93	93	93	.....
62½	52¼	DPF Inc cv5½s87	28	54	53½	53½	.....
77	67½	Duplan cv5½s94	37	67½	67	67½	− ½
112	108	DuqsneLt 8¾s2000	10	108½	108½	108½	+ ½

in the list of outstanding corporation bonds reprinted below show how very badly this type of security can behave in times of inflation.

There are, however, a few exceptions, and because of them not all corporate bonds should be overlooked. These happy exceptions come in two groups.

The most common of these is the bond carrying a bonus of either common stock or the option to buy common stock at a fixed price for many years (see Chapter 10 on warrants). Such an arrangement provides a built-in safety factor in that when the dollar is devalued, although the bond itself will lose a part of its purchasing power, the common stock will likely appreciate a similar amount, thus offsetting the loss. This only applies, however, if the corporation is one which can raise its prices and profit margin when inflation strikes — in other words, to companies selling "things". It particularly does not apply to utilities, who often must receive permission from various government bodies before they can raise their rates.

Thus, certain corporation bonds may be purchased today that give a good yield, a fair degree of safety, plus a bonus of stock or stock options that promise the likelihood of capital gains. There are many such issues, and so there is usually little difficulty in making such purchases.

An excellent example of this type of issue was the 7⅜% 15-year debenture issued by the Chrysler Financial Corporation in May 1971. The yield was good, the safety factor excellent, for this company is one of the largest and most conservative U.S. corporations in its field, and yet each $1,000 bond carried a bonus of 20 5-year options (warrants) to purchase stock in the company. A delightful result of such a purchase was that capital gain could be guaranteed. This could be accomplished through the immediate sale of the bonus stock or stock options. In the case of the Chrysler bonds the stock options could be sold immediately for $12.75 each or $255 in total per $1,000 bond. The bondholder would still get back his $1,000 plus interest in 15 years and would have an immediate 25% capital gain (plus a yield of over 10% on his net invest-

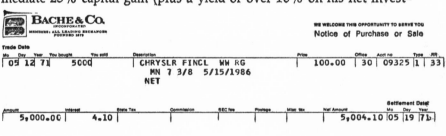

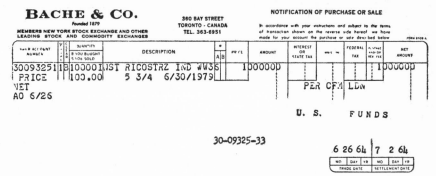

ment!) Even better, because the interest rate was a high 7⅜%, these bonds rose steadily without the warrants and can be sold today for $900. They should be sold immediately, because in the coming year the price of all corporate bonds will undoubtedly fall.

A less common type of corporate bond whose purchase is recommended is one in which interest and principal are payable in more than one currency at the holder's option. Thus, if the United States were to devalue its dollar, the bondholder would be protected because he could take his capital back in another currency. (In actuality U.S. dollars would be received but in an increased amount, depending on the extent of devaluation.) An outstanding example of such an issue was one made in the United States by the American Petrofina Company. This debenture gave a yield of 5½%, and both interest and principal were payable in six different currencies. Because of the fluctuations which have already occurred among these currencies, the debenture in the few years since issue at $1,000 may now be sold for $1,300. This type of security represents the best of many worlds — safety, yield, and capital gain — and should be purchased whenever available, provided that the issuing company is sound.

Because this type of bond is in great demand, there is usually an immediate profit to be made following its purchase. An example was the debenture of the Institute Ricostrz Industries guaranteed by the Italian government and issued in June, 1964, in several countries. This issue, incidentally, illustrates free riding, which is the purchase of securities without putting up any money (see Chapter 11). The contract above shows the purchase of ten such bonds on June 26, 1964. No money was paid, but the selling broker was instructed to deliver the bonds to another broker against payment; that is, payment would only be made when physical delivery of the bonds was effected. Because of the slowness in delivery of all new issues and particularly those from Europe, actual delivery was not made until September 30, 1964. By this time the bonds had moved up considerably in value.

14 KING ST. WEST
TORONTO
TELEPHONE 364-4441

R. A. DALY & COMPANY
LIMITED

630 DORCHESTER BLVD. W
MONTREAL
TELEPHONE: 861-9751

MEMBERS THE TORONTO STOCK EXCHANGE   MONTREAL STOCK EXCHANGE   CANADIAN STOCK EXCHANGE   THE INVESTMENT DEALERS' ASSOCIATION OF CANADA

BOUGHT FOR YOU / OR SOLD TO YOU	SOLD FOR YOU OR / BOUGHT FROM YOU	DESCRIPTION	CODE	PRICE		MO	DAY	YR.	REF.
	10000	I.R.I. CUM WTS 5 3/4%30JUNE79	960484	107.00	US	09	30	64	014
						TRADE DATE			

PRINCIPAL AMOUNT	COMMISSION	ONT. TAX	QUE TAX	U.S. TAX	CURRENCY EXCHANGE	ACCRUED INTEREST	NET AMOUNT	
10,700.00	25.00	3.00		5.00		153.33	10,820.33	US

BI	BR		CK	SMN					SETTLEMENT DATE	MO	DAY	EX.	TB
T81	54	4180	3	25						10	06	5	1
B O.E.	ACCOUNT NO.												

In this very strange transaction a profit of $280 was made without a cent being put up!

Thus among corporate bonds there are many good opportunities for both widow and orphan, but they must be chosen carefully. The three questions to ask are:

a. Is the company sound?

b. Is the yield satisfactory?

c. Does the bond carry a "kicker"; that is, does it carry a bonus, or is it multipay?

If the answer to all three questions is yes, *buy them.*

5. BLUE CHIP STOCKS represent a share in the ownership of the leading companies in North America. These companies are called "blue chip" because they have been in business for decades and have paid dividends consecutively for many years.

U.S. blue chips are a relatively safe investment with excellent possibilities of growth and capital gain. Unfortunately, they also have an excellent chance of going down drastically in any recession because of the tremendous rise such stocks have enjoyed in our past twenty-year market boom. Another disadvantage is the very low yield blue chips now give. In fact, earnings and dividends have not come close to keeping pace with the increase in price of these stocks, and many of them now pay dividends considerably smaller than bank interest. The time to buy such stocks undoubtedly will come again, but they do not represent good value today and should be passed over by the average small investor.

Canadian blue chips are a horse of a different colour. They represent a very special situation now because of the imposition on January 1st, 1972 of a Canadian capital gains tax. The net result of this very heavy tax is that Canadian holders of blue chip stocks, who were largely conservative traders to begin with, are now extremely reluctant to sell their holdings. The result undoubtedly will be a tremendous boom for Canadian blue chips and I have personally been purchasing such stocks since last year. I am convinced that we are going to see a boom in this type of stock similar to the one the U.S.A. saw in their blue chip stocks in the 1920s.

Canadian investors in the widow and orphan class would be well advised to put a substantial portion of their money in the Canadian blue chips. (This advice is not for U.S. investors because of the equalization tax which applies to all except a few exempt issues.) Companies that fall into this category are Dominion Stores, Abitibi, Bank of Montreal, Imperial Oil, Falconbridge, Simpsons, Steel Company of Canada, Texaco of Canada, Traders Finance, and Brights Wines.

6. MUTUAL FUNDS are in many ways the ideal investment for the investor seeking safety, yield and growth, but whose time is fully employed outside of the market and who thus cannot closely watch his investments. A mutual fund takes the money of its shareholders and invests it in many dozens of different securities, thus spreading the risk far wider than any individual could possibly do. There are hundreds of mutual funds, and each of them gives a different emphasis to its investments. Some funds specialize in safety with a high proportion of their funds in bonds; others primarily seek high yields and put most of their money in high dividend stocks and debentures; and some sacrifice both safety and yield in order to purchase only the stocks of companies which are likely to increase in price through growth of the firm. There are, of course, various gradations of the three types of mutual fund, with the vast majority using a combination of the three methods.

Over the past twenty years, performance of mutual funds has varied almost as widely as that of individual stocks, but many of them have given a truly incredible performance. I purchased shares in one fund, the Investment Company of America, 25 years ago. Since that time I have received annual dividends averaging between 10% and 15%, most of which were non-taxable because they were capital gains. (If I were a U.S. citizen, I would have to pay taxes at a low preferential rate on capital gains.) In addition to this my shares, which were then worth $7.57, now have grown to a value of $13.99 each. In 1971, for example,

I received a dividend of 69¢ per share, of which only 39¢ was classified as income and the balance as a capital gain. During that year the company's net asset value increased by 13.8% while the Dow Jones went up only 6.1%. This was not just a lucky year, for in almost every year I.C.A. has outperformed the market. Below is a chart from I.C.A.'s annual report, showing the results of a $10,000 investment in the company's stock. It is hard to believe, but $10,000 invested in this mutual fund 39 years ago would be worth nearly $1,000,000 today.

See the difference time can make in an investment program

If you had invested $10,000 in ICA this many years ago...		...and taken all income dividends and capital gain distributions in additional shares...		...this is what your investment would be worth today
Number of Years	Period Jan. 1 - Dec. 31	Initial Investment Cost	Income Dividends Reinvested	Total Investment Cost	Total Value of Shares Dec. 31, 1971
1	1971	$10,000	$ 288	$ 10,288	$ 10,711
2	1970-1971	10,000	757	10,757	10,987
3	1969-1971	10,000	750	10,750	9,814
4	1968-1971	10,000	1,123	11,123	11,483
5	1967-1971	10,000	1,701	11,701	14,793
6	1966-1971	10,000	1,936	11,936	14,947
7	1965-1971	10,000	2,674	12,674	18,961
8	1964-1971	10,000	3,332	13,332	22,058
9	1963-1971	10,000	4,339	14,339	27,104
10	1962-1971	10,000	3,966	13,966	23,508
11	1961-1971	10,000	5,112	15,112	28,950
12	1960-1971	10,000	5,576	15,576	30,260
13	1959-1971	10,000	6,596	16,596	34,557
14	1958-1971	10,000	9,855	19,855	50,035
15	1957-1971	10,000	8,935	18,935	44,050
16	1956-1971	10,000	10,155	20,155	48,786
17	1955-1971	10,000	13,039	23,039	61,233
18	1954-1971	10,000	20,718	30,718	95,518
19	1953-1971	10,000	21,191	31,191	96,027
20	1952-1971	10,000	24,090	34,090	107,545
21	1951-1971	10,000	28,804	38,804	126,777
22	1950-1971	10,000	34,958	44,958	151,884
23	1949-1971	10,000	38,617	48,617	165,967
24	1948-1971	10,000	39,270	49,270	166,961
25	1947-1971	10,000	39,990	49,990	168,365
26	1946-1971	10,000	39,335	49,335	164,465
27	1945-1971	10,000	54,079	64,079	225,078
28	1944-1971	10,000	66,949	76,949	277,263
29	1943-1971	10,000	89,211	99,211	367,837
30	1942-1971	10,000	104,667	114,667	429,523
31	1941-1971	10,000	97,154	107,154	396,744
32	1940-1971	10,000	95,286	105,286	387,774
33	1939-1971	10,000	96,205	106,205	390,706
34	1938-1971	10,000	122,627	132,627	497,666
35	1937-1971	10,000	75,828	85,828	306,545
36	1936-1971	10,000	107,054	117,054	432,085
37	1935-1971	10,000	196,083	206,083	791,426
38	1934-1971	10,000	245,727	255,727	991,791

The dollar amount of capital gain distributions taken in additional shares in each of the above time periods was as follows (by number of years): (1) $194; (2) $601; (3) $1,089; (4) $1,661; (5) $2,698; (6) $3,426; (7) $5,044; (8) $6,477; (9) $8,424; (10) $7,660; (11) $10,019; (12) $10,987; (13) $13,233; (14) $19,619; (15) $17,770; (16) $20,409; (17) $26,409; (18) $41,853; (19) $42,321; (20) $47,845; (21) $56,861; (22) $68,446; (23) $75,139; (24) $75,872; (25) $76,937; (26) $75,744; (27) $104,524; (28) $129,145; (29) $171,469; (30) $200,308; (31) $185,046; (32) $180,998; (33) $182,607; (34) $233,080; (35) $143,645; (36) $204,162; (37) $373,952; (38) $468,623. See chart and accompanying text on pages 12-13.

The success of any individual mutual fund depends on the financial acumen with which its managers are endowed. In choosing which one to buy, there is a very simple yardstick — past performance. A prospective investor must decide whether he wishes to place his money in a fund specializing in one of the three factors of safety, growth, or yield, or intends to take a blend of the three. Except for an individual in very unusual circumstances, the wisest choice is usually the latter one.

One way *not* to decide which mutual fund to buy is through advice of your stockbroker. Every mutual fund does a great deal of buying and selling of securities through one or more brokers. In return these brokers are expected to advise those clients purchasing mutual funds to buy only into the fund providing the stock business. Under these circumstances impartiality is impossible. Better to seek advice from your banker.

Mutual funds are divided in one other way, and this is where most investors go wrong. There are open-end funds and closed-end funds. An open-end fund is one in which there is no limit to the amount of stock that will be issued by the fund; in fact they will issue just as much as they can sell. Their stock is sold to the public at its net breakup value plus a commission or loading charge which covers the salesman's and broker's commissions. The great advantage of this type of fund is that the stock can be redeemed, that is, sold back to the fund at any time at its breakup value with no commission charged. Most investors who buy mutual funds buy open-end funds.

The closed-end fund is not so common: it is a fund that has a fixed amount of stock which cannot be increased ad infinitum like the open-end fund. Its stocks, except when originally issued, can be purchased like any other stock only from a shareholder who wishes to sell. The fund itself will not redeem its stock from its shareholders. The interesting feature of closed-end funds is that invariably they sell at a discount from their net asset value of anywhere from 20% to 45%! This is one of the few cases where a stock purchaser can be sure of getting a bargain, for he is really buying dollar bills for between 60¢ and 80¢.

The reason that closed-end funds sell at a discount is that theoretically if a fund were to sell a large block of one stock, they would depress the market and so would receive less than the current price for their block. Like so many other market fallacies, this is completely untrue. In actuality many brokers specialize in handling large blocks, and if the company stock is sound, there is no difficulty in selling such blocks at market prices and sometimes even at premiums above the market.

A typical example of a closed-end fund is Argus Corporation C. This company is a strong, well-diversified fund which can be purchased at a considerable discount from its true value. At the time of writing it has a breakup value of $17.50 but can be purchased for $12.

Thus, some mutual funds represent the best possible investment for the individual who cannot afford to take large risks but *is* prepared to take a small risk.

The three questions to ask before making a purchase are:

a. Is the fund closed-end and selling at a large discount from its asset value?

b. Are the individual stocks held in the fund in leading firms in their particular industries?

c. Is the fund's past record a good one?

If the answer to all three is yes, *buy it.*

In summary, there are six types of investments normally available in the "widow and orphan" market. Because of the long upgoing (bull) market associated with the weakening of the U.S. dollar, four of these are not suitable for the investor who cannot afford large risks. This investor should choose his investments among the mutual funds and the special corporate debentures described earlier.

There is one other investment in this class that is highly suitable — the convertible bond. But because this bond is such an important investment method, it will be discussed in a separate chapter.

2
WHICH BROKER SHOULD I USE?

Most people choose a broker because he is a neighbour or an old schoolmate, or belongs to the same golf club. Yet brokers are as different as contractors. There are very good ones and very bad ones, and an individual should choose his broker for the advantages the broker offers. All brokers give service; they execute buy and sell orders. No one broker does this materially better than any other. But there are two advantages some brokers offer and some do not — research and money.

The larger brokerage firms have research analysts who are in close touch with many different corporations. Often they will spot an upward trend in a corporation long before it is obvious to the general public. Several brokers are typical of this group. The analyst for one U.S. broker foresaw an upward earnings boost of Meredith Publishing one year before it took place, and their clients made large profits as a result. Similarly, one Toronto broker who was closely connected with Federal Pacific Pioneer Electric, advised their clients to purchase the stock at $10 and saw it go to $18 within a year. Most brokers cannot afford large analytical services, and many have only one man who works at analysis part time. These brokers should be avoided.

For the day trader in U.S. securities (a speculator who buys and resells a security on the same day) there are tremendous advantages to dealing with a Canadian broker rather than with a United States firm. When dealing with a U.S. broker, up to 70% of the value of the stock must be deposited within three days, but if the same trade is made via a Canadian broker, nothing need be put up. At the end of three days, the speculator merely collects his profits or pays his loss. This procedure is perfectly legal, and many shrewd American speculators follow this system. The best firms to deal with for this type of trading are members of the Toronto Exchange who have Telex communications with New York associates.

A typical example, shown below, involved a $19,000 trade without a penny being put up. The $402 profit was forwarded to the New York speculator three days later.

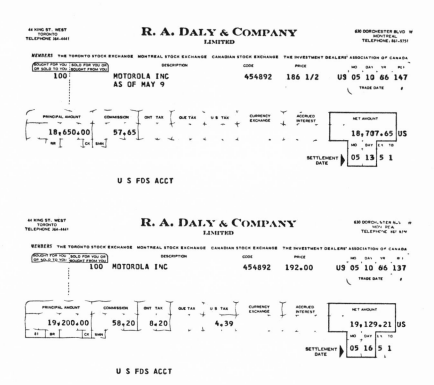

An even better advantage supplied by some brokers is the gift of money. They don't actually send a cheque, but they might just as well. The gift is given in the form of "hot issues". A hot issue is a new security issue which is in such large demand that it immediately begins to trade at a price above that at which it is issued. An example is shown below:

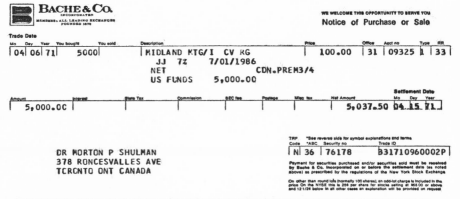

EASTMAN DILLON, UNION SECURITIES & CO.

Except where otherwise indicated by Number 6, 7, 8, or 9, in the "SYM" column, we have this day made the following transaction for your account and risk as your agent, subject to the conditions noted on the reverse side hereof. (Name of other broker or party and time of execution forwarded on request.)

TRADE DATE	QUANTITY BOUGHT (YOU BOUGHT)	SOLD (YOU SOLD)	DESCRIPTION	PRICE	SYM	SORG
03/09/65	200		GNL ANILINE &FLM CCM CTF TO PCHSE SHARES ENCLOSED MUST BE SIGNED &RETURND WITH PAYMENT BY 3 17 65	30.60	6	4 • SEE REVERSE

SETTLEMENT DATE	AMOUNT	STATE TAX INTEREST DIVIDEND S. T. CHG.	FEDERAL TAX	COMMISSION	REG FEE/CTF. AND/OR POSTAGE	NET AMOUNT
03/17/65	6,120.00					*,120.00

ON PURCHASES, PLEASE PAY NET AMOUNT SHOWN ABOVE. ON SALES, PLEASE DELIVER SECURITIES PROMPTLY

020058 PROSPECTUS ENCLOSED

44 KING ST. WEST
TORONTO
TELEPHONE 364-4441

R. A. DALY & COMPANY
LIMITED

630 DORCHESTER BLVD. W
MONTREAL
TELEPHONE: 861-9751

MEMBERS THE TORONTO STOCK EXCHANGE MONTREAL STOCK EXCHANGE CANADIAN STOCK EXCHANGE THE INVESTMENT DEALERS' ASSOCIATION OF CANADA

BOUGHT FOR YOU OR SOLD TO YOU	SOLD FOR YOU OR BOUGHT FROM YOU	DESCRIPTION	CODE	PRICE		MO	DAY	YR.	PL?
	200	GENERAL ANILINE & FILM AMENDED SECURITY OF MAR 9	276717	34 1/4	US	03	11	65	003

TRADE DATE

PRINCIPAL AMOUNT	COMMISSION	ONT. TAX	QUE TAX	U.S. TAX	CURRENCY EXCHANGE	ACCRUED INTEREST	NET AMOUNT
6,850.00	72.26	4.00		10.72			6,763.02 US

BI	BR	CK	SMN			SETTLEMENT DATE	MO	DAY	EX	TB
T81	54	4180	3 25				03	13	5	1

E. & O.E.   ACCOUNT NO.

In that particular trade there was an immediate $640 profit without any investment. The same thing often occurs in bond issues with kickers or convertible bonds (see Chapter 6). An example of this type of hot issue is illustrated below:

BACHE & CO.
INCORPORATED
MEMBERS: ALL LEADING EXCHANGES
FOUNDED 1879

WE WELCOME THIS OPPORTUNITY TO SERVE YOU
Notice of Purchase or Sale

Trade Date

Mo	Day	Year	You bought	You sold	Description	Price	Office	Acct no	Type	RR
04	06	71	5000		MIDLAND MTG/I CV RG JJ 7% 7/01/1986 NET US FUNDS 5,000.00 CDN.PREM3/4	100.00	31	09325	1	33

Amount	Interest	State Tax	Commission	SEC fee	Postage	Misc tax	Net Amount	Settlement Date Mo Day Year
5,000.00							5,037.50	04 15 71

DR MORTON P SHULMAN
378 RONCESVALLES AVE
TORONTO ONT CANADA

TRF Code	*ABC	Security no	Trade ID
N	36	76178	B31710960002P

*See reverse side for symbol explanations and terms

Payment for securities purchased and/or securities sold must be received by Bache & Co. Incorporated on or before the settlement date (as noted above) as prescribed by the regulations of the New York Stock Exchange.

On other than round lots (normally 100 shares), an odd-lot charge is included in the price. On the NYSE this is 25¢ per share for stocks selling at $55.00 or above and 12 1/2¢ below in all other cases an explanation will be provided on request.

PLEASE SEND PAYMENT, INSTRUCTIONS, AND INQUIRIES TO THE BACHE OFFICE WHICH SERVICES YOUR ACCOUNT. TO FACILITATE HANDLING BE SURE TO MENTION YOUR ACCOUNT NUMBER ON ALL TRANSACTIONS.

Trade Date Mo Day Year	You bought	You sold	Description	Price	Office	Acct. no	Type	RR
04 13 71		5000	MIDLAND MTG/I CV RG	101⅛	31	09325	1	33

JJ 7% 7/01/1986
0 150   CDN.PREMI3/16

U.S. FUNDS CONVERTED TO CDN. US. FUNDS 5,040.86

Amount	Interest	State Tax	Commission	SEC fee	Postage	Misc tax	Net Amount	Settlement Date Mo Day Year
5,062.50	4.86		25.00				5,081.82	04 20 71

DR MORTON P SHULMAN
378 RONCESVALLES AVE
TORONTO ONT CANADA

NT0010

TRF *See reverse side for symbol explanations and terms
Code *ABC Security no   Trade ID
34   7617R   331711030010R

Payment for securities purchased and/or securities sold must be received by Bache & Co. Incorporated on or before the settlement date (as noted above) as prescribed by the regulations of the Stock Exchange where transaction was executed.

On other than round lots (normally 100 shares) an odd lot charge is included in the price. On the NYSE this is 25c per share for stocks selling at $55.00 or above and 12½c below. In all other cases an explanation will be provided on request.

RETAIN THIS COPY FOR YOUR RECORDS

These sure profits are given out by most brokers to their clients in proportion to the amount of regular business received from each client. However, not all brokers share equally in these hot issues, and unfortunately some of those who do have a share do not pass them on to their clients but grab the profit themselves.

In the choice of a broker, therefore, the most important single factor is whether the broker has a large participation in hot issues and whether he passes them on to his clients. Some of the largest firms participate in all the hot issues, but because the firms are so very large, the allotments available to any individual client are so small as to be inconsequential.

Examples of how the salesmen of one firm give their customers frequent financial presents are shown below. In a four-month period they forwarded seven different gifts to one physician customer. In each case the stock was part of a "hot issue" which was resold the same day, and the profits ranged from 5% all the way up to 130%.

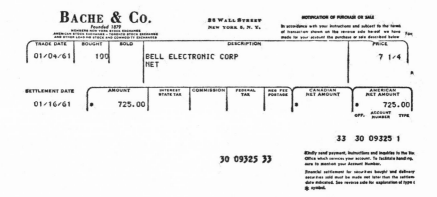

TRADE DATE	BOUGHT	SOLD	DESCRIPTION	PRICE
01/04/61	100		BELL ELECTRONIC CORP NET	7 1/4

SETTLEMENT DATE	AMOUNT	INTEREST STATE TAX	COMMISSION	FEDERAL TAX	REG FEE POSTAGE	CANADIAN NET AMOUNT	AMERICAN NET AMOUNT
01/16/61	725.00						725.00

OFF. ACCOUNT NUMBER TYPE

33 30 09325 1

30 09325 33

Kindly send payment, instructions and inquiries to the Tax Office which services your account. To facilitate handling, sure to mention your Account Number.

Financial settlement for securities bought and delivery securities sold must be made not later than the settlement date indicated. See reverse side for explanation of type & symbol.

W	AS PRINCIPAL WE HAVE PURCHASED FROM YOU
X	AS AGENT WE HAVE PURCHASED THROUGH/TO YOU
Y	AS AGENT YOU HAVE PURCHASED FOR US
Z	AS AGENT WE HAVE SOLD FOR YOU

R. A. DALY & COMPANY
MEMBERS
TORONTO STOCK EXCHANGE
THE INVESTMENT DEALERS' ASSOCIATION OF CAN.

R. A. DALY & COMPANY LIMITED HAVE PLEASURE IN CONFIRMING THE FOLLOWING TRANSACTION EFFECTED WITH YOU SUBJECT TO THE RULES AND REG

CODE	ARRANGED BY	MARKET	DATE TRADE	SETTLEMENT	NO. OF SHARES OR PAR VALUE	DESCRIPTION OF SECURITY	PRICE	GROSS AMOUNT	ACCRUED INTEREST	CO
Z	WMP	N.Y. OC	JAN 4 61	JAN 10	1 00	BELL ELECTRONICS	7.7/8 U.S. FUNDS	787 50		

BACHE & CO.
Founded 1879
MEMBERS NEW YORK STOCK EXCHANGE
AMERICAN STOCK EXCHANGE – TORONTO STOCK EXCHANGE
AND OTHER LEADING STOCK AND COMMODITY EXCHANGES

36 WALL STREET
NEW YORK 5, N. Y.

NOTIFICATION OF PURCHASE OR SALE
In accordance with your instructions and subject to the terms of transaction shown on the reverse side hereof, we have made for your account the purchase or sale described below.

TRADE DATE	BOUGHT	SOLD	DESCRIPTION	PRICE
01/25/61	20		VACUUM ELECTRONICS NEJ	15.00

SETTLEMENT DATE	AMOUNT	INTEREST STATE TAX	COMMISSION	FEDERAL TAX	REG. FEE POSTAGE	CANADIAN NET AMOUNT	AMERICAN NET AMOUNT
02/01/61	$ 300.00					$	300.00

OFF. ACCOUNT NUMBER TYPE

33　30 09325 1

30 09325 33

Kindly send payment, instructions and inquiries to the Bra Office which services your account. To facilitate handling, sure to mention your Account Number.

Financial settlement for securities bought and delivery securities sold must be made not later than the settlem date indicated. See reverse side for explanation of type o ✻ symbol.

W	AS PRINCIPAL WE HAVE PURCHASED FROM YOU
X	AS AGENT WE HAVE PURCHASED THROUGH/TO YOU
Y	AS AGENT YOU HAVE PURCHASED FOR US
Z	AS AGENT WE HAVE SOLD FOR YOU

R. A. DALY & COMPANY
MEMBERS
TORONTO STOCK EXCHANGE
DEALERS' ASSOCIATION OF CAN

CORRECTED CONTRACT AS TO NAME OF CLIENT

R. A. DALY & COMPANY LIMITED HAVE PLEASURE IN CONFIRMING THE FOLLOWING TRANSACTION EFFECTED WITH YOU SUBJECT TO THE RULES AND REG

CODE	ARRANGED BY	MARKET	DATE TRADE	SETTLEMENT	NO. OF SHARES OR PAR VALUE	DESCRIPTION OF SECURITY	PRICE	GROSS AMOUNT	ACCRUED INTEREST	CO
Z	WMP	N.Y OC	JAN 25	JAN 31	20	VACCUUM ELECTRONICS	23.1/2 U.S. FUNDS	470 00		

E. & O. E.

PLEASE NOTE ➙
1. IF NOT ALREADY IN OUR POSSESSION PLEASE ARRANGE FOR DELIVERY OF THE RELATIVE STOCK CERTIFICATES OR B
2. ANY EXPENSE INCURRED THROUGH FAILURE TO DELIVER SECURITIES IN PROPER TRANSFERABLE FORM SHALL BE
3. THIS CONTRACT SHOULD BE PRESERVED FOR TAX PURPOSES. AS INTEREST PAID TO YOU MUST BE REPORTED TO TH
4. WHEN ACTING AS AGENT WE WILL FURNISH THE NAME OF THE OTHER BROKER OR BROKERS INVOLVED IN THE TR
SETTLEMENT MAY BE EFFECTED AT THE BRANCH THROUGH WHICH YOU ARE DEALING. STREET ADDRESS OF WH

BACHE & CO.

Founded 1879
MEMBERS NEW YORK STOCK EXCHANGE
AMERICAN STOCK EXCHANGE – TORONTO STOCK EXCHANGE
AND OTHER LEADING STOCK AND COMMODITY EXCHANGES

86 WALL STREET
NEW YORK 8, N. Y.

NOTIFICATION OF PURCHASE OR SALE

In accordance with your instructions and subject to the terms of transaction shown on the reverse side hereof, we have made for your account the purchase or sale described below.

TRADE DATE	BOUGHT	SOLD	DESCRIPTION	PRICE
02/08/61	50		MIDLAND GUARDIAN CO NET	14.00

SETTLEMENT DATE	AMOUNT	INTEREST STATE TAX	COMMISSION	FEDERAL TAX	REG. FEE POSTAGE	CANADIAN NET AMOUNT	AMERICAN NET AMOUNT
02/16/61	$ 700.00					$	$ 700.00

OFF. ACCOUNT NUMBER TYPE

33 30 09325 1

30 09325 33

Kindly send payment, instructions and inquiries to the Ba: Office which services your account. To facilitate handling, sure to mention your Account Number.

Financial settlement for securities bought and delivery securities sold must be made not later than the settlem: date indicated. See reverse side for explanation of type : ✱ symbol.

W	AS PRINCIPAL WE HAVE PURCHASED FROM YOU
X	AS AGENT WE HAVE PURCHASED THROUGH/TO YOU
Y	AS AGENT YOU HAVE PURCHASED FOR US
Z	AS AGENT WE HAVE SOLD FOR YOU

R. A. DALY & COMPANY

MEMBERS
TORONTO STOCK EXCHANGE
THE INVESTMENT DEALERS' ASSOCIATION OF CAN

R. A. DALY & COMPANY LIMITED HAVE PLEASURE IN CONFIRMING THE FOLLOWING TRANSACTION EFFECTED WITH YOU SUBJECT TO THE RULES AND REG

CODE	ARRANGED BY	MARKET	DATE TRADE	DATE SETTLEMENT	NO OF SHARES OR PAR VALUE	DESCRIPTION OF SECURITY	PRICE	GROSS AMOUNT	ACCRUED INTEREST	CO:
Z	WMP	NY	FEB 16 61	FEB 22	50	MIDLAND GUARDIAN	17.¼ U.S. FUNDS	862 50		

E. & O. E.

PLEASE NOTE ➤

1 IF NOT ALREADY IN OUR POSSESSION PLEASE ARRANGE FOR DELIVERY OF THE RELATIVE STOCK CERTIFICATES OR BC
2 ANY EXPENSE INCURRED THROUGH FAILURE TO DELIVER SECURITIES IN PROPER TRANSFERABLE FORM SHALL BE T
3 THIS CONTRACT SHOULD BE PRESERVED FOR TAX PURPOSES. AS INTEREST PAID TO YOU MUST BE REPORTED TO TH:
4 WHEN ACTING AS AGENT WE WILL FURNISH THE NAME OF THE OTHER BROKER OR BROKERS INVOLVED IN THE TRA

SETTLEMENT MAY BE EFFECTED AT THE BRANCH THROUGH WHICH YOU ARE DEALING. STREET ADDRESS OF WHI

BACHE & CO.

Founded 1879
MEMBERS NEW YORK STOCK EXCHANGE
AMERICAN STOCK EXCHANGE – TORONTO STOCK EXCHANGE
AND OTHER LEADING STOCK AND COMMODITY EXCHANGES

86 WALL STREET
NEW YORK 8, N. Y.

NOTIFICATION OF PURCHASE OR SALE

In accordance with your instructions and subject to the terms of transaction shown on the reverse side hereof, we have made for your account the purchase or sale described below.

TRADE DATE	BOUGHT	SOLD	DESCRIPTION	PRICE
02/20/61	200		SHORE CALNEVAR INC NET	9.00

SETTLEMENT DATE	AMOUNT	INTEREST STATE TAX	COMMISSION	FEDERAL TAX	REG. FEE POSTAGE	CANADIAN NET AMOUNT	AMERICAN NET AMOUNT
02/28/61	$ 1,800.00					$	$ 1,800.00

OFF. ACCOUNT NUMBER TYPE

33 30 09325 1

30 09325 33

Kindly send payment, instructions and inquiries to the Ba: Office which services your account. To facilitate handling, sure to mention your Account Number.

Financial settlement for securities bought and delivery securities sold must be made not later than the settlem: date indicated. See reverse side for explanation of type : ✱ symbol.

R. A. DALY & COMPANY

W	AS PRINCIPAL WE HAVE PURCHASED FROM YOU
X	AS AGENT WE HAVE PURCHASED THROUGH/TO YOU
Y	AS AGENT YOU HAVE PURCHASED FOR US
Z	AS AGENT WE HAVE SOLD FOR YOU

MEMBERS
TORONTO STOCK EXCHANGE
THE INVESTMENT DEALERS' ASSOCIATION OF CANA

R. A. DALY & COMPANY LIMITED HAVE PLEASURE IN CONFIRMING THE FOLLOWING TRANSACTION EFFECTED WITH YOU SUBJECT TO THE RULES AND REG

CODE	ARRANGED BY	MARKET	DATE TRADE	SETTLEMENT	NO OF SHARES OR PAR VALUE	DESCRIPTION OF SECURITY	PRICE	GROSS AMOUNT	ACCRUED INTEREST	COM
Z	WMP	NYOC	FEB 20 61	FEB 24	2 00	SHORE CALNEVAR	10.¼ U.S. FUNDS	2 050 00		

E. & O. E.

PLEASE NOTE →
1. IF NOT ALREADY IN OUR POSSESSION PLEASE ARRANGE FOR DELIVERY OF THE RELATIVE STOCK CERTIFICATES OR BO
2. ANY EXPENSE INCURRED THROUGH FAILURE TO DELIVER SECURITIES IN PROPER TRANSFERABLE FORM SHALL BE T
3. THIS CONTRACT SHOULD BE PRESERVED FOR TAX PURPOSES. AS INTEREST PAID TO YOU MUST BE REPORTED TO THR
4. WHEN ACTING AS AGENT WE WILL FURNISH THE NAME OF THE OTHER BROKER OR BROKERS INVOLVED IN THE TRA

SETTLEMENT MAY BE EFFECTED AT THE BRANCH THROUGH WHICH YOU ARE DEALING, STREET ADDRESS OF WHI

R. A. DALY & COMPANY

W	AS PRINCIPAL WE HAVE PURCHASED FROM YOU
X	AS AGENT WE HAVE PURCHASED THROUGH/TO YOU
Y	AS AGENT YOU HAVE PURCHASED FOR US
Z	AS AGENT WE HAVE SOLD FOR YOU

CORRECTED CONTRACT*

MEMBERS
TORONTO STOCK EXCHANGE
THE INVESTMENT DEALERS' ASSOCIATION OF CAN

R. A. DALY & COMPANY LIMITED HAVE PLEASURE IN CONFIRMING THE FOLLOWING TRANSACTION EFFECTED WITH YOU SUBJECT TO THE RULES AND REG

CODE	ARRANGED BY	MARKET	DATE TRADE	SETTLEMENT	NO OF SHARES OR PAR VALUE	DESCRIPTION OF SECURITY	PRICE	GROSS AMOUNT	ACCRUED INTEREST	COM
Z	WMP	NYOC	MAR 3 61	MAR 9	15	LEASEWAY TRANSPORTATION	24.¼ U.S. FUNDS	363 75		

E. & O. E.

PLEASE NOTE →
1. IF NOT ALREADY IN OUR POSSESSION PLEASE ARRANGE FOR DELIVERY OF THE RELATIVE STOCK CERTIFICATES OR BC
2. ANY EXPENSE INCURRED THROUGH FAILURE TO DELIVER SECURITIES IN PROPER TRANSFERABLE FORM SHALL BE T
3. THIS CONTRACT SHOULD BE PRESERVED FOR TAX PURPOSES. AS INTEREST PAID TO YOU MUST BE REPORTED TO THI
4. WHEN ACTING AS AGENT WE WILL FURNISH THE NAME OF THE OTHER BROKER OR BROKERS INVOLVED IN THE TRA

SETTLEMENT MAY BE EFFECTED AT THE BRANCH THROUGH WHICH YOU ARE DEALING, STREET ADDRESS OF WHI

BACHE & CO.

Founded 1879
MEMBERS NEW YORK STOCK EXCHANGE
AMERICAN STOCK EXCHANGE – TORONTO STOCK EXCHANGE
AND OTHER LEADING STOCK AND COMMODITY EXCHANGES

86 WALL STREET
NEW YORK 8, N. Y.

NOTIFICATION OF PURCHASE OR SALE

In accordance with your instructions and subject to the terms of transaction shown on the reverse side hereof, we have made for your account the purchase or sale described below

TRADE DATE	BOUGHT	SOLD	DESCRIPTION	PRICE
03/03/61	15		LEASEWAY TRANSPORT NET	15.00

SETTLEMENT DATE	AMOUNT	INTEREST STATE TAX	COMMISSION	FEDERAL TAX	REG FEE POSTAGE	CANADIAN NET AMOUNT	AMERICAN NET AMOUNT
03/09/61	$ 225.00					$	$ 225.00

OFF. ACCOUNT NUMBER TYPE

33 30 09325 1

30 09325 33

Kindly send payment, instructions and inquiries to the Bac
Office which services your account. To facilitate handling,
sure to mention your Account Number.

Financial settlement for securities bought and delivery
securities sold must be made not later than the settleme
date indicated. See reverse side for explanation of type s
* symbol.

BACHE & CO.
Founded 1879
MEMBERS AMERICAN STOCK EXCHANGE
AMERICAN STOCK EXCHANGE - TORONTO STOCK EXCHANGE
AND OTHER LEADING STOCK AND COMMODITY EXCHANGES

86 WALL STREET
NEW YORK 5, N. Y.

NOTIFICATION OF PURCHASE OR SALE

In accordance with your instructions and subject to the terms
of transaction shown on the reverse side hereof, we have
made for your account the purchase or sale described below.

TRADE DATE	BOUGHT	SOLD	DESCRIPTION	PRICE
03/08/61	25		MARLEY CO NET	19 1/2

SETTLEMENT DATE	AMOUNT	INTEREST STATE TAX	COMMISSION	FEDERAL TAX	REG FEE POSTAGE	CANADIAN NET AMOUNT	AMERICAN NET AMOUNT
03/16/61	487.50						487.50

OFF. ACCOUNT NUMBER TYPE

33 30 09325 1

30 09325 33

Kindly send payment, instructions and inquiries to the Bache
which services your account. To facilitate handling, be
mention your Account Number

BACHE & CO.
Founded 1879
MEMBERS NEW YORK STOCK EXCHANGE AND OTHER
LEADING STOCK AND COMMODITY EXCHANGES

NOTIFICATION OF PURCHASE OR SALE

In accordance with your instructions and subject to the terms of transaction
shown on the reverse side hereof, we have made for your account the
purchase or sale described below

YOUR ACCOUNT NUMBER	QUANTITY B YOU BOUGHT S YOU SOLD	DESCRIPTION	PRICE A/B	AMOUNT	INTEREST OR STATE TAX	Commission	FEDERAL TAX	POSTAGE REG. FEE	NET AMOUNT
300093251 ONT$ .25	25	MARLEY CO	3 23.00	57500	100	1075	24		56276

U. S. FUNDS

30 09325 33

33

Send payment, instructions and inquiries to the Bache Office
which services your account. To facilitate handling please mention
your Account Number

Financial settlement for securities bought and delivery of securities sold must be
made not later than the settlement date indicated. See reverse side for explanation of A/C Type and *symbol

Mar. 16/61	Mar. 22/61
NO DAY YR	NO DAY YR
TRADE DATE	SETTLEMENT DATE

BACHE & CO.
Founded 1879
MEMBERS NEW YORK STOCK EXCHANGE
AMERICAN STOCK EXCHANGE - TORONTO STOCK EXCHANGE
AND OTHER LEADING STOCK AND COMMODITY EXCHANGES

86 WALL STREET
NEW YORK 5, N. Y.

NOTIFICATION OF PURCHASE OR SALE

In accordance with your instructions and subject to the terms
of transaction shown on the reverse side hereof, we have
made for your account the purchase or sale described below.

TRADE DATE	BOUGHT	SOLD	DESCRIPTION	PRICE
04/05/61	15		ALBERTO CULVER CO NET	10.00

SETTLEMENT DATE	AMOUNT	INTEREST STATE TAX	COMMISSION	FEDERAL TAX	REG FEE POSTAGE	CANADIAN NET AMOUNT	AMERICAN NET AMOUNT
04/13/61	150.00						150.00

OFF. ACCOUNT NUMBER TYPE

33 30 09325 1

30 09325 33

Kindly send payment, instructions and inquiries to the Bache
Office which services your account. To facilitate handling,
sure to mention your Account Number.

W	AS PRINCIPAL WE HAVE PURCHASED FROM YOU
X	AS AGENT WE HAVE PURCHASED THROUGH/TO YOU
Y	AS AGENT YOU HAVE PURCHASED FOR US
Z	AS AGENT WE HAVE SOLD FOR YOU

R. A. DALY & COMPANY
MEMBERS
TORONTO STOCK EXCHANGE
THE INVESTMENT DEALERS' ASSOCIATION OF CANA

R. A. DALY & COMPANY LIMITED HAVE PLEASURE IN CONFIRMING THE FOLLOWING TRANSACTION EFFECTED WITH YOU SUBJECT TO THE RULES AND REG

CODE	ARRANGED BY	MARKET	DATE TRADE	DATE SETTLEMENT	NO OF SHARES OR PAR VALUE	DESCRIPTION OF SECURITY	PRICE	GROSS AMOUNT	ACCRUED INTEREST	COM
Z	OFFICE	NYOC	APR 6 61	APR 12	15	ALBERTA CULVER	23.00 U.S. FUNDS	345 00		

E. & O. E.

PLEASE → NOTE
1 IF NOT ALREADY IN OUR POSSESSION PLEASE ARRANGE FOR DELIVERY OF THE RELATIVE STOCK CERTIFICATES OR BO
2 ANY EXPENSE INCURRED THROUGH FAILURE TO DELIVER SECURITIES IN PROPER TRANSFERABLE FORM SHALL BE T
3 THIS CONTRACT SHOULD BE PRESERVED FOR TAX PURPOSES AS INTEREST PAID TO YOU MUST BE REPORTED TO THE
4 WHEN ACTING AS AGENT WE WILL FURNISH THE NAME OF THE OTHER BROKER OR BROKERS INVOLVED IN THE TRA
SETTLEMENT MAY BE EFFECTED AT THE BRANCH THROUGH WHICH YOU ARE DEALING. STREET ADDRESS OF WHI

In addition to intentional gifts of money as described above, brokers occasionally send gifts that are quite unintentional.

For some strange reason, brokers do not appear to take the same care in controlling their cheques as do other financial institutions, and all too often they quite unintentionally send out rather substantial financial bonuses. To draw from my own experience, about once a year I have received large cheques to which I was not entitled from a number of brokers. These have varied from $500 to $25,000. I have reproduced a copy of one such strange "gift" below. In this case the broker owed me about $50, so it wasn't just a matter of adding a couple of extra zeros.

Other investors have told me of having this same experience. Of course, the money must be returned eventually, but it certainly can cause excitement for a while.

Sad to say, brokers are equally careless with the money in customers' accounts. I made a purchase through a usually reliable Toronto firm of $5,000 worth of Sunshine convertibles — total cost $4,800. Unfortunately the broker made the slight error of charging my account $482,430.00!

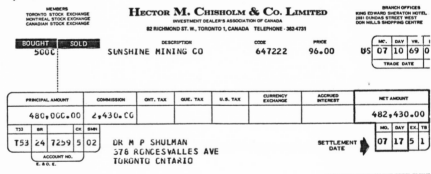

There is one source of undeserved money that does not always have to be returned — the unearned dividend. A few brokers have built up a substantial extra source of income by registering in their own names all stocks being shipped to other brokers or even to customers. In many cases, particularly if the stock does not pay dividends, the registration will not be changed, and the stock certificate may be put away in a safety deposit box and forgotten. Months or years later when dividends are declared on these stocks, they will be sent to the person in whose name ownership is registered. The dividends must, of course, be given to the rightful owner if a claim is made by him, but all too often the true owner is unaware of the dividend and makes no claim.

Any person buying and selling securities should at the time of payment instruct his broker that the security be registered in his name before it is delivered. This will ensure that all future dividends are received. In addition it will result in the improper receipt of numerous undeserved dividends. For example, on March 2, 1966, I sold my holdings in Diversified Metal Corporation. Yet on May 2, 1966, I received this dividend cheque.

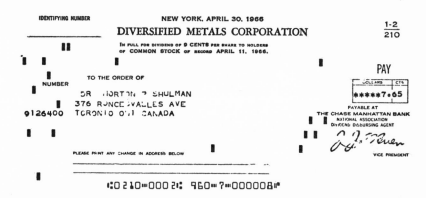

The most honest individual in the world could not return this cheque to its true owner, for his identity is unknown. My stock was sold by one broker to another broker acting for a third broker. It would take a Sherlock Holmes to trace the present holder of the stock. I must, therefore, keep the dividend, and if it is claimed by its true owner or his broker I will forward it to him. Experience has shown that about one-third of these dividends are never claimed. Far better that you should receive these funds than your broker.

The rules in picking a broker who will give the greatest return on your investment dollar are:

1. The broker should be a member of the New York Stock Exchange or the Toronto Stock Exchange.

2. The broker should underwrite stock issues or convertible bonds or "kicker" bonds with reasonable frequency. This can be ascertained by a daily glance at the Wall Street Journal.

3. The broker should give active clients participation in "hot issues" at least four times a year. If he doesn't, get another broker.

In summary, choosing the right broker is as important as choosing the right lawyer and for the same reasons — the best broker means more dollars in the bank. A broker with many hot issues can easily increase one's overall income by 10% to 20%.

3
WHICH TO BUY— U.S. OR CANADIAN SECURITIES

When I wrote "Anyone" in 1966 I came to the reluctant conclusion, "It is with difficulty that I as a Canadian must recommend, other factors being equal, 'Buy American'." I am happy to be able to say that now in 1972 that situation has changed considerably and although I am not yet able to recommend "Buy Canadian" at least I am able to say "Buy Ontarian."

No U.S. exchange has encouraged promoters. The U.S. exchanges' problems involve only the quality of the companies listed, for some of the smaller exchanges have been tempted to list stock of some relatively shady companies. You are far less likely to lose money if you limit yourself to stock listed on the New York Exchange, which has the most stringent listing rules and keeps the closest eye on its stocks.

The Canadian problem is that, unlike the U.S.A. we have no national securities commission and although the various provinces have fairly similar security laws they are administered very unevenly. As a result crooked stockateers move from province to province, using as their base the area that gives them the least trouble. For many years Ontario was North America's home to the worthless stock promoters, but a series of flamboyant stock collapses culminating in 1966 in the Atlantic Acceptance & Prudential Finance disasters prodded the government into taking action, tightening up the securities regulations and more important enforcing them. A few stockateers were even sent to jail.

The result was a mass exodus of these gentlemen to British Columbia, and from 1967 to 1971 that province became the mecca for long-distance stock salesmen. In 1969 I lectured to a group of 250 doctors in Sacramento and found that over three-quarters of them had been contacted by Vancouver stock salesmen during the previous four months. Over half of those contacted had actually purchased worthless mining stocks or vastly overpriced junior industrials. In 1971 the word went through the grapevine that the British Columbia government had received so many complaints that it was about to crack down, and again a mass movement took place, this time to Montreal, where the Quebec Securities Commission was welcoming salesmen who would never be licensed elsewhere. As an example of their laxity, as late as 1972 the Quebec Securities Commission was vigorously rejecting the idea of reporting of insider stock trading, a requirement taken as a matter of course everywhere else.

That is the current situation. The unfortunate part of it is that the non-expert cannot tell the crooked from the honest company, so in order to play safe he must avoid all Quebec-based securities. It is a good rule of thumb:

1. never to buy securities listed only on Montreal's Canadian Stock Exchange.

2. never to buy securities listed only on the Vancouver Stock Exchange.

3. never to buy unlisted Canadian securities.

The situation is quite different in relation to stocks listed on the Toronto Stock Exchange. Regulations there are now strictly enforced, and although Toronto is not yet up to New York Stock Exchange standards, it has at least approached those of the American Exchange.

Most important, Canadian markets have been very weak in relation to the U.S. stock market during the past ten years because of President Kennedy's imposition of the interest equalization tax. This 15% tax which U.S. purchasers must pay on most Canadian stock purchases has caused a lag in Canadian stock prices which is far in excess of 15%.

The result is that high-grade Canadian securities now sell at significantly lower price earning multiples than do their U.S. equivalents and so have become outstanding buys. Unfortunately there are few of my favourite convertible bonds available in Canada and these, because of their scarcity, tend to be overpriced, but for that portion of your capital which you intend to put in stocks, there are incredible Canadian opportunities available today. For Canadians it has now finally become not only patriotic to invest at home but also profitable. Even Americans with the 15% equalization tax find that there are many great opportunities in Canada today; e.g. in November 1971 a sales motivation firm owned by Harvey Kalef, a Canadian Horatio Alger, went public at $3.10 per share.

PITFIELD, MACKAY, ROSS & COMPANY
LIMITED

MEMBERS
ALL STOCK EXCHANGES IN CANADA
THE INVESTMENT DEALERS ASSOCIATION OF CANADA
WE CONFIRM THAT YOU HAVE
NOUS CONFIRMONS QUE VOUS AVEZ

MEMBRES
DE TOUTES LES BOURSES AU CANADA
DE L'ASSOCIATION DES COURTIERS
EN VALEURS MOBILIERES DU CANADA

BOUGHT ACHETÉ	SOLD VENDU	DESCRIPTION	PRICE PRIX	MO. DAY JOUR YR. AN. REF #
	4000	N.S.I.MARKETING LTD. SECONDARY PRIMARY	458729 3.10	09 14 71 4956

PROSPECTUS ENCLOSED

PRINCIPAL AMOUNT MONTANT PRINCIPAL	COMMISSION	PROVINCIAL TAXES TAXES PROVINCIALES	US TAXES TAXES E U	EXCHANGE ECHANGE	INTEREST INTERET	NET AMOUNT MONTANT NET
12,400.00	301.20					12,701.20

T82 41 0187 9 HE
ACCOUNT NO
NO DE COMPTE   SMN VEND

DR MORTON P SHULMAN
378 RONCESVALLES AVENUE
TORONTO 154 ONTARIO

HM

MOIS MO   JOUR DAY   TB   EX
09   17   A   T
SETTLEMENT DATE DF RÈGLEMENT
TORONTO

SETTLEMENT SHOULT HE MADE AT THE
ABOVE OFFICE
PAIEMENT DOIT ETHE FAIT AU BUREAU
CI HAUF MENTIONNE

SEE REVERSE SIDE FOR CODE EXPLANATION AND CONDITIONS TO WHICH THIS TRANSACTION IS SUBJECT.
VOIR AU VERSO CODE DES EXPLICATIONS ET CONDITIONS SOUS RESERVE DE CETTE NEGOTIATION.

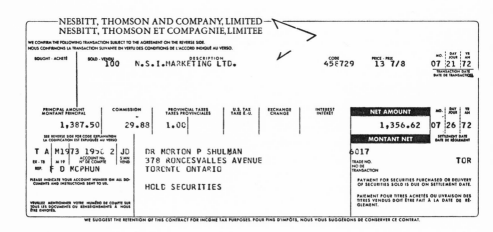

NESBITT, THOMSON AND COMPANY, LIMITED
NESBITT, THOMSON ET COMPAGNIE, LIMITEE

WE CONFIRM THE FOLLOWING TRANSACTION SUBJECT TO THE AGREEMENT ON THE REVERSE SIDE.
NOUS CONFIRMONS LA TRANSACTION SUIVANTE EN VERTU DES CONDITIONS DE L'ACCORD INDIQUÉ AU VERSO.

BOUGHT - ACHETÉ	SOLD - VENDU	DESCRIPTION	CODE	PRICE - PRIX	MO. DAY JOUR YR. AN
	100	N.S.I.MARKETING LTD.	458729	13 7/8	07 21 72

TRANSACTION DATE
DATE DE TRANSACTION

PRINCIPAL AMOUNT MONTANT PRINCIPAL	COMMISSION	PROVINCIAL TAXES TAXES PROVINCIALES	U.S. TAX TAXE É.-U.	EXCHANGE CHANGE	INTEREST INTERET	NET AMOUNT	MO. DAY JOUR YR. AN
1,387.50	29.88	1.00				1,356.62	07 26 72

MONTANT NET

SETTLEMENT DATE
DATE DE RÈGLEMENT

SEE REVERSE SIDE FOR CODE EXPLANATION
LA CODIFICATION EST EXPLIQUÉE AU VERSO

T A M1973 1950 2 JD
EX - TB   M 19   ACCOUNT No N° DE COMPTE   S MN VEND
REP.   F D MCPHUN

DR MORTON P SHULMAN
378 RONCESVALLES AVENUE
TORONTO ONTARIO

HOLD SECURITIES

6017
TRADE NO.
NO DE
TRANSACTION

TOR

PAYMENT FOR SECURITIES PURCHASED OR DELIVERY
OF SECURITIES SOLD IS DUE ON SETTLEMENT DATE.
PAIEMENT POUR TITRES ACHETÉS OU LIVRAISON DES
TITRES VENDUS DOIT ETRE FAIT À LA DATE DE RÈ-
GLEMENT.

PLEASE INDICATE YOUR ACCOUNT NUMBER ON ALL DO-
CUMENTS AND INSTRUCTIONS SENT TO US.

VEUILLEZ MENTIONNER VOTRE NUMÉRO DE COMPTE SUR
TOUS LES DOCUMENTS OU RENSEIGNEMENTS À NOUS
ÊTRE ENVOYÉS.

WE SUGGEST THE RETENTION OF THIS CONTRACT FOR INCOME TAX PURPOSES. POUR FINS D'IMPÔTS, NOUS VOUS SUGGÉRONS DE CONSERVER CE CONTRAT.

The stock languished for a few weeks slightly below that figure and then U.S. investors began to compare its 10 times earnings price with U.S. motivations firms which trade at 20 to 30 times earnings. The Americans began to buy and the stock rose steadily.

To sum up:

1. For Canadian investors that portion of your funds going into common stocks should go into high grade industrials listed on the Toronto Stock Exchange.

2. For U.S. citizens, most of your money should go into U.S. convertible bonds but there are some great opportunities on the Toronto Stock Exchange for at least a part of your funds.

4
THE PENNY
STOCK MARKET

Consolidated Denison went from 20¢ to $50.

Quemont went from 3¢ to $20.

Pyramid went from 10¢ to $19.

The dream of every stock-market gambler is to buy just such a vision — to invest $1,000 and see it turn into $500,000. Because of these dreams, thousands of men have become millionaires — not by buying penny stocks, but by selling them. It is now standard promoter practice to pay a few hundred or a few thousand dollars to buy a property within a short distance of a producing mine or a "hot" prospect and then to issue up to a million dollars' worth of stock at anywhere from 30¢ to a dollar to the gullible public. Of every million dollars' worth of stock issued, far less than half will be used for actual exploration of the property, and in some cases none of the money is so used. A portion of the cash will go into the treasury of the company, a large amount will go to the telephone and telegraph companies to pay for the long-distance calls to the suckers, and the vast majority will go to make new millionaires of the promotors.

The myth of the fortunes made from the penny stock that finds a rich ore body and goes to $20 or $30 has been carefully fostered by a mining industry which depends on the promotion type of financing for its vigour. Unfortunately, it is a complete myth. *There is not a single member of the public living in North America today who has made a sizable sum of money by investing in the penny mining market.*

The Irish sweepstakes persuade millions of North Americans to make a donation to Irish hospitals by giving back a portion of the "take" and by making a few of their benefactors rich beyond their dreams. The penny mining market has never made a member of the public rich, and yet through extremely clever publicity has persuaded the supposedly intelligent professional classes of North America to continue to donate millions annually to this very uncharitable group. How do they so successfully perpetrate this same fraud year after year?

The routine is as formalized as a ballet. The promoter either forms a new company or purchases control of an existing company listed on a Canadian stock exchange. A typical example was Fax Mines,* a company with a listing on a Canadian stock exchange trading at 5¢. The

* Fax Mines, Jenny Mines, Jerrett Motors, Canadian Jefferson Securities, Edward Collins, George Crawford, Fred Gora, Henry Severn, Heather Investment Services, and Strang Advisory Services are fictitious names used in this and the following chapter to illustrate an often-repeated situation. Any resemblance to living persons or firms is purely coincidental.

company had no assets and had sold its total capitalization of 5 million shares. A well-known Canadian promoter, Edward Collins, purchased one million shares of the company's stock for $70,000 from the original organizer of the company. This gave him effective control of the company, as the remaining four million shares were widely distributed, with no individual holding more than ten thousand shares. A promoter never attempts to move a stock when in this situation, because the other shareholders may begin to sell their stock to him. Instead, Collins called a special meeting of the shareholders, which because of the company's inactivity was attended only by himself and his associates. At this meeting he called in all of the company's stock and changed the company's name to get rid of the old tired Fax Mines image. The shareholders were given one share in the new company for every 10 shares they had held previously. The new company, Jenny Mines, had an authorized capital of five million shares, but there were now only 500,000 outstanding, of which 100,000 were held by Collins.

At this time there was a very active uranium boom in Canada. Several companies near Elliot Lake had discovered ore bodies and were going into production to supply ore to the United States. Collins arranged for his brother-in-law, George Crawford, to purchase a piece of bush land ten miles from Elliot Lake and 25 miles from the proven mines. Crawford paid $250 to the prospector who staked the property and promptly sold the land to Jenny Mines for $50,000.

Jenny Mines had no money, however, so Collins underwrote (purchased) 200,000 shares of stock from the treasury of the company at 25¢ a share so as to supply the $50,000. The company then announced that in return for this underwriting they had granted Collins one-year options to purchase another $1,500,000 shares at prices ranging from 30¢ to $1.00.

At this point Crawford returned the $50,000 to his brother-in-law. These men now had reached the point where, by laying out $250, they had received 200,000 shares of company stock plus options on an additional 1.5 million.

Next, Collins paid $3,000 to an employee of a large trust company who had access to the files listing the shareholders of several large mines for whom the trust company acted as transfer agent. For his $3,000 he received 12,000 names and addresses of individuals who were then holders of successful mining stocks. The "trust" company employee didn't have to copy out all these names, for his firm had every name on a mailing plate, and the employee merely ran all the plates through the machine, thus producing a master list in one hour of overtime. (Another promoter did not wish to spend the $3,000 and rented a third-floor office on Bay Street from which he entered a trust company's office at midnight while the janitor was kept busy with a bottle of whisky. No one at the trust company ever suspected, although the promoter grumbled that he always left the plates much neater than he had found them.)

The 12,000 investors now began to receive a well-printed, glossy "information bulletin" sent out by Collins' brokerage house, which he grandly called "Canadian Jefferson Securities". The weekly bulletin expansively and optimistically described the uranium boom then going on in Canada and pointed out some of the extraordinary price changes that had occurred; stock of some companies had literally quadrupled or better in days. The third bulletin described in loving detail the romantic story of Gunnar Mines, a legitimate company which had jumped in a few days from $2.50 to $13. Along with this bulletin was a stamped postcard. The receiver was invited to sign and return it in order to receive, with no obligation, full information on a new exciting prospect near the successful mines described earlier. This company was "about to begin drilling", which could very likely send its price from its then 39¢ to over $10.

Promoters consider a 3% return from a promotional mailing to be satisfactory, and Collins expected to get back 350 to 400 postcards. To his amazed delight, he received 1,600 signed postcards, probably due to the front-page publicity given the Canadian uranium strike and the atomic bomb.

Within a few days these 1,600 individuals, practically all of whom were in the United States, received a long-distance call from Toronto which went like this: "This is your Canadian broker calling. My name is Fred Gora, and I want to tell you about what will probably be the greatest opportunity in your lifetime — to get in on the ground floor of a great Canadian mine before the sharks up here know about it. The name is Jenny Mines, and she probably has such a big uranium ore body that you can stick Gunnar and Consolidated Denison in one corner of it and you wouldn't even see them. The price is only 39¢, and although I'd like to offer you more, the president of our firm will only allow me to sell 1,000 shares to new customers. The idea is, we'll make you money on this one and then try to do more business at some future date. You want to check with your banker? Well, of course, go right ahead, but I have only been alloted 25,000 shares to sell to new clients, and you represent my last thousand. I have over 300 more people I haven't phoned yet, and my last call was to a banker in New York City; he wanted 20,000 shares, and I could only give him one. Jenny is listed on the stock exchange, you know, and we're only distributing stock at this low price because they insist on a wider distribution before it moves over $1.00. Okay, I'll send out a contract to you tonight. Please put a cheque in the mail for $390. You don't even have to pay the regular stock exchange commission."

As a result of these 1,600 calls, 400,000 shares were sold, and payment was received for 350,000. Collins now needed more stock for his "clients" and so exercised his options on Jenny Mines at 30¢. Ten days later the 400 original phone purchasers received a second call: "This is Fred Gora phoning from Canada, bringing good news about Jenny Mines. The outlook for the company has improved so much that Jefferson Securities have put another $100,000 in their treasury. The stock has been very active on the stock exchange and has now moved up to an all-time high of 65¢. Some very good news is going to be released tomorrow.

I am not allowed to reveal it yet, but I can tell you this, that it will put the price of the stock much, *much* higher. Because you are now a regular client, the president has given me permission to sell you a small amount of stock at today's price; this is only because you showed faith in us before, when Jenny was 39¢. We have very little available, and only to our regular clients, but I have managed to squeeze out a maximum of 3,000 shares for you — and frankly the president said to try to talk you down to half of that, but I want to make this money for you so that we will do a lot of business in the future. So just put your cheque in the mail for $1,950, and you can skip the commission. Jenny Mines is going to make all of us very rich men."

In the meanwhile, Eddy Collins had really put $100,000 in the treasury of Jenny Mines in order to exercise his stock option, but he had no intention of leaving it there. Jenny Mines now hired "Crawford and Company" to do a magnetometric survey of the property for the sum of $85,000, two-thirds of which was immediately passed back to Collins under the table. Strangely enough, this was the good news that Fred Gora had predicted, and the company now made a public announcement that the survey was under way and would be followed by diamond drilling.

The stock continued to move higher on the stock exchange, reaching $1.00 three weeks later. By this time Collins had twelve salesmen working the phones, busily selling Jenny Mines all over North America. He exercised further options, paying Jenny Mines $250,000 for further blocks of stock at higher prices. Needless to say, most of this money quickly found its way back to Collins via the drilling company that Jenny Mines hired.

This drama was rapidly reaching its climax, and a crescendo of stock selling occurred. Announcement of the imminent drilling was made to the *Northern Miner*, advertisements were placed in the mining and daily press with a map showing the proximity of Jenny Mines to successful mines, and a tremendously high-pressure phone campaign was conducted to sell Jenny Mines at $1.00. "Jenny closed at $1.10 today. We are letting you have it at 10¢ under the market." Unfortunately, the clients did not understand the unintentional pun in that sentence.

Friday, January 28, 1963, Jenny closed at $1.20 on the stock exchange. Saturday morning Eddy Collins paid off his salesmen. They received an average of $9,000 each for the ten weeks' work. Fred Gora, his best salesman, had earned $21,000. They smiled and shook hands, and the salesmen went to look for another similar promotion.

Fred Gora boarded a plane for Vancouver with his $21,000 in $100 bills in a breast pocket. He soon fell asleep in his aisle seat, and the thick packet of bills fell into the aisle. The stewardess could not believe her eyes and hurried forward to give the money to the pilot. His first thought was of dope pushing, and he radioed ahead to ask the Royal

Canadian Mounted Police to meet the plane at Calgary. Some minutes later Gora awoke, and feeling the absence of his money pack, became volubly upset until the stewardess calmed him and returned the money.

When the plane landed in Calgary, the R.C.M.P. quickly whisked Gora into a private office and began a polite but insistent cross-examination as to the source of the money. Gora swears that when he refused to talk, the police corporal blurted out, "Mr. Gora, we are aware that one of your acquaintances has been smuggling hog bristles from Communist China into the United States via Canada. This is a very serious offence. We insist on knowing if your money is from this source."

The amazed swindler burst out laughing and replied, "Hog bristles! Are you kidding? This is my pay for selling moose pasture to American investors!" The constable apologized and escorted Fred Gora back to his airplane.

On Monday, January 31, Jenny Mines opened with no bid-offered at $1.00. The first trade was at 60¢, and within twenty minutes the stock sold down to 14¢, where it remained for several days while short traders (professionals who had sold stock they didn't own in the expectation of just such a collapse) bought back the stock they had sold over $1.00. Jenny then gradually declined to 3¢, and it has traded in a 3¢ to 6¢ range since that time.

Collins made a gross profit of 2½ million dollars, out of which he had to pay just under $400,000 to his various associates. He decided for reasons of health to close Jefferson Securities on February 1, then moved to Nice, where he rented the large villa that he still occupies today. Strangely he did not dissipate his illgotten wealth in the vice traps of Nice but, being a hard working individual, opened a new business. This was an advisory service, giving market advice to European investors who were interested in North American securities — but more about this type of swindle in another chapter.

Unbelieveable as this story sounds, it has been repeated hundreds of times in the past decade, and some individuals have fallen for the same fable many times. Doctors are the prime suckers, for they have excess cash with no business to put it in; they are too rushed to properly investigate any stock; and they are trusting by nature. There is probably not a doctor in all of North America who has not been stuck at least once by Eddy Collins or others of his ilk. Dentists and lawyers are a close second, but chartered accountants seem to fare better. Widows and orphans are never stuck by these operators, who avoid them like the plague, not because of innate decency, but because widows scream to the authorities and the press. The professional or businessman rarely publicly complains, because he cannot bear to have his own greed and stupidity exposed.

And indeed there is no limit to the greed and stupidity of these lambs who think they are wolves. At 11 p.m. one very cold January night, I received a phone call from a lawyer friend who said he had to see me that night on a very urgent financial matter. He explained that he had two clients with him, dentists who had invested their entire savings of $85,000 in a fantastic once-in-a-lifetime proposition, and that he intended to invest his own modest savings in the morning but first wanted my opinion.

Twenty minutes later, three excited men arrived at my home and poured forth this fantastic story: An unbelievably large iron ore deposit had been discovered in Liberia; the Sheik of Kuwait had agreed to put up twenty million dollars to finance the development and production of the ore, which was then to be shipped to Kuwait, where it was to be used in a new process for refinement of oil under the Kuwait desert. The twenty million was already in deposit in a Liberian bank, and the deal was to be closed in just five days, but the promoters and developers of the property had run short of ready cash and needed just $30,000 to pay the legal fees and close the deal. In return for loaning this $30,000, the two dentists had been given the secret information that Ross Metals,* an unlisted penny stock trading at 30¢, was for tax reasons to be given full title to the iron property. When this news was released to the public, the stock would be worth about $50 per share. To prove the truth of all these statements, the previous week one of the dentists had actually been flown to Liberia and had not only seen the property but had been introduced to the Sheik of Kuwait himself (or a reasonable facsimile). That week the dentists had purchased 200,000 shares of Ross Metals at 30¢.

When I expressed, as gently as possible, my doubts about this "deal of the century", the dentists' reaction was violent. They jumped to their feet, accused me of wanting to discourage them so that they would sell their stock cheaply while I bought it up, then stamped angrily from the house. I learned that night never to try to talk sense to individuals in love with their dreams. They will not tolerate anyone shattering them.

One month later the promoters of Ross Metals had sold all their stock, and it quickly fell to 2¢. The property in Liberia unfortunately did not have enough ore to warrant going into production, and the pseudo-Sheik of Kuwait had disappeared. Interestingly enough, the two dentists are still mad at me. I guess they have to blame someone other than themselves.

Fortunately, not all penny stocks are swindles. But, as a general rule, if the stock is being sold over the phone, the chance of the client's making money is about nil.

Even those promoters who are honest (and most promoters and honesty have difficulty going together) cannot offer their clients a decent break. For even if every penny that goes into the company's treasury is spent on exploration and development, the chance of producing a mine is close to nil. Of the thousands and thousands of penny prospects that have been explored in all of North America since the war, less than half

* Name changed.

a dozen have ultimately turned into a mine and paid dividends greater than their cost. Unfortunately, even the most conscientious promoter must siphon off over half of the money he receives in order to pay the fringe expenses involved in promotion and sale of these mining stocks.

It is, of course, far easier to give advice than to follow it, and although I have no trouble turning down the phone promoter, I find it very difficult to say no to the friend with the "hot tip"; and money is usually just as lost on a hot tip as with the promoter. The information is all too often either false or planted. A recent personal experience illustrates the temptations and pitfalls of the hot tip, even when, as in this case, the stock being tipped was an honest, legitimate one.

One evening John Hay, a mining engineer friend, phoned excitedly after the market had closed. "Mort, I have exciting news! International Copper is trading in Vancouver at 65¢. Tomorrow at two o'clock the company is going to announce a 2% copper find plus an 85¢ underwriting, and the stock is going to be listed on the Vancouver exchange. I have the information straight from a director of the company. I'd like you to buy some stock first thing in the morning, and we'll split the profits. There's no chance of this information being wrong, because he knows I can't afford to lose and he wouldn't give me bad information."

It would be a rare individual who could refuse such a story, apparently straight from a director of a mining company, and next morning I purchased one thousand shares of International Copper at 60¢.

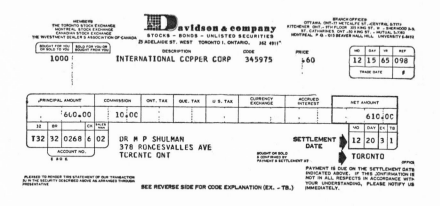

By 11 a.m. the stock was down to 55c, and I was mentally berating my own ignorance when John phoned to reassure me that all was well and that at 2 p.m. the announcement would be made. Sure enough, at 1.30 the stock began to move up, and at 2 p.m. I sold it at 84¢.

At 2:15 John Hay phoned frantically, "I've made a terrible mistake, I gave you the name of the wrong company! Let's get out and take our loss!" When I told him that I had already sold at a profit we both broke up with laughter.

The moral is that if you make money on a hot tip, it's an accident.

What about those penny mines that do find ore and go up so beautifully? Five years ago a typical penny dreadful was being sold over the phones at 35¢ while drilling was being done on the property. To the amazement of the promoter, a huge ore body was found, which meant that the stock was worth 20 to 30 times the price it was being sold for. No news of this strike was released by the promoter, because to his dismay he had sold almost all his stock. Instead, he went to work buying back all the stock from the phone customers at 50c per share. After he had it all back, he released the news, and the stock moved up to its present level of $60.

At least the clients made a little money on that one!

The classic penny stock story happened to a Toronto doctor four years ago. This man saw his holding of 250,000 shares of a two-bit stock rise all the way to $65, but he didn't sell a share all the way up and he ended up blowing the entire $16 million dollar profit.

The name of the company is Brilund and it was a typical Toronto mining promotion with the exception that the promoter did not cover his tracks very well as he removed the $1 million cash then in the treasury. He was charged and went to jail and in the aftermath Brilund stock fell from $2 to 2¢.

One of the largest "investors" in Brilund was a wealthy Toronto physician who had been conned into purchasing over 200,000 shares of stock between $1.50 and 2.00. It looked like his money was gone, but a miracle took place in the form of another Brilund shareholder, a tough American who felt that the Canadian bank in which Brilund's account had been deposited had not taken the proper precautions to prevent theft by the promoter. This U.S. citizen bought control of the apparently defunct company and on behalf of Brilund sued the bank for a million dollars. To the amazement of all the onlookers Brilund won the suit and got back its million dollars and the stock now quickly moved back to $2.50.

Now the real miracle took place. Brilund's new president went to Africa and for a few dollars purchased the exploration rights to a huge area where prospectors had searched unsuccessfully for diamonds for years. A few weeks later diamonds were found just outside the area. The stock soared; in four months it went all the way up to $65.

Every day our doctor's broker phoned him frantically urging him to sell but he steadfastly refused, certain the stock was going to $500 per share. In fact he bought more stock until his average cost rose to $7 per share.

Sad to say, no diamonds were found on Brilund's property and the stock slowly and steadily slipped downwards. Today it trades at $7 and the doctor still has his 250,000 shares.

There is one general rule in relation to penny mining stocks. *Don't buy them.* The odds are impossible.

There is, however, one exception to this rule. It is a very important one and should not be overlooked.

There are some low-priced mining stocks that have made spectacular market moves and in which no promotion was involved; for example, Pine Point went from $2 to $83, and Mattagami from $3 to $22. The trouble with this type of stock is that it is uncommon; the move is gradual, unspectacular, unadvertised; and the public never buys it until *after* it has made the big move. How can these situations be recognized early? A description of such an issue will show the points to look for.

A typical example was Newconex Holdings. This was a company formed in 1962 by giant Consolidated Goldfields of South Africa. Goldfields had been increasingly nervous about their concentration of funds in South Africa and England and, deciding to place some of their funds in safer political arenas, created subsidiaries in the United States, Australia, and Canada. These subsidiaries were set up in such a way that their shareholders literally could not lose.

Newconex originally issued 700,000 shares of stock at $5 each, of which 450,000 were purchased by Goldfields themselves, and the remaining 250,000 were sold to the public by a highly reputable Canadian stock broker, Nesbitt Thomson & Company. The $3.5 million thus raised was all placed in the Newconex treasury. Each of the 700,000 shares carried as a free bonus two options (warrants) entitling the holder to purchase 2 additional shares of Newconex at $5 at any time within a five-year period.

Simultaneously, Goldfields concluded a unique agreement with Newconex which ensured Newconex's financial success. This unprecedented agreement obliged Goldfields through a wholly owned subsidiary to begin an active program of exploration in Canada. All losses were to be borne by Goldfields, all worthless properties were to be kept by Goldfields, but Newconex was given the right to take over any successful finds from Goldfields within one year, at cost! This meant that Newconex was now an exploration company with all the possibilities of sudden upward surges in the stock that could occur with an ore find, but without any of the dangers of attrition of capital through exploration expense. In other words, this was a company that could not lose!

One would have expected a tremendous rush from the public to buy the stock, for it is not too often that a speculator is given the chance to gamble without any risk of loss. There was no rush; in fact, there was no public buying at all. Nesbitt Thomson & Co. sold the 250,000 shares available to their clients, arranged for the stock to be listed on the Toronto Stock Exchange, and then worried no further about it. Newconex stock slowly drifted downward and in a few weeks was trading at $4.25 with the two warrants still attached. The warrants themselves were trading at $1.00, and so the stock alone was valued by the buying public at only $2.25. Yet this stock had $5 in cash behind every share, plus a guarantee against loss by Goldfields.

During the next three years, Goldfields spent close to one million dollars on exploration and found nothing. Newconex was sitting with $3.5 million dollars, which they invested in stocks and bonds following the advice of Nesbitt Thomson and Company. They invested the funds remarkably well and within three years had increased their assets by over 50%. Each share now had cash and liquid assets behind it of $8.00. The disinterest of the public continued and the stock offered on the exchange was slowly bought up by two or three wealthy, knowledgeable investors and investment funds. The warrants continued to trade around $1 while the stock hung being between $4 and $5. It is interesting to note that even experts find difficulty in buying value when no promoter is spreading glamour about, and by the end of 1964 practically all of Nesbitt Thomson's clients had sold their stock. Goldfields, however, was not unaware of the tremendous value building up in Newconex, and they purchased 50,000 more shares of the company stock from Canadian Gas and Energy, a closed-end mutual (see Chapter 1) fund that had purchased the stock near its lowest prices on the Toronto stock exchange.

Goldfields now compared the results Newconex had achieved in comparison with the other subsidiaries in the United States and Australia and decided that the Canadian company had not done well enough. They requested the president's resignation and brought in Mr. Bill Robinson from Canadian Gas and Energy as the new president. By September, 1965, Newconex had become a beehive of activity. It had crews exploring in many areas of Canada (at Goldfields' expense), and it was busy examining many companies offered to it for sale.

One company that approached Newconex was Pyramid Mining, who owned a very strategic piece of ground in the North West Territories, right next to the huge Pine Point Mine. Pyramid needed money to explore this property, and Newconex agreed to supply this in return for a block of Pyramid stock.

All this activity had not appreciably affected the price of the Newconex stock, which now had liquid assets equal to $8.50 per share but which continued to trade around $5.

There is always a critical point in the stock history of under-valued mining situations like Newconex where the public suddenly sees a situation which has been obvious for years but which no one has looked at. The critical day for Newconex was October 7, 1965. On that day the *Northern Miner* ran this item on the front page:

Newconex, Conwest Share At Pine Point

Newconex Canadian Exploration, exploration a r m of Newconex Holdings, is getting into the Pine Point area in a big way.

At mid - week, the Northern Miner was able to confirm with company officials that it now holds about a 50% participation with Conwest and Central Patricia in that team's substantial and well regarded holdings which almost surround Pine Point Mines.

Conwest, which will continue as the operator, has been carrying out extensive geophysical work on this key ground all summer. Tentative plans are to drill this winter.

This was the first public notice that Newconex was busily searching for a mine, and the following week the *Miner* wrote up as exciting news what the whole mining fraternity had been ignoring for three years.

The Conwest-Central Patricia team, starting this week to drill some well regarded anomalies in the Pine Point area on ground they have held for years, new-highed at $6.75 and $1.82 respectively. But the market didn't take too much note of an exclusive story in this paper last week which revealed that Newconex Holdings as a full partner, now probably holds the largest single interest in this project, although it did gain 45¢ to reach its former all-time high of $6.15. This figure is still well below its liquid breakup value which now stands at about $8.50 per share. A unique feature of the Newconex set up permits the company to purchase anything found by its exploration arm for $15,000. The tab for this arm, Newconex Canadian Exploration, is picked up by the parent Gold Fields Mining & Industrial Ltd. of London, Eng. In other words, Newconex Holdings, the T.S.E. listing, doesn't have to spend its money on exploration. And it has a pretty capable associate in Conwest. On the other hand, this association could make available almost unlimited funds in the event of a success at Pine Point or elsewhere. **Newconex Warrants,** which give the right to buy Newconex stock at $5 per share till Feb. 28, 1967, gained 40¢ on the week to $1.65 on volume of 79,200 shares. Floating supply of both stock and warrants is unusually light, which makes for a rather explosive situation marketwise.

* * *

That did it! First the mining people, then the public, jumped in. The two contracts below illustrate the effect the sudden awakening produced:

HECTOR M. CHISHOLM & CO. LIMITED

MEMBERS
TORONTO STOCK EXCHANGE
MONTREAL STOCK EXCHANGE
CANADIAN STOCK EXCHANGE

GROUND FLOOR
82 RICHMOND STREET WEST
362-4731

TORONTO 1, CANADA

BRANCH OFFICE
KING EDWARD SHERATON HOTEL
363-3074

TO ⌐

Dr. M. Shulman,

WE HAVE THIS DAY **BOUGHT** FOR YOUR ACCOUNT ON ☑ THE TORONTO STOCK EXCHANGE ☐ THE CANADIAN STOCK EXCHANGE ☐ THE UNLISTED MARKET DATE Oct. 30/65 VALUE Oct. 5/65

BROKERS ON REQUEST	SHARES	DESCRIPTION	PRICE	AMOUNT	COMMISSION	TAX	TOTAL
Daly	200	Newconex Holdings	5.10	1020.00	30.00		1050.00

E. & O.E.

PURCHASES OR SALES ARE MADE WITH THE DISTINCT UNDERSTANDING THAT ACTUAL DELIVERY IS CONTEMPLATED, AND ARE SUBJECT IN ALL RESPECTS TO THE BY-LAWS, RULES AND CUSTOMS OF THE STOCK EXCHANGE WHERE THE ORDER IS EXECUTED AND TO THE CUSTOMS OF THE BROKERAGE BUSINESS. IT IS AGREED THAT ALL SECURITIES CARRIED FROM TIME TO TIME IN THE CUSTOMER'S MARGINAL ACCOUNT, OR DEPOSITED TO PROTECT THE SAME, MAY BE LOANED BY US OR MAY BE PLEDGED BY US ON OUR GENERAL LOANS, EITHER SEPARATELY OR TOGETHER WITH SECURITIES OR OTHERS, AND EITHER TO SECURE ADVANCES WITHIN OR IN EXCESS OF THE AMOUNT DUE US THEREON. IT IS ALSO AGREED THAT WE RESERVE THE RIGHT TO CLOSE TRANSACTIONS (WITHOUT DEMAND FOR ADDITIONAL MARGIN OR ANY OTHER NOTICE WHATSOEVER) ON A STOCK EXCHANGE OR SIMILAR INSTITUTION, OR AT ANY PUBLIC OR PRIVATE SALE, WHENEVER WE DEEM IT NECESSARY FOR OUR OWN PROTECTION BY REASON OF INSUFFICIENT MARGIN OR OTHERWISE.

HECTOR M. CHISHOLM & CO. LIMITED

WE HAVE THIS DAY SOLD FOR YOUR ACCOUNT ON	☐ THE TORONTO STOCK EXCHANGE	☐ THE CANADIAN STOCK EXCHANGE	☐ THE UNLISTED MARKET	DATE Nov. 4/65	VALUE Nov. 9/65		
BROKERS ON REQUEST	SHARES	DESCRIPTION	PRICE	AMOUNT	COMMISSION	TAX	TOTAL
Bong	200	Newconex Holdings	9.25	1850.00	40.00	2.00	1808.00

How can other Pyramids or Newconexes be recognized before their stock has moved 'way up in price? These mining prospects all have five features in common:

a. They are never sold over the phone.

b. No promoter recommends their purchase.

c. Their treasuries all contain substantial funds.

d. From 25 to 80% of their stock is held by one or more large producing mining firms.

e. The amount of stock issued to the public is small, usually less than one million shares.

There are always a few such stocks available, trading at very low prices, and their history has been almost universally a good one. But these stocks are purchased primarily by knowledgeable people in the mining business and not by the public. These are the only situations in the mining market where the purchaser is almost sure of making a profit.

What this chapter boils down to is, never buy tips or promotions; buy value and wait.

Value in the mining field in stocks under $10 is represented by Sunshine Mining at $9.50, Newconex at $5, Conwest at $8.50, and Campbell Chibougami at $6. None of these companies are being promoted; no one is getting a rake-off, and you'll get a fair run for your money. They are not for the widow or orphan, but for the businessman with a little extra money I heartily recommend them.

Yvanex Developments is an example of the type of gambling stock that is perfect for the person who is willing to risk losing a few dollars in the hope of making a big strike. The company first issued stock to the public in Toronto in August in 1972 at 48 cents a share and it fitted the six criteria perfectly. The stock is not promoted over the phone, in fact there is no promoter as such; there is ample money in the treasury to carry out the company's program; and most of the shares are being held for investment by a subsidiary of giant International Minerals of New York.

The company was set up by International Minerals in partnership with Getty Mining, a subsidiary of Getty Oil, to search for base metals in Canada. This is the type of penny stock gamble where the purchaser for once gets an even break — with Getty and International Minerals running the show we know that the exploration money will go into exploration and we also know that if a find is made the shareholders will not have it stolen from them.

This is the type of chance I like to take in penny stocks — the risk is 48 cents a share, but if the company finds an ore body the profit could be many times that.

In summary the investor should stay away from all penny stocks, while the speculator should stay away from most penny stocks. If you are going to gamble in the penny market, pick a subsidiary of one of the big companies.

5
ADVISORY SERVICES

"Our recommendations outperformed the Dow average by 37%."

"Do you own any of the stocks listed below? If so, send for our free analysis."

"Kelly warrants went from 5¢ to $32. You can learn how to make equally large profits."

These are come-ons to lure investors into subscribing to market letters and, more important, into following their advice. Market letters are the prime weapon of so-called advisory services. Many of them are crooked.

The weak market from 1966 to 1971 literally decimated the ranks of the advisory services. Over 90% of them went out of business from dispensing bad advice and gradually losing their clients (as the clients lost their money). However, since the market began to turn up again in late 1971 and the suckers have once again begun to venture back to the stock exchange, a new crop of advisors has arrived to guide the uninformed and the foolish. You can be certain that you would do better financially buying stocks blindly rather than following the advice of these gentlemen.

Advisory services should not be confused with information

services such as Standard & Poor's and/or Moody's. Firms like these specialize in selling detailed information about companies whose stocks are publicly traded. On the basis of this information, the sophisticated investor can invest his money more intelligently. There has never been any suggestion of hanky-panky among the information companies.

The advisory service is an organization presumably set up to dispense unbiased information and advice. Unfortunately, the economics of such an organization make it extremely difficult for it to be run honestly. Membership dues, which run anywhere from $5 to $500 per year, entitle the member to receipt of the weekly or biweekly market letter, plus varying amounts of individual advice on request. The average advisory service has a clientele of approximately 2,000 subscribers, and it immediately becomes apparant that the average fee of $25 per year will not yield enough gross revenue even to pay the advertising expenses.

Advertising costs are terribly high in this field, and there is an average cost of $25 to secure each subscription. Direct mail advertising is the least expensive way to get clients, but 1,000 pieces of mail bring in an average of only 10 one-year subscriptions. Newspaper advertising is even less productive, and full-page ads in the financial section have on occasion brought in only two or three subscriptions. Inasmuch as the owners of these advisory services must make money in order to remain in business, it soon becomes necessary for them to establish new sources of income. Such sources are always available.

It is an interesting fact that the written word is many times more influential than the spoken one, and written words for which clients are paying soon develop awesome powers. It is not unusual for a market letter with a circulation of 2,000 to produce buying of $200,000 or $300,000 in a stock following a one-page recommendation.

The PFR market letter (one of the better letters whose honesty has never been questioned) recommended the purchase of Campbell Chibougamau stock in December, 1965. Campbell is a junior Canadian copper mine listed on the American Stock Exchange and the Toronto Stock Exchange; it traded then at about $5 a share. Within two trading days, Campbell had traded over 100,000 shares, equivalent to over half a million dollars, and its price had jumped to over $7.00.

With powerful distribution of this type available through market letters, it is not surprising that dishonest promoters with stock to sell are attracted to them.

An additional factor making these advisory services easy marks for the dishonest is the complete lack of training necessary in order to begin an advisory service. Youths with absolutely no market knowledge have been granted licenses to start such services, and as a result their advice has often been quite unusual. It is interesting that mature intelligent investors would carefully read and follow market letters written by boys to whom they would not have given a second of time in person.

The casual way in which market letters and advisory services are begun has produced some ludicrous situations. One of the most successful letterwriters developed a large devoted clientele by getting all his market ideas from the comics, and his average was better than many who used more orthodox methods. Another market advisor bases his advice on the current situation of the stars, but he has no more stars in his eyes than have his clients.

This situation in which untrained individuals reached positions of tremendous stock placing power, yet still had difficulty in making money, inevitably resulted in stock promotors paying large sums of money in order to have the advisor recommend the purchase of their stocks. In some cases the promoter actually buys the advisory service and keeps the advisor on as a figurehead.

Before going into the details of this type of swindle, we should draw a distinction between the various types of market letters. There are three:

a. Least effective is the type which is distributed free by an individual promotion broker in an attempt to sell his own stocks. These letters may describe other stocks, but only as a come-on to show the great profits which the promoter intimates can be made in his own issue. (See Chapter 4 on penny stocks for details about this type of letter.)

b. Individual reputable stock brokers often issue free to their clients an advisory letter, distributed at regular intervals, recommending the purchase of individual stocks that the broker feels are undervalued. As a general rule, such recommendations are honestly given, and the stocks often do merit purchase. Unfortunately, a very serious abuse of these letters is now a common occurrence. Because advice of this type will often be sent to thousands of clients simultaneously (particularly when issued by the larger stockbrokers), there is often a rapid pouring into the exchange of buy orders for the stock involved, producing an immediate rise in its price. Knowing that this will occur, certain junior employees (and some not so junior) have developed a substantial sub rosa income by phoning a friend the day before the recommendation is issued to the firm's clients and having the friend purchase a block of the stock, which is sold the following day after client buying begins and the stock moves up. Because this practice has now become so very common, investors should beware of such recommendations, particularly if they have had a recent price rise.

c. The other form of market letter is the one which creates the most abuse. Subscriptions to the service are purchased on a yearly basis. The service represents itself as doing independent research and supplying unbiased advice which theoretically should enable the purchaser to improve his market performance. Humbug! Occasionally one of these services will publish a report showing that its recommendations have outperformed the market, but often these apparent good results are achieved by comparing a stock at its bid price the day before a recommendation, and no client is able to buy it at this price) with its price after it has been recommended and considerable buying has forced the price up.

Incidentally, there is one way that the nimble trader can make money from the very large advisory services. Some of the largest ones will forward their recommendations to clients by telegram in return for an additional fee. Because there is usually a price rise following these recommendations, immediate purchase of small quantities of the stock when the telegram arrives with sale the next day, regardless of the price, is often profitable. During a bull (upgoing) market, a doctor friend managed to perform this trick once a month for a year, showing a profit on eleven of the trades. Two of the trades are illustrated below. This practice is not recommended to the average speculator, however.*

Delivery Phone:
EMpire 8-7137
EMpire 4-9986

TELEX - LATIMER, TORONTO - 02-2565

TORONTO, ONT.
Confirmation Phone:
EMpire 3-8921

W. D. Latimer Limited
Security Dealers
244 BAY STREET   Nov. 2-61
Date

We have this day SOLD TO YOU

Please have cheques made payable at par in Toronto

Broker	Quantity	Security	Price	Amount	Brokerage	Tax Que. Prov.	Total
	500	Steadmans	8½	4250.00			4250.00
	700	"	8 5/8	6037.50			6037.50

Delivery Phone:
EMpire 8-7137
EMpire 4-9986

TELEX - LATIMER, TORONTO - 02-2565

TORONTO, ONT.
Confirmation Phone:
EMpire 3-8921

W. D. Latimer Limited
Security Dealers
244 BAY STREET   Nov. 2-61
Date

We have this day BOUGHT FROM YOU

Please have cheques made payable at par in Toronto

Broker	Quantity	Security	Price	Amount	Brokerage	Tax Que. Prov.	Total
	1000	Steadmans	9.00	9000.00		10.00	8990.00
	550	"	9 1/8	5018.75		5.50	5013.25
E. & O.E.							

* These two legitimate companies were recommended by an honest advisory service.

CODE		
A	AS PRINCIPAL WE HAVE SOLD TO YOU	
B'	AS AGENT WE HAVE SOLD THROUGH FROM YOU	
C	AS AGENT YOU HAVE SOLD FOR US	
D¹	AS AGENT WE HAVE PURCHASED FOR YOU	

R. A. DALY & COMPANY

MEMBERS
TORONTO STOCK EXCHANGE
THE INVESTMENT DEALERS' ASSOCIATION OF CA

R A DALY & COMPANY LIMITED HAVE PLEASURE IN CONFIRMING THE FOLLOWING TRANSACTION EFFECTED WITH YOU SUBJECT TO THE RULES AND R

CODE	ARRANGED BY	MARKET	DATE TRADE	SETTLEMENT	NO OF SHARES OR PAR VALUE	DESCRIPTION OF SECURITY	PRICE	GROSS AMOUNT	ACCRUED INTEREST	C.
D	OFFICE	NYO:	MAR 30 61	APR 7	1 00	INSTRUMENTS FOR INDUSTRY	6.½ U.S. FUNDS	650 00		

E & O E

PLEASE NOTE →
1 IF FUNDS ARE NOT ALREADY IN OUR POSSESSION PLEASE ARRANGE FOR PAYMENT DIRECT CR AGA NST DELIVERY
2 WHEN CARRYING SECURITIES FOR CLIENTS WE RESERVE THE RIGHT OF PLEDGING THE SECURITIES AND RAISING M CONVENIENT TO US CHARGING INTEREST ACCORDINGLY
3 THIS CONTRACT SHOULD BE PRESERVED FOR TAX PURPOSES AS INTEREST PAID BY YOU MAY BE OFFSET AGAINST
4 WHEN ACTING AS AGENT WE WILL FURNISH THE NAME OF THE OTHER BROKER OR BROKERS INVOLVED IN THE TRA
SETTLEMENT MAY BE EFFECTED AT THE BRANCH THROUGH WHICH YOU ARE DEALING STREET ADDRESS OF WI

CODE		
W¹	AS PRINCIPAL WE HAVE PURCHASED FROM YOU	
X	AS AGENT WE HAVE PURCHASED THROUGH TO YOU	
Y	AS AGENT YOU HAVE PURCHASED FOR US	
Z	AS AGENT WE HAVE SOLD FOR YOU	

R. A. DALY & COMPANY

MEMBERS
TORONTO STOCK EXCHANGE
THE INVESTMENT DEALERS' ASSOCIATION OF CA

R A DALY & COMPANY LIMITED HAVE PLEASURE IN CONFIRMING THE FOLLOWING TRANSACTION EFFECTED WITH YOU SUBJECT TO THE RULES AND R

CODE	ARRANGED BY	MARKET	DATE TRADE	SETTLEMENT	NO OF SHARES OR PAR VALUE	DESCRIPTION OF SECURITY	PRICE	GROSS AMOUNT	ACCRUED INTEREST	C
Z	OFFICE	NY	MAR 30 61	APR 7	1 00	INSTRUMENTS FOR INDUSTRY	0.00 U.S. FUNDS	1 000 00		

E & O E

PLEASE NOTE →
1 IF NOT ALREADY IN OUR POSSESSION PLEASE ARRANGE FOR DELIVERY OF THE RELATIVE STOCK CERTIFICATES OR
2 ANY EXPENSE INCURRED THROUGH FAILURE TO DELIVER SECURITIES IN PROPER TRANSFERABLE FORM SHALL BE
3 THIS CONTRACT SHOULD BE PRESERVED FOR TAX PURPOSES AS INTEREST PAID TO YOU MUST BE REPORTED TO T
4 WHEN ACTING AS AGENT WE WILL FURNISH THE NAME OF THE OTHER BROKER OR BROKERS INVOLVED IN THE T
SETTLEMENT MAY BE EFFECTED AT THE BRANCH THROUGH WHICH YOU ARE DEALING, STREET ADDRESS OF WI

There is one special profit-making device that is used by Canadians subscribing to large U.S. advisory services. Because many U.S. and Canadian holidays do not coincide, on about six Mondays a year U.S. markets are closed while Canadian markets are open, and on those days there is no U.S. mail delivery but there is one in Canada. The large advisory services send their market letters out on weekends so that their

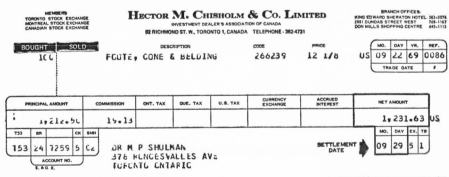

clients all receive them simultaneously on Monday morning. On these special Mondays when the U.S. subscribers, who represent 95% of the purchases, cannot get their market letter the Canadians have a one-day jump on them.

American investors should take care in purchasing recommended interlisted securities following a holiday. They should remember that the Canadians already had first crack at them.

The subscription services can be subdivided into four subtypes:

1. The strictly honest service giving honest advice for a fee. There are a few of these in existence, but unfortunately it is impossible for the ordinary investor to distinguish them from their not-so-honest cousins. The problem facing the honest service is that, in order to make a financial go of the business, it must develop a large paying clientele, and the cost of so doing is prohibitively high.

One of my friends, thinking that a strictly honest letter *had* to be a success, opened such a service. After two years he found that he had recommended 40 stocks of which 36 had gone up. He had 800 clients and he was earning $20 a week. He closed the service and took a job as a customer's man. During the two years he was publishing, he had over one dozen offers of financial support from various promoters. The honest advisor either does not buy any securities or else lists any securities which he purchases in his advisory letter.

2. The semi-honest service giving what they consider to be good advice on a variety of industrial and mining securities. This type of advisor never takes a payoff, but he ensures his financial success by buying up blocks of the stock he intends to recommend and then resells it to his own clients. He never does this under his own name but hides the transaction by using a friend or relative. This type of advisor never gets rich, because he usually recommends basically sound issues which rarely have a large percentage improvement in price in such a short interval.

Occasionally one of these services gets its comeuppance. The owner of Strang Advisory Service purchased a block of stock in Webb

& Knapp (Canada) at $2.00 and then recommend its purchase to his clients. It immediately jumped to $2.50, and the advisor was happy to dump his stock and make a nice $15,000 profit. In the following weeks Webb & Knapp continued to move higher, and when it reached $3, the advisor began to sell it short, knowing that it had gone up only because of his recommendation and so expecting an imminent drop. When it reached $3.50 he sent out an urgent telegram to all his clients, recommending profit-taking through immediate sale of Webb & Knapp. His clients sold all right, but the stock continued to move higher, reaching $4.75 one week after his urgent sell advice. Unfortunately for our advisor, what he did not realize was that a much larger New York based service had just recommended purchase of Webb & Knapp!

The stock that had been sold short was bought back at a net loss of just under $20,000. After the advisory services and the short selling were finished, the stock gradually slipped back to $2, which was what it was worth through all the gyrations.

A surprising number of these advisors are chartists, who choose their recommendations by study of the volumes traded and prices recorded of an individual stock over a period of time. A chartist will make a daily record of many stocks, in each case producing a graph showing volume and price. He will study those graphs, looking for certain telltale signs which will indicate to him a "breakout is coming" or "topping is occurring" or "the long-term trend line has been broken". On the basis of this "information" he will recommend purchase or sale of the security involved. This method of forecasting price movements has proven almost as accurate as that of studying the stars or the comics, but unlike these latter methods, charting has thousands of adherents. The theory upon which charting is based is that the market itself cannot be fooled, and all future price movements are forecast by increased or decreased buying and selling. By studying past price movements, they believe that they have discovered certain repeating patterns. It's something like the man who says that since there were 25 years between the beginning of the first and second world wars, a third war should have started in October, 1964. The fact that it didn't doesn't shake his conviction. He believes that this is just an exception.

Chartists have an equally blind faith, and some of them are so blinded by their delusion that they will actually buy stock in a company after studying a chart without knowing the company's earnings or even what business it is in! This mass delusion has been instrumental in producing several millionaires; not the chartists, but those who prey on them. One wealthy New Yorker who runs the markets on several stocks has carefully studied the chart system and has developed a specialty of trading his controlled stocks so as to produce the patterns which a chartist believes indicates a move upwards. Using this unique method, he has sold several million dollars worth of overvalued stocks. He is the only person I have ever met who boasts of the value of charts and can prove it!

3. The individually owned advisory service in which the majority of the recommendations are legitimate, except that every few weeks a "clinker" is thrown in. This clinker is a stock in which a promoter wishes to produce buying in order to sell some of his own position. He will pay the adviser either on a volume basis or a flat rate. The flat rate can vary anywhere from a few hundred dollars up to $25,000 for an all-out recommendation in a well-regarded advisory sheet. The volume basis used to be the most popular method; the promoter was required to pay a fee varying from 15 to 25% of the price of the stock on every share traded in the four days following the recommendations. This method fell into disuse because, alas, there is truly no honour amongst these gentlemen, and the promoters soon found that a great deal more stock was trading than they were selling. What was happening was that the advisor had placed a number of phoney buy and sell orders which cancelled each other out but increased the volume of trading tremendously.

Inasmuch as these advisory services intended to remain in business and hoped to sell a great many more stocks to the same clients, they naturally did not wish to see their recommended stocks collapse, for this would make future sales immeasurably more difficult. Thus the price paid for the recommendation would vary a great deal, depending on who was the promoter. One gentleman still active in the promotion field was well known for selling every possible share after a service had recommended one of his stocks and then letting the price of the stock collapse. He managed to get control of a wide group of companies, varying all the way from furniture stores to mining prospects, but every one of his enterprises ended disastrously for the shareholders. In one case he paid $25,000 to a flourishing advisory service to recommend the purchase of one of his mining prospects trading at 80¢. Over the next two days he sold out his entire position, pocketed over a quarter of a million dollars, and made no further effort to support the price of the stock. It rapidly declined to 10¢, and the advisory service never completely recovered from the loss of confidence which resulted.

On the other hand, there are other promoters who look at the longer picture, and who will at least make some effort to support their stocks after a recommendation is made. These men find it cheaper to do business with owners of market letters than do the more ruthless operators. One of these promoters owns about a dozen small mining companies, each in a different branch of the industry — silver, gold, copper, lead, and zinc. Because each of these different metals has its periods of popularity, he concentrates on selling the particular group which is then "hot". He describes himself whimsically as, "Just a grocer. When they want apples I sell them apples, and when thy want bananas I sell them bananas. I keep them all on the shelves, and sooner or later someone wants to buy them." This man uses advisory services frequently and for several years paid a weekly retainer of $300 to one service to ensure that the owner did not close any deals with other promoters!

The various companies owned by this last promoter are all basically sound, none of them has collapsed, and actually the buyers of these stocks would not be making nearly as bad an error as most persons buying through the advice of a market letter. The real trouble is that the stocks are all overpriced when they are recommended.

4. The type of advisory service most dangerous to the public is the one that is deliberately set up by a promoter as a "front" to get rid of worthless or overpriced stocks. Sometimes huge sums of money are spent in building up such a service through widespread advertising, or alternatively, a well-established service may be purchased outright. In either case the story is the same — several weeks or even months of carefully restrained recommendations of a large number of high-grade securities followed by an all-out recommendation of the stock that the promoter wishes to sell.

These tactics can be very effective, and although it may take $100,000 or more to build up such a service, it is possible for the organizers to take in in excess of a million dollars in a matter of two or three days.

Jerrett Motors stock was distributed in just such a way. This was a company set up to market a new type of low gas-consumption automobile engine that the promoter, Henry Severn, claimed would revolutionize the market. Severn was a handsome, charming man with considerable experience in distribution of stocks in various companies in Europe and the Middle East. When he arrived in New York, he was on the wanted list of the police of France and Turkey for stock fraud. His first step was to buy control of Jerrett Motors, a small, privately owned firm that had been supplying automobile parts to several auto manufacturers for years. Their sales had never exceeded $1,000,000 per year, and net profit had been only $15,000 in the preceding year. Management was happy to sell control of the company for $120,000.

Henry Severn now "went public". He announced that Jerrett Motors had purchased for $500,000 the North American rights to distribute a new type of automobile engine that provided the same service as current models, consumed one-tenth the gasoline, and would sell for less than $100. The business world was electrified by this announcement, and Severn had no difficulty in persuading Lawford and Company, a small but reputable broker, to underwrite and distribute a public issue of one million shares of stock at $1.75 per share. The 1¾ million dollars thus placed in the treasury was immediately depleted by $500,000, which Severn said was being forwarded to the inventor in France. The vice-president of Lawford and Company went on the board of Jerrett to represent and protect Lawford's customers.

Eddy Collins (remember him from the penny stock fraud?) meanwhile had set up a stock advisory service whose market letter was mailed from London. In dozens of European and U.S. newspapers, ads appeared offering an all encompassing advisory service for only $10 per year. The advertisements listed ten stocks that "Heather Investment Services" had recommended in the past year which had doubled in price.

Collins offered as a "free" service to evaluate all stocks held by new clients and promised that those who followed his advice would double their money by spring.

The response to the series of ads was phenomenal, and within four months Heather Investment Services had a paid circulation of over 5,000. The service then began to recommend the purchase of Jerrett Motors. In the advisory letters, the history of I.B.M. was related in detail: How the company had brought new inventions to the marketplace and how their stock had gone from $5 to $800. Every week this line appeared: "An investment of $1,000 in I.B.M. grew in 10 years to $200,000." Heather Investment Service stressed that Jerrett Motors now had a new invention that was going to capture the entire automotive market; they suggested that the large auto manufacturers were desperately trying to buy control, and that the stock could very easily go to $100 per share in weeks.

The clients bought, and Jerrett stock went up in a few weeks to $4 per share. Now Collins was able to write in his bulletin, "I said Jerrett Motors would double in 2 months and it has. Now I say it will double again in the next month. This is the I.B.M. of 1964, and before this year is out the stock may very well trade at $1,000." This brought in about 200,000 shares of buying, and within three weeks the stock was up to $10.

By now the directors of Lawford and Company were becoming nervous. Their persistent requests to see the invention were answered by a private showing of a small automobile engine, which because of "technical difficulties", they were not allowed to operate. They were promised, however, that there would be a public demonstration within a few days. Their requests for an accounting as to where the million dollars withdrawn from the treasury for "development purposes" had been spent received only vague answers, and their representative was voted down when he demanded an outside audit. Lawford and Company had no choice. Their vice president resigned from Jerrett's board, and Lawford phoned all their clients to whom they had sold Jerrett stock and advised them to get rid of it. They could have saved themselves the trouble; their clients were all sophisticated investors and had already sold practically all of their holdings. Strange rumours of looting of the company's treasury and a question as to the actual existence of the engine itself were already circulating on Wall Street, and Lawford's clients had been happy to triple their money and get out.

Now began the most reprehensible part of the whole scheme. Eddy Collins had a list of the securities held by 4,000 of his subscribers, and he began a mail and then a phone campaign to urge them to sell all these excellent securities and replace them with stock of Jerrett Motors, which had quadrupled just as he had predicted and which he said was certain to move up astronomically during the next few weeks.

His campaign was highly successful, and a deluge of buying of Jerrett stock followed. It continued to move higher, reaching $24 by late spring.

Henry Severn was meanwhile selling his stock as fast as the orders poured in and had by now disposed of close to 1 million of his 1½ million shares. He had now run into a problem in the form of short selling. This is the sale of stock not owned by the seller in the belief that the stock will go down and can be repurchased at a lower level. The rumours about the company had increased to loud rumbles after the resignation of Lawford's vice president, and professional traders were selling Jerrett stock at a rapidly increasing rate. There was now a total short position of over 200,000 shares, and the short selling was now almost equal to the buying pouring in from Collins subscribers. In order for Severn to get rid of the remaining half million shares he now took a final two steps. He placed full-page ads in the financial press, announcing the placing of the engine on retail sale the following month, and he announced that Jerrett Motors had received a takeover offer equivalent to $110 per share from Instrument Controls, a Canadian firm. Instrument Controls was a dummy corporation with no assets that Severn had set up for this very purpose a year earlier.

Although the announcements brought in about 100,000 shares of buying, to Severn's dismay it also produced almost as much short selling, and he now decided to take one final irrevocable step before closing down the operation.

Severn took a one-day trip to Nice which he spent in consultations with Collins. When he returned in New York the following morning, the plans had been settled. Three days later twenty-four stock exchange members received special delivery letters from Geneva. Enclosed in each was a certified cheque for $120,000 on the nonexistent "Royal Bank of Geneva" plus a letter ordering the immediate purchase of 4,000 shares of Jerrett Motors. The letters were signed "Henry Da Silva, Royal Bank of Geneva". Five of the brokers were sufficiently suspicious to phone or wire Geneva before placing the orders. The other nineteen, unfortunately, were not so cautious. By 11 a.m. they had bought 76,000 shares of Jerrett at $25 per share. At 11:10 a.m. the exchange, now aware of the fraud, began to phone every member to warn them. The brokers tried to dump the Jerrett stock, and by 11.30 a.m. it was down to 75¢.

The next day Henry Severn disappeared, and three months later Jerrett declared bankruptcy. The company had been thoroughly looted and had no assets. The miracle engine had never existed. Henry Severn has not been heard from since, but is believed to be living in Rio de Janeiro. Edward Collins closed down his London advisory service and returned to Nice. He has purchased his villa and is reported anxious to invest in any promising business.

The clients who bought Jerrett have surprisingly little bitterness toward Collins. A number of them have remarked, "We had received good advice — after all, the stock did go up tenfold. If only we had sold out!"

In summary, it is too difficult for the ordinary investor to tell the good letter from the dishonest one and the good recommendations from the bad, so the best advice that can be given in connection with advisory letters is *Don't:*

Don't subscribe.
Don't read them.
Don't follow their advice.

If an investor or speculator needs advice, the place to go is to a reputable broker. The New York exchange is now policing its members sufficiently closely that membership in that exchange is the best guarantee of impartiality in giving advice.

⑥
CONVERTIBLE
BONDS

What must we seek in order to find the ideal investment?

First, there must be absolute security of capital.

Second, there must be an adequate yield of dividends or interest.

Third, there must be the possibility, or better still, the likelihood, of large capital gains.

Fourth, this security must be one that can be easily sold very quickly and turned into cash, that is, it must be liquid.

This ideal investment is found *only* in the field of convertible bonds. The convertible bond is the single most important type of investment possible, for it combines the best features of both the bond and stock markets.

A stock represents ownership in a firm and as such will vary in value, depending on how well the firm is doing. A bond, on the other hand, is a loan from the bondholder to the firm, and unless the firm goes bankrupt, the bond will always be worth its face value. It may not always be possible to sell it for its face value, but every bond is a loan for a fixed period of time, and when that time has run out, the firm must repay the face value of the loan.

The advantages of a bond over a stock are safety of capital and a sure income. The disadvantages are the absence of any hope of capital gain plus the lack of protection from inflation, or devaluation of the dollar. The advantages of stock over bonds are the excellent possibility of capital gains plus the protection against inflation or devaluation. The disadvantages are the complete lack of safety of capital and the absence of a sure income. The convertible bond is an amalgam of the advantages of both bond and stock with elimination of the disadvantages.

What is a convertible bond? It is a bond with the added feature that it can be changed into stock at the holder's option at any time;

in other words, it is convertible. It is easiest to explain by taking a specific example. Rittersporn Dairies wishes to raise $10 million and issues ten-year convertible bonds to that total face value. The bonds pay 5¾% annually. Each $1,000 bond is convertible into one hundred shares of Rittersporn Dairies at any time during the bond's life. Rittersporn Dairies stock was selling at $8 per share at the time of the bond issue. Inasmuch as the $1,000 bond can be changed into one hundred shares of stock, this would put a cost of $10 per share on each share of stock, so obviously there is no point in making the conversion if the stock is selling at less than that on the open market. If, however, a year later Rittersporn has used the $10 million judiciously, the company's earnings may well have had a very big jump, and the stock that was selling at $8 previously now may have moved up to $15. Because each bond can be converted into one hundred shares of stock, the bond which cost $1,000 a year earlier is now worth 100 X $15 or $1,500 — a capital gain of 50% in one year. If, on the other hand, things do not go well with Rittersporn and the stock sells down to $2 per share, the bondholder has lost nothing, for he is still holding his bond and drawing his 5¾% interest.

Thus the holder of a convertible bond can gain if the company's stock goes up but cannot lose if it goes down. Many a stockholder would like to be in this happy position. I know of several millionaire investors who buy only convertible bonds.

There is one unique set of circumstances that can force down the price of a convertible bond, at least temporarily. There are two factors holding up the price of the bond: its convertibility into common stock and its rate of income as a straight bond. In order for the bond to fall in resale value there must be a combination of a collapse of the price of the stock plus a general rise in bond interest rates, i.e. a simultaneous collapse of both the bond and stock markets.

This unlikely combination took place in the world money markets from 1967 to 1970, and many holders of convertible bonds saw the value of their bonds fall to as low as 50% of face value (if they had held the equivalent stocks at the same time they would have lost a much higher percentage of face value). In 1971-2, however, all of these bonds made massive recoveries because even in cases where the stock's price did not go back up, as world interest rates fell once again the bond's value as a straight bond rose.

The airline bonds were good examples of this temporary disaster. Eastern Airlines in 1968 issued 8% convertible bonds due in 1988. Over the next three years the price of Eastern's stock plummeted from $30 all the way to $14. The price of the convertible bond fell to $800. However by September 1972 that bond was back to $1,100. People who bought at a discount made huge profits. Straight purchasers made as much as 40% on their investments in one year. Margin (credit) purchases made as much as 350% profit in one year.

What firms issue convertible bonds and why? Dozens of issues of this type come out yearly. There is not an industry that has not had convertible bonds, and there is hardly a leading corporation that has not issued them at some time. There are three reasons for issuing a convertible bond rather than an ordinary one. The first is to enable the issuer to pay a lower interest rate. Naturally a convertible bond is easier to sell than an ordinary one, and so it is possible to pay an interest rate 1/2% or even 1% lower than otherwise. This can mean a saving of millions of dollars over the life of the bond. Second, the overall trend of stock prices is upwards, resulting in conversion of most of these bonds into stock before they become due. It is, of course, not necessary for the borrowing firm to repay any bonds that are converted and so this is often a way to avoid raising the money to redeem the bonds. Third, many firms have a small stock capitalization and a large bond debt. But issuing convertible bonds that are ultimately changed into stock, they succeed in increasing the size of their stock base; they have more stock and thus more shareholders. Any firm interested in public relations is anxious to have many shareholders as possible, because shareholders tend to be very faithful customers.

Examples of convertible bonds that have proven very profitable to their owners are shown below. The best type of convertible bond is one in which there may be a wide fluctuation in the price of the stock, such as a pipeline, as this will make it more likely for the bond to go up.

In this particular example the Westcoast bonds went up on the day of issue and there was a sizeable profit without any investment. On other convertible pipeline bonds large fortunes have been made from small investments.

(It should be noted that although bonds are issued in denominations of $1,000, they are always quoted in units of 100 for brevity. Thus on the previous contract, although the bonds were sold for $1.052.50 each, the sale price was quoted at 105¼.)

A few years ago Interprovincial Pipeline made an issue of convertible debentures at $1,000 each before the company began to pipe oil.

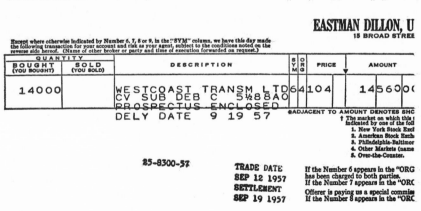

After four years the company's earnings were zooming upwards, as was the bid on the stock, and the convertible debentures sold up to $5,000 each. Because the risk on these bonds is minimal, they can be purchased by putting up only 10% deposit (or margin) instead of the 50% required on stocks. Thus each bond can be purchased with $100 down payment. At the time of issue, a Toronto gynecologist invested $5,000 in these bonds on margin, for which he received a face value of $50,000 worth of bonds. The remaining $45,000 was supplied by the bank. When the doctor sold out five years later, he made a net profit of $200,000 from his $5,000 investment.

Some utility and pipeline convertibles have proven to be tremendous financial successes, and the result is that they all become hot issues when first brought out, a happy situation for those who do not wish to keep the bonds but are pleased to make an immediate profit without any investment.

In this example the El Paso bonds went up 1¼% in the hour after being issued, and there was a $100 profit without any investment.

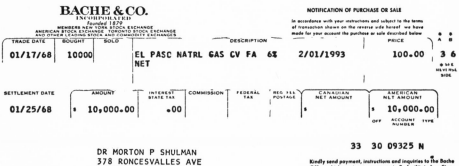

HECTOR M. CHISHOLM & CO. LIMITED

INVESTMENT DEALER'S ASSOCIATION OF CANADA
82 RICHMOND ST. W., TORONTO 1, CANADA   TELEPHONE · 362-4731

BRANCH OFFICES
KING EDWARD SHERATON HOTEL   363-3074
2881 DUNDAS STREET WEST   769-1167
DON MILLS SHOPPING CENTRE   445-1113

BOUGHT	SOLD	DESCRIPTION	CODE	PRICE		MO.	DAY	YR.	REF.
	10000	EL PASO NATURAL GAS CO. CONV. 6⅜FEB 1/93	948380	101.25	US	01	30	68	136
						TRADE DATE			#

PRINCIPAL AMOUNT	COMMISSION	ONT. TAX	QUE. TAX	U.S. TAX	CURRENCY EXCHANGE	ACCRUED INTEREST	NET AMOUNT	
10,125.00	25.00	3.00				1.67	10,098.67	US

T53	BR		CK	SMN			MO.	DAY	EX.	TB
T53	24	7259	5	02	DR M P SHULMAN 378 RONCESVALLES AVE TORONTO ONTARIO	SETTLEMENT DATE	02	02	8	1

ACCOUNT NO.
E. & O. E.

WE ARE PLEASED TO RENDER THIS STATEMENT OF OUR TRANSACTION WITH YOU IN THE SECURITY DESCRIBED ABOVE AS ARRANGED THROUGH OUR REPRESENTATIVE.

U S FUNDS ACCT   SEE REVERSE SIDE FOR CODE EXPLANATION (EX.—TB.)

PAYMENT IS DUE ON THE SETTLEMENT DATE INDICATED ABOVE. IF THIS CONFIRMATION IS NOT IN ALL RESPECTS IN ACCORDANCE WITH YOUR UNDERSTANDING. PLEASE NOTIFY US IMMEDIATELY.

In some cases where no investment is made the profits can be amazingly high. Bache underwrote an issue of convertible bonds of Helmerich & Payne in January, 1968. They were issued at $1,000 each and within half a day were trading at just under $1,060.

BACHE & CO.

INCORPORATED
Founded 1879
MEMBERS NEW YORK STOCK EXCHANGE
AMERICAN STOCK EXCHANGE   TORONTO STOCK EXCHANGE
AND OTHER LEADING STOCK AND COMMODITY EXCHANGES

NOTIFICATION OF PURCHASE OR SALE

In accordance with your instructions and subject to the terms of transaction shown on the reverse side hereof, we have made for your account the purchase or sale described below

TRADE DATE	BOUGHT	SOLD	DESCRIPTION			PRICE	* A	* B
12/21/67	10000		HELMERICH&PAINE CV NET	JD 5⅜	12/01/1987	100.00	3 SEE REVERSE SIDE	6

SETTLEMENT DATE	AMOUNT	INTEREST STATE TAX	COMMISSION	FEDERAL TAX	REG. FEE POSTAGE	CANADIAN NET AMOUNT	AMERICAN NET AMOUNT
01/03/68	$ 10,000.00	.00			$		$ 10,000.00

OFF   ACCOUNT NUMBER   TYPE

DR MORTON P SHULMA=
378 RONCESVALLES AVE   30-09325-33
TORONTO ONT CANADA

33   30 09325 E

send payment, instructions and inquiries to the Bache which services your account. To facilitate handling,) to mention your Account Number.

al settlement for securities bought and delivery of securities)st be made not later than the settlement date indicated. verse side for explanation of type and * symbol.

525

HECTOR M. CHISHOLM & CO. LIMITED

INVESTMENT DEALER'S ASSOCIATION OF CANADA
82 RICHMOND ST. W., TORONTO 1, CANADA   TELEPHONE · 362-4731

BRANCH OFFICES
KING EDWARD SHERATON HOTEL   363-3074
2881 DUNDAS STREET WEST   769-1167
DON MILLS SHOPPING CENTRE   445-1113

BOUGHT	SOLD	DESCRIPTION	CODE	PRICE		MO.	DAY	YR.	REF.
	10000	HELMERICH & PAYNE CONV. DTO3JAN68 5⅜1DEC87	954123	106.00	US	01	16	68	210
						TRADE DATE			#

PRINCIPAL AMOUNT	COMMISSION	ONT. TAX	QUE. TAX	U.S. TAX	CURRENCY EXCHANGE	ACCRUED INTEREST	NET AMOUNT	
10,600.00	25.00	3.00				26.39	10,598.39	US

T53	BR		CK	SMN			MO.	DAY	EX.	TB
T53	24	7259	5	02	DR M P SHULMAN 378 RONCESVALLES AVE TORONTO ONTARIO	SETTLEMENT DATE	01	22	8	1

ACCOUNT NO.
E. & O. E.

ARE PLEASED TO RENDER THIS STATEMENT OF OUR TRANSACTION TH YOU IN THE SECURITY DESCRIBED ABOVE AS ARRANGED THROUGH IP REPRESENTATIVE.

U S FUNDS ACCT   SEE REVERSE SIDE FOR CODE EXPLANATION (EX.—TB.)

PAYMENT IS DUE ON THE SETTLEMENT DATE INDICATED ABOVE. IF THIS CONFIRMATION IS NOT IN ALL RESPECTS IN ACCORDANCE WITH YOUR UNDERSTANDING. PLEASE NOTIFY US IMMEDIATELY.

Profit $600!

Although clients of other firms received small allotments, the best allotments went to the customers of the various underwriters. An individual ordering and receiving $50,000 worth of these debentures would have made a one-day profit of $3,000.

Another excellent reason to buy convertible bonds is their resistance to decline even when all other bonds are falling. During recent years there has been an overall rise in interest rates. This in turn has produced an equally steady fall in the market price of outstanding bond issues, with the prominent exception of most convertible bonds. The very fact of their convertibility tends to hold up their price level even when all other bonds fall.

Below is a list of outstanding convertible bonds quoted in a recent paper:

CONVERTIBLES

Ackl 7½ 15 Jun 1988	87.00	89.00
Alla Gas 7½ 1 Feb 1990	133.50	135.50
BlocB 6½ 15 Oct 1988	85.00	87.00
ConsG 5½ 1 Feb 1989	100.00	102.00
Dynasty 7 1 April 1987	77.00	82.00
Emco 7 1 Aug 1991	106.50	108.50
Scurry Rain 7¼ 1 May 1988	91.00	93.00
Simps S 4½ 15 Oct 1988	96.00	100.00
TrCP 5 1 Dec 1989	99.00	102.00
Wcoast 7½ 1 Jan 1991	125.00	127.00

Unlike ordinary bond lists in the above paper, none of the high-grade convertible bonds in the list has had a serious drop.

Convertible bonds in less seasoned enterprises are naturally more volatile.

In 1969 an exploratory speculative company, Crystal Oil, listed on the American Stock Exchange, issued high yield 7% convertibles at $1,000 each.

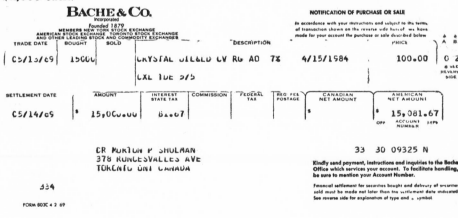

Within three days I was able to sell my bonds at a 26% profit.

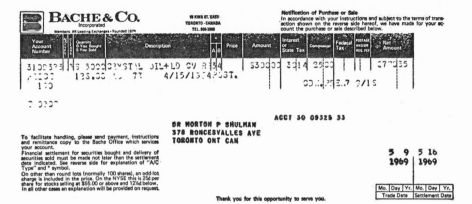

I was quite pleased with myself until I glanced at their price five months later and saw that they were trading at $1,800 each. Subsequently the price of speculative oil stocks plunged and the bonds fell all the way down to $800. I wish that I had repurchased them there. Today they are back up to $1,100.

In some cases like this one, the price of the bond went up even before the bill for payment had arrived.

The convertible bonds of more seasoned companies are a much more attractive investment, however, because although the profits may be somewhat less, the risks are almost nil.

Greyhound Coach Lines in March, 1958, issued 5½% convertible debentures at $1,000 each.

In the next six months the stock market action was poor, Greyhound did not appear to be doing any better, and its stock dipped downwards. Yet the bonds held up and were worth $1,020 at the end of this difficult period.

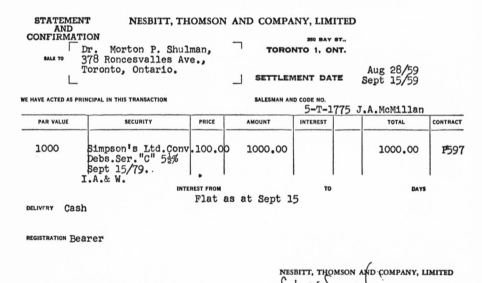

In September of 1958 a widow friend purchased ten of these debentures, for which she paid $10,200. She drew 5½% interest for three years and then resold them for $17,000. This was truly the ideal investment for "widow and orphan".

Some first-grade companies have seen their convertible debentures do even better. A Simpson (Sears Roebuck) convertible issued in 1959 for $1,000 and paying 5½% was worth $1,800 six years later.

One less common type of convertible debenture is occasionally issued by the company which is just beginning to have public ownership. Because no one is quite sure how much the stock will earn, it may be difficult to sell stock publicly at a reasonable price. The issuing corporation gets around this by issuing convertible debentures.

For example, in 1957 Canadian Utilities, the Manitoba Power Company, decided to seek shareholders in order to have funds for expansion. 5¾% convertible debentures were issued at $995 each.

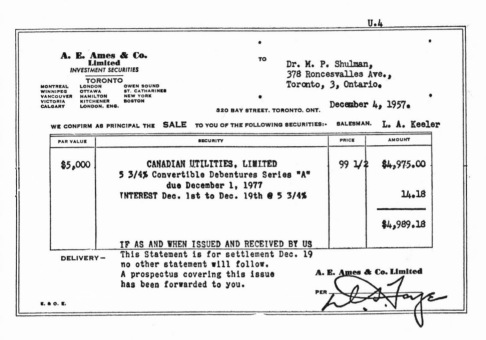

Because this was a utility, earnings did not move up spectacularly as did some of our other examples, but they did move up slowly and steadily. By 1959 the debentures were worth $1,145 each, plus interest.

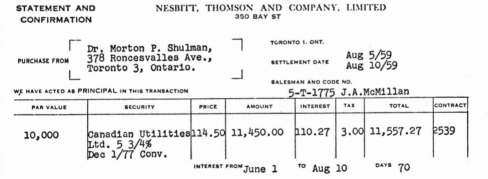

Growth continued at the same rate of 7% per year plus the 5¾% interest, and the same widow mentioned earlier sold her Canadian Utilities debentures in 1962 for $1,360 each. Some widows do better than their advisors!

In times of falling interest rates, buying convertible bonds can be very exciting. 1971 was such a time and because the rates were falling so rapidly, bonds often rose even though the price of the company's stock did not move at all. Itel was an example of such a situation.

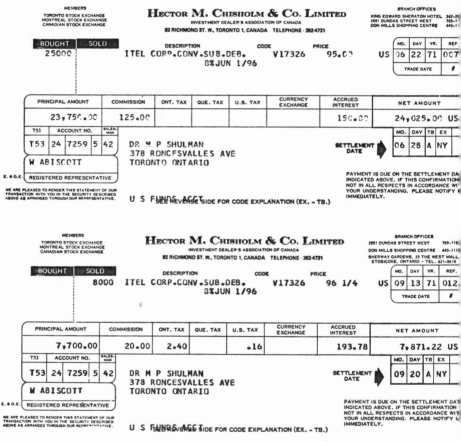

There is really only one pitfall to watch for in investing in a convertible bond. It must be remembered that when any bond is bought, money is being loaned by the purchaser to the corporation issuing the bond. Therefore, one should not purchase a convertible bond from any corporation from whom one would not purchase an ordinary bond, because the danger in any loan is that the borrower will not be able to repay his loan. As in any other business, an excellent criterion of whether a loan will be repaid is whether previous loans have been repaid.

A simple yardstick by which to judge a company's convertible bonds is the name of the underwriting broker. If he is a member of a major stock exchange who is doing a moderate amount of underwriting, he will not imperil his reputation by issuing stock in an unsound corporation.

One other important matter to consider is the conversion price of the stock, that is, how many shares are received if the bond is converted into stock. If the figure is ten shares per $1,000 bond, the purchaser will be paying $100 per share if he converts. This conversion figure is usually 10% to 15% above the current price of the stock. If it is more than 20% above the current stock price, then the stock must move up a long way before the conversion feature will have any value, and the bond should not be bought. The closer the conversion figure to the current price of the stock, the more attractive is the bond.

Thus the basic rules in buying convertible bonds are as follows:
1. The underwriter should be a member of a major stock exchange.
2. The company should have a record of earnings and should have assets well in excess of the face value of the bonds.
3. The company should be in an industry where there is a possibility of growth.
4. The conversion price of the bond should be within 15% of the current price of the stock.
5. The interest paid by the bond should be within 1% of that paid on non-convertible corporation bonds.

There are several dozen such issues every year. When buying them you cannot lose. By confining your investments only to this type of issue and diversifying among a number of convertible bonds, you are certain of large profits plus good income. *Buy them!*

7
CONVERTIBLE PREFERRED

Convertible bonds are ideal investments. Convertible preferred are *almost* ideal, and they should not be overlooked, for they offer great possibilities of capital gains with a limited risk.

Ownership of a company is represented by common stock, which gives both the privileges and danger of ownership. The privileges are the right to vote and appoint the management of the company plus the reward of participating in increased profits. The danger is the possibility of losing money if the company does not do well and earnings fall. Preferred stock is a compromise security between high risk common stock and low or no risk bonds. Preferred stockholders receive a fixed annual dividend, which is usually higher than the yield paid to the company's bondholders, but they do not have a vote unless their dividend is in arrears, and they do not participate in any increase in earnings. Unlike a bondholder, a preferred stockholder cannot be certain of getting his capital back on a fixed date, for preferred stock does not run for a specified length of time, although it can be redeemed if the company so decides. Normally preferreds are only redeemed when money is freely available and can be borrowed by the company for less interest than is being paid on the outstanding preferred.

The preferred shareholder has two advantages over the common stockholder. The preferred dividends must be paid every year before the company considers any payment to its common shareholders. These preferred dividends are usually cumulative, and if one year a firm cannot pay its preferred dividend, it must save up the missed money in succeeding years and pay off all missed preferred dividends before beginning any payments on its common stock. The other advantage is that in any windup, bankruptcy, or dissolution of the company, preferred shareholders must be paid the value of their stock in full before anything can be paid to the common stockholders. However, preferred shareholders rank behind bondholders and all other creditors in such a windup.

Thus the preferred share has two real advantages:

1. Temporarily increased yield.
2. Preference over the common share in receipt of dividends and in case of a windup of the company.

These relatively minor advantages do not compensate for the very serious disadvantages:

1. No participation in increased company earnings as with common stock.
2. No certainty of capital return as with bonds.
3. The likehood of preferred stock being redeemed if interest rates fall.
4. No protection against inflation.

Therefore, the wise investor will normally completely avoid preferred stocks, with one major exception — the convertible preferred.

Just as the convertible bond was developed to meet some of the drawbacks of bonds, similarly convertible preferred stock was developed for the company that wished to issue preferred stock but found that to do so would require a terribly high interest rate. Instead, prospective buyers can be attracted by the lure of convertibility. A convertible preferred stock carries the right to convert it into common stock, thus giving the relative safety and assured yield of the preferred stock plus the possibility of making capital gains if the common stock goes up.

A typical example of a convertible preferred was issued by Allis Chalmers in May 1965. Money was becoming tighter at that time and yields were rising. Rather than pay 5% or more for the necessary money, Allis Chalmers issued a 4.2% convertible preferred at $100 per share.

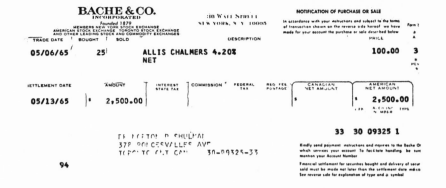

Each share of this new preferred was convertible into three and a half shares of Allis Chalmers common stock, which was then trading on the New York Stock Exchange at $28 per share. If the common stock were to move up in price over $30 per share, it is clear that the convertible feature would have given the preferred an increased value over its $100 issue price. If, for example, the Allis Chalmers common stock doubled to $56 per share, the convertible preferred would be worth almost $200 per share.

What happens to convertible preferreds when the common stock goes down? Immediately after Allis Chalmers made their issue, the general stock market weakened, and Allis Chalmers common stock quickly lost 20% of its value. The preferred certainly went down, but not nearly as much, and at its worst it lost only 6%, going to $94 per share. This is because the assured 4.2% dividend plus the convertibility feature put a floor on the stock price and acted to retard its fall.

However, the delightful feature of convertible preferreds is that although they do not fall nearly as fast as their common stock, they do go up just as quickly. Thus when the Allis Chalmers common stock recovered to $34, the preferred quickly jumped to $120 per share.

This is a perfect example of how, by buying a convertible preferred, one can enjoy a good yield, relative safety, and still make a capital gain. In other words, it is possible to have the advantages of common stock without the very serious risks normally entailed.

There is one pitfall which buyers of convertible preferreds must avoid — the purchase of common stock disguised as convertible preferred. This not uncommon ploy is used to issue a so-called preferred stock that carries the same high risk as ordinary common stock. It must be remembered that preferred stock is preferred only in relation to the company's common stock and is safe only in relation to the financial worth of the common stock. If a company's net worth is $100,000,000 after the value of all outstanding debts including bonds is deducted, and if in addition there is outstanding $20,000,000 worth of preferred stock, this leaves a value of $80,000,000 to the common stock. This $80,000,000 serves to protect the preferred shareholders and would have to be dissipated before there was any risk to the preferred. In such a circumstance, the preferred is quite safe. On the other hand, if a company's net worth is $25,000,000 after the face value of all debts is deducted and there is the same $20,000,000 worth of preferred outstanding, then the common stock has a value of only $5 million. In this case a loss of 5 million by the company would immediately imperil the preferred, which has very little protection. Preferreds of this type will fluctuate just as wildly and widely as any common stock. There are certain circumstances under which common stocks can be very profitable, but it should be remembered that the risk is just as great as any possible profit and that such risk is unnecessary when so many other safe, high-potential profit situations are available.

An example of a convertible preferred which carried all the risks of common stock was the issue of Rockower 6% cumulative redeemable convertible 1st preferred on November 8, 1961, at $10 per share.

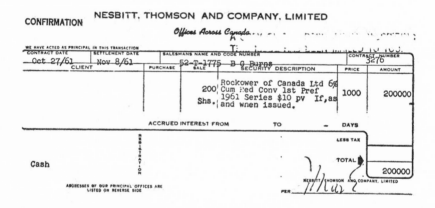

This company was engaged in the sale of clothing through outlets in the Tower Discount Stores. There was no common stock in the hands of the public, as it was all held by principals and management of Rockower. The equity represented by the common stock was very small, so that the convertible preferred behaved as irrationally as any common stock could. In late 1961 the stocks of discount houses were behaving very well; their sales and stocks were soaring, and optimism for the future was unlimited. Within two months Rockowers preferred stock soared up over $28.

In retrospect it is quite clear that Rockower was never worth anywhere near $28, but excesses of enthusiasm had made investors and speculators lose their heads. Suddenly everyone was shaken back to reality by the sudden collapse of many discount chains.

Although this did not really affect Rockower in any way, the loss of optimism for the stock engineered a rapid rush to sell, and within a year Rockower prefererd was down to $5.

<table>
<tr><td>TELEPHONE
EM. 4-5161.</td><td>No. 7479</td><td colspan="2">JACKSON, McFADYEN SECURITIES LII
MEMBERS:
TORONTO STOCK EXCHANGE
MONTREAL STOCK EXCHANGE
CANADIAN STOCK EXCHANGE
THE INVESTMENT DEALERS' ASSOCIATION OF CANADA
11 ADELAIDE ST. WEST — TORONTO 1, ONTARIO</td></tr>
<tr><td colspan="4">WE HAVE THIS DAY BOUGHT FOR YOUR ACCOUNT AND RISK ON THE TORONTO STOCK EXCHANGE
(SUBJECT TO THE RULES AND REGULATIONS OF THE EXCHANGE WHERE EXECUTED)   DATE</td></tr>
</table>

VALUE DATE	CLIENT'S NAME	SHARES	SECURITY	PRICE	AMOU
FEB 6 65		200	ROCKOWER OF CDA-PFD 5.3/8		1 C

Interestingly, those who sold Rockower at $5 were just as wrong as those who bought at $28. Rockower itself was never in danger of going bankrupt and it gave a 12% yield when selling at $5. Gradually confidence returned, and the stock slowly moved upward to its current level of $15.

This story has been related only to show what should *not* happen with a preferred. If a preferred is really preferred as to safety and earnings, it can fluctuate upwards as did Rockower but should never plunge to 50% of its issue price. Let us now look at a proper convertible preferred. There are hundreds to choose from.

In late January, 1964, Federal Pacific Electric, a large U.S. manufacturer of heavy electrical equipment, decided to sell off part of their Canadian subsidiary, F.P.E. Pioneer Electric, as requested by the Canadian Minister of Finance of all U.S. parent firms. Federal Pacific intended to keep control of the subsidiary, so they retained all of the B common stock and issued to the public A, or partially preferred, stock plus a 5½% $50 convertible preferred. This issue was initially made in the form of units consisting of 2 convertible preferred shares at $50 and 5 shares of Class A at $10, each unit selling for $150.

NESBITT, THOMSON AND COMPANY, LIMITED

Forward with Canada

CONTRACT DATE	SETTLEMENT DATE	SALESMANS NAME AND CODE NUMBER		CONTRACT NUMBER
Jan 22/64	Feb 4/64	B.G.Burns 52 T 1775		10634
ACTING AS PRINCIPAL WE HAVE TO DAY	BOUGHT FROM YOU	SOLD TO YOU	SECURITY DESCRIPTION	PRICE	AMOUNT

ACTING AS PRINCIPAL WE HAVE TO DAY	BOUGHT FROM YOU	SOLD TO YOU	SECURITY DESCRIPTION	PRICE	AMOUNT
Dr. Morton P. Shulman, 378 RoncesvallesAvenue, Toronto,Ontario.		20 units	FPE Pioneer Electric Ltd. Each Unit consistng of 2 5½% Cum Conv 1st pfd shs Series A PV $50 per sh & 5 class A shs Comm NPV If as and when issued	15000	300000

ACCRUED INTEREST FROM   TO   -   DAYS

	LESS TAX	
COPY OF THE PROSPECTUS DESCRIBING HIS ISSUE HAS BEEN MAILED TO YOU.	TOTAL	
		300000

NESBITT, THOMSON AND COMPANY, LIMITED

PER

This issue illustrates a number of basic points in investing in the market, particularly in the preferred field, and it is the perfect illustration of a "can't-lose" situation. It involved free riding, hot issues, and spin-offs, which are discussed in other chapters, and it presented an ideal convertible preferred which could only go up.

An examination of the prospectus when the company first made this issue was an unusual delight. The company stock had been previously held completely by its U.S. parent, which had had some troubled years. The Canadian subsidiary, however, had had only good years, and each year its earnings increased. In addition future prospects were excellent, and the company had a large backlog of orders.

The capitalization of F.P.E. was very unusual. It consisted of common shares called B shares; A shares, which were preferred as to a 56¢ dividend; and a 5½% convertible first preferred.

The A shares held preference to the B shares in initial dividends, being entitled to 56¢ per share per annum before the B received any payment. If the company declared dividends on the B shares in excess of 56¢ per year, the A had to receive an equal amount above this preferred 56¢. Thus the A stock was actually a participating preferred — preferred as to dividends, but participating in increased earnings if the company did well.

The B stock was all held by the parent U.S. company; the parent company was taking the primary and major risk. This in itself was a good reason to buy the A stock.

There were, however, far more important reasons. In 1963 the company had earned 90¢ per combined A and B share. Of this, the A shares had been paid 56¢ each, while the B shares received only 4¢. The excess 52¢ the B had not received was returned to the company's treasury where it was of value to both classes of stock, thus increasing the true earnings of the A stock to about $1.50.

Thus the A stock was preferred as to dividends, would participate in any improvement in the company's fortunes, paid a 5.6% dividend, and yet was being issued at only $10, less than seven times earnings. Comon stock in growth companies like this one usually trade at twenty or twenty-five times earnings and give a yield of between 3 and 4%. Therefore this A stock was an outstanding buy.

The convertible preferred was even more outstanding. This stock, issued at $50 (p. 64), gave a yield of 5½% and was convertible into 4 shares of Class A stock. Earnings of the company per preferred share was $12, so the stock was being issued at less than five times earnings. So here we had a preferred whose earnings were so high that there was literally no risk in its purchase, giving a 5½% yield and, even more remarkable, being convertible into a Class A participating stock.

It was obvious that these stocks were being issued at prices far below their true worth, yet the public interest was almost nil. I think the reason is that this type of issue is considerably more complicated than the average type of glamour stock which the public flocks to buy in order to get "action" more quickly. Unfortunately, the action is often in the wrong direction.

The units traded for only a very few days before being split up into their A stock and convertible preferred components. During these few days the free riders who had bought the units in order to grab a quick profit dumped them thereby giving long-term investors a wonderful chance to buy them cheaply.

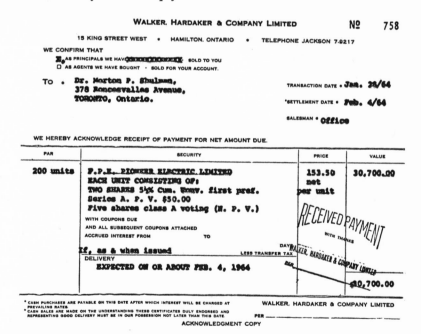

In February the units ceased to trade and their two components began to sell separately, the Class A at $10⅛ and preferred at $52¾.

Although these prices were higher than the issue price, they were still very obviously ridiculously low to anyone who had taken the trouble to study convertible and participating preferreds. Fortunately for the rest of us, the public ignored these stocks completely, and they continued to be available at these very low prices for months.

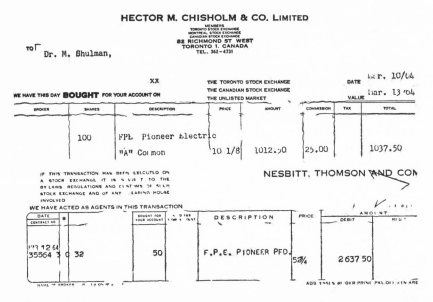

HECTOR M. CHISHOLM & CO. LIMITED

MEMBERS
TORONTO STOCK EXCHANGE
MONTREAL STOCK EXCHANGE
CANADIAN STOCK EXCHANGE
82 RICHMOND ST WEST
TORONTO 1. CANADA
TEL. 362-4731

TO Dr. M. Shulman,

XX   THE TORONTO STOCK EXCHANGE   DATE Mar. 10/64
WE HAVE THIS DAY **BOUGHT** FOR YOUR ACCOUNT ON   THE CANADIAN STOCK EXCHANGE
THE UNLISTED MARKET   VALUE Mar. 13 '64

BROKER	SHARES	DESCRIPTION	PRICE	AMOUNT	COMMISSION	TAX	TOTAL
	100	FPE Pioneer Electric "A" Common	10 1/8	1012.50	25.00		1037.50

IF THIS TRANSACTION HAS BEEN EXECUTED ON A STOCK EXCHANGE IT IS SUBJECT TO THE BY LAWS REGULATIONS AND CUSTOMS OF SUCH STOCK EXCHANGE AND OF ANY CLEARING HOUSE INVOLVED

NESBITT, THOMSON AND CO.

WE HAVE ACTED AS AGENTS IN THIS TRANSACTION

DATE CONTRACT NO		BOUGHT FOR YOUR ACCOUNT		DESCRIPTION	PRICE	DEBIT	CREDIT
MR 12 64 35564 3 0 32		50		F.P.E. PIONEER PFD.	52 3/4	2 637 50	

By the end of 1964 the company's sales and earnings had jumped considerably. Earnings per Class A and B shares were now up to $1.10. True earnings per Class A share were actually much higher, because the B shares were still not receiving an equal share of the dividends. The original underwriting broker now began to recommend the purchase of these stocks to its clients, and they began to creep higher. The public, however, continued to ignore F.P.E. and by May, 1965, the Class A was still available at $13 per share and the preferred at $58.50.

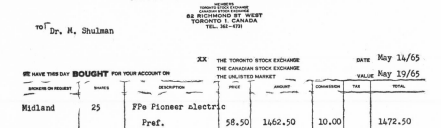

HECTOR M. CHISHOLM & CO. LIMITED

MEMBERS
TORONTO STOCK EXCHANGE
CANADIAN STOCK EXCHANGE
82 RICHMOND ST WEST
TORONTO 1. CANADA
TEL. 362-4731

TO Dr. M. Shulman

XX   THE TORONTO STOCK EXCHANGE   DATE May 14/65
WE HAVE THIS DAY **BOUGHT** FOR YOUR ACCOUNT ON   THE CANADIAN STOCK EXCHANGE
THE UNLISTED MARKET   VALUE May 19/65

BROKERS ON REQUEST	SHARES	DESCRIPTION	PRICE	AMOUNT	COMMISSION	TAX	TOTAL
Midland	25	FPe Pioneer Electric Pref.	58.50	1462.50	10.00		1472.50
	75	"	59.00	4425.00	30.00		4455.00

By the summer of 1965 considerable buying began to come into F.P.E. from a number of friends to whom I pointed out this great opportunity, and the Class A moved up to 15½ and the preferred to $62.

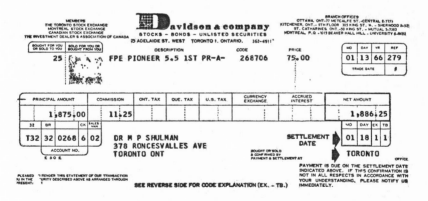

HECTOR M. CHISHOLM & CO. LIMITED

MEMBERS
TORONTO STOCK EXCHANGE
CANADIAN STOCK EXCHANGE
82 RICHMOND ST WEST
TORONTO 1. CANADA
TEL. 362-4731

TO ⌐ Dr. M. Shulman

XX   THE TORONTO STOCK EXCHANGE   DATE   Aug. 9/65
E HAVE THIS DAY **BOUGHT** FOR YOUR ACCOUNT ON   THE CANADIAN STOCK EXCHANGE
THE UNLISTED MARKET   VALUE   Aug. 12/65

BROKERS ON REQUEST	SHARES	DESCRIPTION	PRICE	AMOUNT	COMMISSION	TAX	TOTAL
Chis	50	F.P.E. Pioneer Electric Pref.	62.00	3100.00	22.50		3122.50

E. & O.E.   HECTOR M. CHISHOLM & CO. LIMITED

At the end of the 1965 F.P.E. brought out its annual report, showing that earnings per combined Class A and B shares were now at a record $1.60, while sales were at a new peak and the company now had a backlog of orders larger than ever before.

Suddenly and belatedly, as always happens with these issues, the general public became aware of F.P.E. Pioneer Electric, and generalized buying poured into the stock. The Class A sold up to $19 and the preferred to $75.

MEMBERS
THE TORONTO STOCK EXCHANGE
MONTREAL STOCK EXCHANGE
CANADIAN STOCK EXCHANGE
THE INVESTMENT DEALER'S ASSOCIATION OF CANADA

Davidson & company

STOCKS – BONDS – UNLISTED SECURITIES
25 ADELAIDE ST. WEST TORONTO 1, ONTARIO.   362-4911

BRANCH OFFICES
OTTAWA, ONT.-77 METCALFE ST.-CENTRAL 8-7171
KITCHENER, ONT.- 9TH FLOOR 305 KING ST. W. - SHERWOOD 8-5111
ST. CATHARINES, ONT.-50 KING ST. - MUTUAL 5-7303
MONTREAL, P.Q. - 1013 BEAVER HALL HILL - UNIVERSITY 6-8493

BOUGHT FOR YOU OR SOLD TO YOU	SOLD FOR YOU OR BOUGHT FROM YOU	DESCRIPTION	CODE	PRICE	MO	DAY	YR	REF
25		FPE PIONEER 5.5 1ST PR-A-	268706	75.00	01	13	66	279
					TRADE DATE			#

PRINCIPAL AMOUNT	COMMISSION	ONT. TAX	QUE. TAX	U.S. TAX	CURRENCY EXCHANGE	ACCRUED INTEREST	NET AMOUNT
1,875.00	11.25						1,886.25

32	BR	CK	SALES MAN
T32	32 0268	6	02

ACCOUNT NO.
E & O E.

DR M P SHULMAN
378 RONCESVALLES AVE
TORONTO ONT

SETTLEMENT DATE

BOUGHT OR SOLD & CONFIRMED BY
PAYMENT & SETTLEMENT AT

MO	DAY	EX	TB
01	18	1	1

TORONTO
OFFICE

PLEASED TO RENDER THIS STATEMENT OF OUR TRANSACTION
NU IN THE CURITY DESCRIBED ABOVE AS ARRANGED THROUGH
PRESENT: T

SEE REVERSE SIDE FOR CODE EXPLANATION (EX. – TB.)

PAYMENT IS DUE ON THE SETTLEMENT DATE INDICATED ABOVE. IF THIS CONFIRMATION IS NOT IN ALL RESPECTS IN ACCORDANCE WITH YOUR UNDERSTANDING, PLEASE NOTIFY US IMMEDIATELY.

At these levels the Class A stock had given a capital gain of 90% in less than two years and the preferred 50%. Yet during this time both stocks had given a yield of 5½%, and even more amazing, the Class A carried very little risk and the prefered absolutely none. Here was another situation where everyone made money.

The free riders made a profit without any investment, speculators in hot issues did the same; those who bought early made money; those who bought late made money; those who held on made more; those seeking income received a high yield; those seeking security ran no risk; those seeking capital gains did many times better than those who bought the average common stock. Unusual? Yes — but not unique. There are opportunities like this every year in the United States and Canada. In some cases the profits are unbelievably high. In no case should the risk involve more than 10% of the invested capital.

In March 1972 Trans Canada Pipe Lines issued a 5.3% convertible preferred stock at $50 per share.

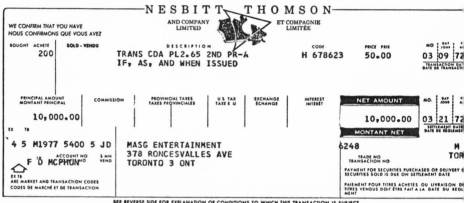

Each preferred share was convertible into 1 1/10 common shares.

Through conversion, the common stock would cost approximately $45½ per share, so there was no point in immediate conversion because the common was trading at only $42 per share. The beauty of this type of issue is that if and when the common moves up, the preferred will move up with it because for the next ten years it can be converted on the same fixed basis. If, on the other hand, the common should fall, the preferred's value will tend to hold up because it is protected by its very reasonable dividend.

Because convertible preferreds offer all the best features of investment with few of the drawbacks, they are greatly sought after when new issues appear. As a result there are great opportunities to make an immediate capital gain without taking any risk or making any investment, because regardless of their ultimate course these stocks usually sell up to a premium immediately after being issued. Trans Canada convertible preferred was no exception. It was issued March 1, 1972 at $50 per share and on March 2 it sold at $53 per share.

Because of the likelihood of large capital gains without the danger of loss of capital, convertible preferreds are ideal subjects for free rides (see Chapter 11) as well as for investors and speculators. Intelligently chosen, such a purchase must be a successful one.

In summary, convertible preferreds can be ideal investments. Here are the points to look for in such a purchase:

1. The company must have a large common stock investment so as to give safety to its preferred.

2. The conversion price should be no more than 15% higher than the current price of the common stock.

3. The yield of the convertible preferred should be a reasonably high one — certainly no more than 1% below current yields on non-convertible preferreds.

4. The company must be a sound one with a record of earnings and possibilities of growth.

If these four factors are present, large profits will result.

8

THE STOP LOSS

Several years ago a book was written about stop loss selling that became a best-seller. It purported to show how judicious use of the stop loss would minimize losses and maximize profits. The theory is very simple, and on paper it appears so certain of success that thousands have attempted to emulate the example described by the writer.

The stop loss is a requirement that a stock *must* be sold if it sells at a certain price. Thus if a stop loss order is placed to sell General Motors at $100, the broker must sell it when it reaches that price. Normally the stock would be priced higher than $100 when the order is placed, although this is not always so. Thus a broker holding such an order would not check with his client even if the order had been placed months before, but would automatically sell the General Motors at the best bid as soon as one sale had occurred at the $100 figure. The client who had placed the stop loss order may not receive $100 per share, however, for the stock will be immediately sold at the best bid then available, which might be lower than $100.

The stop loss theory is that stocks will either go up or go down and that, of course, the investor wishes to keep the ones which will go up and get rid of the ones which are going down. Therefore, at the time of purchase of each stock, a stop loss open order is placed, so that if the stock were to decline a certain percentage, the broker would automatically sell it. For example, one buys 100 shares of General Motors at $105 per share and simultaneously puts in a stop loss order at $100. If the stock reaches that point, it will be automatically sold, producing a loss of $500 plus commission and thus preventing a larger loss if the stock continues to decline. On the other hand, if the stock loss does not go down to $100, it will not be sold, and if it begins to climb, new stop losses are put in at higher figures. Thus if the stock reaches $110, a stop loss is put in at $105 so that the worst than can happen is that the stockholder breaks even; if the stock reaches $115, a stop loss is put in at $110, thus guaranteeing a profit, and so on upwards. It certainly sounds like an excellent idea, and it can be summed up in an old market maxim, "Cut your losses and let your profits ride." Unfortunately, as with so many other theories and maxims, if one attempts to follow this one, disaster may result.

The stop loss is a very handy tool under certain circumstances, but to base a whole stock market philosophy upon it is equivalent to giving an army an unlimited supply of antitank guns but no other weapons and then directing it to fight a war. It may win, but it probably won't.

There are two circumstances in which the stop loss will work; these are the stocks that go straight up and the stocks that slowly go straight down. Unfortunately, they form a very small minority of the many securities traded.

Most stocks follow a zigzag pattern, with an overall trend in one direction or another, and in these cases, which unfortunately form the vast majority, the stop loss system leads straight to bankruptcy.

Let us take an example. In early 1965 Molybdenum, listed on the American exchange, appeared to have very bright prospects. The company was the largest producer of molybdenum in the world, and it appeared that its earnings were due to take a sharp move upward. It was predicted that within one year new mine and company developments would justify a price over $60 for the stock, which was then trading at $40. The individual who purchased the stock at that time and put in a stop loss was quickly sold out, for the stock slipped to $33. If our stop loss believer tried again when the stock rallied to $35 he would again lose, for Molybdenum then slipped to $28. In the latter part of the year the company's predicted boom did occur, and the stock did sell up over $60. Lots of people made money. A very, very few lost; they had used the stop loss system and in effect they had been whipsawed.

If one looks over the entire list of stocks on the New York exchange the pattern we find is up-down-up-down with some stocks ending much higher than they began, some much lower, and most a little higher or lower. This whipsaw action results in the stop loss believer being sold out on any weakness and not being in on the recovery. Those who follow the system faithfully, selling on weakness and buying on strength, can actually buy a stock like Brunswick, which after one year is at exactly the same price, and yet find themselves having lost their entire capital through the repeated whipsaw action.

If a security has been purchased for yield and safety there is, of course, no reason to put in a stop loss. The stop loss is normally considered when a stock has been bought in the hope of making a capital gain.

Presumably before buying such a security the prospective buyer will have decided why he is buying it; his reasons would normally be either that the company stock is reasonably priced in relation to its earnings with the prospect of further growth and increase in earnings, or else that the price of the stock is low in relation to its assets. In either case there is no reason to put in a stop loss, for if the company stock was attractive for either of the above reasons when trading at $50, it should be even more attractive at $45. Rather than selling out in panic, the investor should be buying more at the lower price and averaging down his cost.

If thus the stop loss can be eliminated from stocks purchased for safety, yield, or capital gain on a reasoned basis, there is only one group left where it should be used. This is the stock purchased for capital gain on hope and whose current price cannot be justified on known facts. These are the stocks bought on hot tips or because of rumours of a takeover. Inasmuch as the person buying for these reasons is going to lose his money anyway, he might just as well use the stop loss. After all, it doesn't matter much how you lost it after it's all over.

If all this hasn't been enough to discourage the use of the stop loss, there are three further reasons which can be added:

1. The first is human forgetfulness. There is not a broker in North America who has not had the distressing experience of phoning a client to tell him that an old stop loss order has just been exercised and having the client cry, "Oh no, I sold that stock weeks ago and forgot all about the stop loss!" The person using many stop losses needs a secretary to keep track of them, for there is nothing easier to forget than an unexecuted order which has been placed months earlier. In such cases the broker will buy back the stock, but the client must bear the loss.

2. Stop loss orders must be executed immediately when the stated selling price has been reached. Often there is not a good bid available, and the order must be executed at the best available bid. If the stock is inactive or there are a number of stop loss orders at the same price, the stock may be sold far below the stop loss figure. When Rollins Broadcasting was whipsawing in 1964, its overall move took it from $14 to $150, but in the middle of this upward move there was a one-day reaction from $64 down to $55. A stop loss put in at $61 was actually executed at $57, because the few other bids between $61 and $57 were filled by other orders. Thus the person who thinks he is protecting a profit may actually be ensuring a loss.

This same experience has occurred with many other stocks. Shortly after being listed on the American Exchange, Computer Application tumbled from $30 down to $15¾. A stop loss put in at $21 was executed at $18½. The stock subsequently recovered its entire loss, but this didn't help those poor speculators who had been wiped out by relying on the stop loss.

3. Stop loss sales can be cumulative, and this is their greatest evil. Stock exchanges attempt to prevent too many stop loss orders accumulating in any one stock, but periodically such a disaster does occur in stocks that have had large percentage rises. The usual story is that in a company like Rollins, there will be a radical change which produces greatly increased earnings plus a large, rapid increase in the price of the stock. Because the market action appears so exciting, many stockholders hang on past the point where reason tells them the stock is fully priced. On the other hand, because current earnings and assets cannot possibly justify such a price for the stock, these shareholders attempt to protect themselves by putting in a stop loss order slightly under the current market price. As the stock continues to move up, more and more stop loss orders come in until there is at last a ladder of stop loss orders which may look like this on the floor of the exchange:

Current price of Rollins — $150.
Stop Loss Orders:

700	$149½
1,000	149
400	148
2,000	147
1,000	146
8,000	145
2,000	144
1,200	143
900	142
600	141
10,000	140

The specialist running the market on that particular stock at the exchange is very aware of the powder keg he is sitting on. If selling begins to come in at $150, rather than attempt to support the stock and take the risk of large financial loss, he may very well let it fall. Now the nightmare that stop loss can produce develops rapidly. The moment that Rollins trades at $149½, seven hundred shares must be automatically sold at the best possible price. As this stock is sold it produces a sale at 149, which thus automatically requires the immediate dumping of another thousand shares, and so on down the ladder. At round numbers like 145 or 140 huge amounts of stock are poured in to be sold, because it is more common for an individual to enter a stop loss at a round number.

When a stop loss order binge like this is completed, the stock may have lost one-third of its value and its shareholders up to two-thirds of their capital. Now a new evil enters the picture. Because the stock has fallen so far in price, all those shareholders holding their stock on margin will now receive a call from their brokers demanding more margin. (Margin buying of stock means that the shareholder does not have enough money to buy all the stock he wishes, and so he puts up only a certain amount, usually 50%, and borrows the rest from the broker.) This call for margin in turn produces more selling from those shareholders not wishing or able to put up more capital, and this in turn sets off more stop losses, which in turn produce more margin calls, which in turn set off more stop losses. It can be a pretty horrible picture, and although no one likes to remember it, it has happened before and can happen again.

The moral is, beware of stop loss orders.

There is only one circumstances in which the use of a stop loss can be truly justified — when the individual is leaving the country on vacation and cannot remain in touch with his investments.

With this sole exception, *do not use stop loss orders.*

9
PUTS AND CALLS

Puts and calls are options to buy or sell stock. They are the wildest form of gambling possible in the stock market. Two-thirds of those purchasing options lose their entire investment within six months. One-sixth make rapid profits unimaginable in any other field, sometimes multiplying their investment thirtyfold within a year.

Even though puts and calls offer such possibilities of riches or ruin, they are the least-understood branch of the stock market and are too often used when they should be ignored and forgotten when they are most useful. To explain puts and calls it is first necessary to define a few terms.

A call is an option to buy a stock at a predetermined price for a definite period of time. This can vary anywhere from ten days to one year, but most calls are sold for six months and ten days, with a minority sold for 95 days or 35 days.

A put is an option to sell a stock and can be sold under the same time period as a call.

A straddle is a put and a call on the same stock at the same price.

A spread is a put and a call on the same stock at different prices.

A strap is two calls and a put on the same stock at the same price.

A strip is a call and two puts on the same stock at the same price.

These options are sold to the public through put and call brokers, most of whom are located in New York. These firms specialize only in puts and calls and normally do not handle any other form of brokerage. There is a bitter rivalry between the dozen put and call brokers because of a shortage of sellers of these options. The only thing that brings these brokers together is outside criticism, which they will band together to ward off. The rest of the time they vie strongly with one another in the keenest of competition.

Ninety-five percent of options sold are calls. The remaining 5% are puts. Spreads, straddles, straps, and strips are rarely sold to the public. Put and call brokers normally do not finance their own options; they are not selling options to the public on stocks they own themselves, but they primarily sell options which they have purchased from other members of the public.

These firms do not work on a commission like most other brokers, however. Instead they buy options and resell them for as high a markup as possible. In order to conceal from their clients the size of the markup, they have developed a stratagem known as conversion. They rarely buy puts or calls, which is what they sell. Instead they purchase primarily straddles, but also straps, strips, and spreads, and they change these into calls.

The mechanism by which this is done is highly ingenious. If a put and call broker has received an order for two six-month calls on Ampex, he will sell them for $500 each. He will then buy from a client one six-month straddle on Ampex, for which he will probably pay $575. A straddle consists of one call and one put. He has an order for two calls so he must change the one put into a call. He does this by simultaneously purchasing one hundred shares of Ampex stock, which he holds until the option runs out. If the Ampex goes up, the two calls will be exercised; the broker already owns one call, and he also owns 100 shares of Ampex, which he gives up at the option price to satisfy the second call. If Ampex goes down the calls are, of course, not exercised. The broker gets rid of his 100 shares of stock by exercising the put which he received when he bought the straddle. Thus it doesn't really matter to the put and call broker whether the stock goes up or down. At the end of the six months, regardless of what Ampex is selling for, the calls will have run out and he will be rid of the stock either through its being called from him or by his selling it to the individual who sold him the straddle. In either case his profit is exactly the same — the $1,000 he received for the two calls, less the $575 paid for the straddle, less the carrying charges for the money spent on buying and holding the Ampex for six months. In other words there is a net profit of about $350.

The reason that the broker does not just buy two calls from a client when he receives an order to sell calls is that, in order to make the same profit, he would only be able to pay the client $325 for each call, and the advertised sale price of $500 would soon cause cries of outrage. The broker persuades his client to sell the straddle by pointing out that in six months the Ampex will be either higher or lower; it obviously cannot be both and therefore the client is receiving the $575 for only one option, as the other will not be exercised. In effect he says, "Ampex is $25 today. If you buy the stock today and the call is exercised you will end up having sold your stock for $30.75. If, on the other hand, the put is exercised, you will end up buying another 100 shares of stock for only $19.25. In either case you must be ahead of the game." This sounds very logical, but unfortunately there are flaws in the logic.

Who buys puts and calls and why? The various put and call brokers all issue a little booklet explaining the uses and values of these options. They list a number of reasons to purchase options, most of which are not too sensible. "To protect profits after a long rise buy a put. If the stock continues to rise you will still participate in the profit. If, on the other hand, it should fall you are completely protected." Completely true, but there are much cheaper ways to protect your profits, for example, by selling if the stock dips to a certain predetermined figure. Because the premium for a put is quite prohibitive for profit protection purposes, less than 1% of options are sold for the numerous reasons listed in the booklets. The two reasons which are not listed and which actually produce 99% of option buying are these:

1. 5% of option buying comes from employees, officers, or directors of firms who may have information of a favourable nature concerning major progress or increases in profits, before such information is generally available to shareholders and the public. The advantage of buying options instead of stock is tenfold, for by laying out the same amount of money much higher profits can be made. In 1962 Shell Oil decided to expand in Canada by taking over the Canadian Oil Company. Canadian Oil was then trading for $35 per share, and the Shell board of directors had voted at their directors' meeting to offer the equivalent of $55 for every share of Canadian Oil.

At that time I was a partner in a firm which had sold large number of options to put and call brokers in previous years. Suddenly we were swamped with requests to buy thirty-day calls on Canadian Oil for which we were offered $3.50 per share, a huge sum when considering that a ninety-five-day call normally would sell for about that figure. These orders all emanated from New York and were unlimited; that is, they offered to buy any size.

The advantage to the buyer was obvious. If he bought 1,000 shares of Canadian Oil, his outlay would be $35,000. When the offer was announced he would get $55,000 for his stock, making $20,000 profit. On the other hand if he were to spend the same $35,000 for options on Canadian Oil at $3.50 each, he could buy options on 10,000 shares, on which his profit would now be $10,000 x the rise in prise of the stock: $16.50 or a profit of $165,000.

This is actually what did happen. Options were purchased on many thousands of shares. The profits were immense.

A more recent example caused considerable public furor. Texas Gulf Sulphur made a huge copper discovery near Timmins. The first hole was drilled in November, 1963. Between November, 1963, and March 30, 1964, a number of calls on Texas Gulf Sulphur stock were purchased by employees. A statement was made by the company on April 12, 1964, that the drilling was too preliminary to make a decision as to whether or not an ore body existed. On April 16 the company reported 25,000,000 tons of indicated ore. During this four-day period, no calls were purchased by insiders. The stock went from $20 to $80.

The option purchasers made $60,000 for every $3,000 investment. If they had bought the stock, they would have made only $9,000 on the same investment.

2. The second buyer, who produces the vast majority of option volume, is a gambler. This is the individual who, for one of a hundred different reasons, believes that a stock will go up. He has no inside knowledge, but from his studies of the particular company or stock he thinks that a move in the stock is imminent. Often he does not have the funds to purchase the stock itself but can afford the much smaller price for an option. For example, Brunswick in 1965 had had severe setbacks due to the collapse of the bowling industry, and the Brunswick stock slipped to an all-time low of $7.00. Thousands of options were now sold to various speculators who either felt that the company was going to go completely under and bought puts or else believed that the company would successfully diversify and overcome its troubles and so bought calls.

It is one of the facts of the market that these option buyers are more often wrong than right. It has been my experience that over two-thirds of option buyers are wrong, and the stock goes in the wrong direction. Thus two-thirds of the capital spent in buying options goes straight down the drain. This is not as bad as it seems, however, for the individual option represents only a small portion of the price of the same amount of stock, and the dollar loss on an option is often much smaller than the loss on an equivalent amount of stock, even though the percentage loss may be higher.

To take an example, Universal Match in 1960 was trading at $50 per share. Those who bought six-month calls, for which they paid $800 per one hundred shares, lost 100% of this, or $800. If, however, the same purchaser had bought one hundred shares of stock that slipped all the way from $50 down to $15, he would have lost $3,500. This case illustrates the one great honest advantage of options. They should be purchased in cases where the company under consideration is undergoing a massive expansion or other change which may or may not work out well. In these cases it is better to gamble a little money through a call than to buy the stock itself and risk losing much more.

Syntex at the beginning of 1966 was in exactly the same position. The stock, because of its birth control pill, moved vigorously from $70 to $210 and was then split. Earnings were increasing astronomically, and the future of the company appeared bright indeed. It was expected that the Vatican would shortly announce permission for Roman Catholics to use the Pill, and Syntex would be the prime financial gainer in such a change. But what if the Vatican decision was to put off, or worse, to turn down the Pill? In such a case a six-month call option is the ideal compromise. Rather than invest $21,000 in buying one hundred shares of stock, the cautious speculator bought an option for $2,000, thus limiting his loss but not hindering his possible profit.

This is the sensible use of options, to enable a speculator to gamble in highly volatile stocks while at the same time limiting the risk to small amounts of capital.

Who sells options? This is the best-kept secret of the business, and put and call brokers guard the names of their sellers as closely as the United States government guards Fort Knox. Sellers are the lifeblood of puts and calls; there are not enough of them, and the few sizeable ones are continuously courted by the brokers as Guinevere was by Lancelot. In 1958 a young broker, Wilfred Posluns, formed a partnership with me to sell these options. Soon several New York put and call brokers were phoning long distance each day, forwarding expensive presents, and offering invitations to visit New York and indulge in the various pleasures available in that city. In our innocence we thought that this was because of our delightful personalities!

The shortage of sellers is due to three reasons:

The first is the vast amount of money necessary to sell options. Let us suppose that a new seller wishes to sell only one option per day. Before his first option runs out in six months he will have sold 135 options, for which he will have received $25,000 in premiums. At this point he will have sold options on $285,000 worth of stocks, which he will either have bought or must remain prepared to buy.

The second reason is that an option seller must enjoy the ancient art of bargaining. Because there is no fixed price for options, put and call brokers will try to buy from their sellers as cheaply as possible. Thus for a straddle on Ampex for which they could afford to pay up to $800 and make money and which they really expect to buy for $600, they will initially bid $400 and will then bargain with their seller until they finally agree on a price. In today's fixed price society this bargaining is almost impossible for many people. We complained many times to the New York dealers that this method was demeaning and undignified. We begged them to give us their best price at once so as to save time, but they just laughed and continued as before. I really think that the striking of the bargain gives them as much pleasure as the actual profit.

One day I accepted a price as initially offered by a partner of one of the largest New York put and call brokers. The dismay in this man's voice was equivalent to that of the hawker in an Arabian bazaar whose first price has been accepted — perhaps a little more profit but not nearly so much fun.

The third reason is that, despite the huge investment in selling puts and calls, there is no guarantee of financial success. In fact it is just as easy to lose money as make it in this risky business. The reason is that most options are sought on highly volatile stocks, and the seller of options soon finds that some of his stocks go 'way up and some go 'way down. Unfortunately unlike the buyer of these stocks or options, the ones that go up do not counterbalance the ones that go down, because the option seller does not get the profit on the ones that do go up. Regardless of how much a stock goes up or down, the seller receives only the option price. But in those stocks that go 'way down, the seller can be stuck with his original stock purchase, which he dare not sell until the option has run out and in which he can take a very severe loss.

In order to successfully sell options of this type, the seller must have an intimate knowledge of the market and must also keep in close touch with the individual stocks on which he has sold options in order to protect his investments. Thus most option sellers, if they have sold a call on, say, Ampex at $25 for a premium of $2 per share, and if the price falls the full limit of their option, will sell their stock, hoping to at least break even on that particular deal. They hold their position on the stocks that go up and make the full option as profit.

This system works fairly well most of the time. When it doesn't work, the results can be disastrous, as in whipsawing stocks. Whipsawing occurs when a stock moves up and down over a broad price range several time during the life of an option. Although the stock price may finally end up exactly where it started, the option seller can lose huge sums in the meantime. Molybdenum is the horrible example that always comes to my mind. In 1958 I was the veteran of two years of option selling and had quite convinced myself that I knew all there was to know about the business. Molybdenum was trading quietly at $45 on the American exchange, and I was very happy to sell puts and calls on the stock, slowly at first, and then when the weeks went by, much more rapidly. Then slowly but steadily Molybdenum began to slip, going down at the rate of 50¢ per day. When it got to $40 I began to unload my stock. When it reached $35 I got rid of all of it. Then to my dismay the stock began to climb again at the same rate. When it reached $40 I started to buy again. At $45 I was buying rapidly. At $50 I completed my buying. Now with only one month left for the options to run, to my horrified disbelief the stock began to fall. When the options finally all ran out Molybdenum was $45, exactly where it had started. The balance sheet was somewhat depressing. Premiums taken in $12,000 — Carrying charges $2,000 — Loss on trading $36,000. Overall loss $26,000. To my partner's credit he didn't say a word. I learned the most important single fact to be remembered when selling options. Never sell an option in a company with whose stock and business you are not familiar.

The one group who can make money by selling options are very wealthy people who have a constant large portfolio. By selling options against this portfolio, they can significantly increase their earnings without increasing their risk.

All others would do well to avoid this very dangerous speculation There have been some very spectacular bankruptcies occur as a result of large scale option selling.

In summary, leave option selling for someone else. Option buying can be very profitable under certain limited circumstances, but in general put and calls can be summed up in one word: *Avoid!*

There is one very important exception to this rule. In 1971 a new type of option became available: the purchase of calls on commodities. These calls offer the chance to make huge sums of money with practically no investment. As you can see in Chapter 16, commodity trading is the fastest, most honest and wildest form of gambling available anywhere. It offers possibilities of large profits, but even greater possibilities of being wiped out within hours of making your initial purchase. By purchasing an option you retain your chance to make the profits but you limit your risks to a small sum.

As an example, On December 8, 1971 I purchased for $387.50 an option on one silver contract at its then price of $1.40¾ good for 60 days.

FRIEDBERG & CO. LTD.

FOREIGN EXCHANGE DEALERS
COMMODITIES FUTURES BROKERS
FINANCIAL SERVICES

34 ADELAIDE ST. W.
TORONTO 1, ONTARIO, CANADA
TEL. (416) 864-1195
CABLE ADDRESS FRIEDCO TORONTO

December 8, 1971

Dr. Morton Shulman
378 Roncesvalles
Toronto, Ont.

Dear Dr. Shulman:

We confirm sale to you today of Call option $387.50 on 10,000 ounces of .999 minimum purity at 140.75 per troy oz.

Please notify us if you wish to exercise option no later than 2:00 P.M. February 8, 1972. Upon exercise, we agree to deliver to you the warehouse receipts anytime between February 8th and February 15th.

Please sign and return copy of this confirmation. Payments should be made to Friedberg & Co. Ltd.

Yours truly,

Albert D. Friedberg

Dr. Morton Shulman

If silver had gone straight down I might have lost my $387.50 but I would have had 60 days in which silver could turn around and recover my investment. In contrast, if I had purchased a silver contract outright my down payment would have been $750 and if silver had fallen I would have lost the entire $750 in two or three days with no 60-day chance to recover.

Silver however rose, going to $1.44 only two days later. I then sold one silver contract, recovering my initial investment with the potential profit, but I did *not* exercise my call because I hoped that silver would fall back. Sure enough it did, and one week later I was able to buy back the silver contract for $140 that I had sold at $144. I now had received back my $387.50 but still owned the call option.

Silver now began to rise again and on January 11 I was able to sell a silver contract at $149.40. Of course I did not exercise my option for I hoped for another fall in the price of silver before the option ran out in February.

FRIEDBERG & CO. LTD.

34 ADELAIDE ST. WEST
TORONTO 1, ONTARIO
Tel. (416) 864-1195
Cable Address: FRIEDCO Toronto

CONFIRMATION

DATE 11/1/72   ACCOUNT NO.

TO   Dr. Morton Shulman
     Masg Entertainment Corp.
     378 Roncesvalles
     Toronto, Ont.

WE HAVE THIS DAY MADE THE FOLLOWING TRADES FOR YOUR ACCOUNT AND RISK   as agents

BOUGHT			SOLD		
QUANTITY	COMMODITY	PRICE	QUANTITY	COMMODITY	PRICE
			1	Silver March '72 on Comex	$149.40

NOTICE It is understood and agreed that all futures transactions made by us for your account are either hedges or contemplate actual delivery and receipt of the property and payment therefor; and that all property sold for your account is sold upon the representation that you have the same in your possession actually or potentially. These transactions are made in accordance with and subject to the rules, regulations and customs of the exchange where made and also in accordance with and subject to Federal and State laws. It is understood and agreed that we reserve the right to close out transactions without notice when the margins on deposit with us (1) are exhausted or (2) are inadequate in our judgment to protect us against price fluctuations or (3) are below the minimum margin requirements under the rules and regulations of the exchange relating thereto

N.B.—Any apparent error should be immediately reported by telegraph or telephone, otherwise this account will be considered approved by you. Name of other party to contract furnished on request.   E. & O.E.

For the person who loves to gamble with little risk this is the ideal place. I heartily recommend the purchase of puts or calls on commodities. It is easy to make many trades using such an option as your protection, and so to make a great deal of money.

10
WARRANTS

Warrants are options to buy stock. They differ from calls in that calls are short-term options which are created and sold by individuals, whereas warrants are longer-running options issued by a company itself. Another major difference is that warrants are usually listed on a stock exchange and can always be resold, but calls once purchased normally cannot be resold. The advantage of a call is that it can be purchased on any stock; the advantage of a warrant is that because it was not created to satisfy an individual request, it is much cheaper.

Warrants are without doubt the most volatile security that can be purchased. It is not uncommon for the warrant on a stock to go up as much as tenfold while, during the same period, the stock itself has merely doubled. In Chapter 2 there was a detailed write-up on Newconex, showing how the stock went from $5 to $9 in one month. Yet in the same period Newconex warrants went from $1 to $5. It is this rapid jump in price that gives warrants their great attraction, for it presents the possibility of huge profits from small investments. The rapid price gain is due to *leverage*.

Leverage is the first thing to look for in assessing a warrant; leverage refers to the amount that a warrant will move up if the stock doubles in price. For example, when Newconex stock was trading at $5, its warrant was trading at $1 and presented the right to buy stock at $5. At this level the warrant had no real value but presented a potential value if the stock moved above $5. When the stock moved up to $9, the warrant now had a real value of the market price ($9) less the option price of $5; in other words the warrant now had a real value of $4. If the stock moved to $10, the warrant would have a real value of $5. Thus if the stock doubled from $5 to $10, the warrant would go up at least five times, from $1 to $5. Its *leverage factor* would be 5:1.

The major reason for buying a warrant is its leverage. The leverage figure should never be less than 2:1. Ideally it should be at least 3:1 or 4:1. Normally the highest leverage is found in warrants that have no real value, that is, where the stock is trading at or below the option price of the warrant (for example, Newconex before it moved up above $5). Once the warrants develop real value, their leverage rapidly disappears. If the leverage is less than 2:1, the warrant should not be bought, regardless of all other circumstances.

Let us now consider Newconex stock at $9 while the warrant is at $5. If the stock doubles to $18, the warrant would be worth $13, so the leverage is now less than 3:1. On higher-priced warrants there may be no leverage at all, in that a doubling of the stock price will not more than double the warrant price.

Volatility is the second thing that should be considered in assessing a warrant. There is no sense in buying a warrant with excellent leverage if the stock is a very stable one with no chance of moving up in price. The stock must have potential volatility, in that there must be a good possibility of a fast upward move due to increased earnings or some major change in the company's business. If the company stock does not have volatility or potential volatility, the warrant should not be bought, regardless of how cheaply it is priced.

Time is the third factor to consider in buying a warrant. Practically all warrants have a fixed life and are due to expire on a certain date, varying anywhere from one to twenty years after issue, although a very few are perpetual and never expire. The longer the warrant has to run, the more valuable it is, and as the time of expiry approaches the warrant will gradually lose any premium in its price and slip downward to its real value. If that real value is zero, the warrant may expire without having any value, and so this pitfall must be avoided. *When a warrant is purchased, there should be sufficient time remaining in its life to allow its stock to move up enough to increase the value of the warrant by at least 100%.* As a general rule it is unwise to purchase any warrant that has less than two years to run, and it is best to purchase warrants that have a minimum of five years of life remaining.

If these three factors are all considered before a warrant is purchased, financial profits are certain. Members of the public lose vast sums every year by ignoring one or more of these factors. Warrants present the greatest financial opportunities in the market and also the greatest risks. The risks are unnecessary ones.

An ideal example of the perfect warrant was that of the Investment Company of America. This is a mutual fund which has perpetual warrants outstanding, each of which allows the purchase of eleven shares (approximately) at the price of $10.48 each. In 1954 these warrants were trading at $3¼, having moved up from 50¢. The three factors of leverage, volatility, and time were all favourable, and the warrants were an obvious buy (p. 83).

The leverage in this warrant was truly outstanding. The stock was then trading at about $8. If it were to double to $16, the warrant would have a real value of $16 less $10.48 (the option price) multiplied by 11, because each warrant allowed the purchase of eleven shares of stock. This would give a real value of $60.50. The warrant was then trading at $3.25, so the leverage factor was an amazing 18:1. I have never seen a higher leverage factor.

The time factor was also the best possible one, for the warrants were perpetual; they would never run out. This is very rare.

The volatility factor was the weakest of the three in this case. Because the Investment Company of America is a mutual fund, its value would, of course, move up with a strong market. However, the company follows the practice of paying out all its realized gains in distributions to its shareholders. This slows the rate of growth but does not completely

IN ACCOUNT WITH

DOHERTY ROADHOUSE & CO.

255 BAY STREET
TORONTO

-1

DR. M. SHULMAN
378 RONCESVALLES AVE.
TORONTO ONT.
109-B.

DATE	No. OF SHARES BOT. OR RECEIVED	No. OF SHARES SOLD OR DELIVERED	STOCK	PRICE	DEBIT	CREDIT	BALANCE
1954 MAY-JUNE			BALANCE				5,96800
16.	100.		INV. CO. OF AMER. WTS.	3/¾	32679		
	200.		DO	03⅝	72788		
	100.		DO	03⅝	36394		
	400.		DO	03⅝	1,45576		14,26045
17.	200.		INV. CO. OF AMER. WTS.	03⅞	77744		
		200	ONT. JOCKEY CLUB WTS.	74		14400	14,89389
21.	200.		INV. CO. OF AMER. WTS	400	80200		

FOR AUDIT PURPOSES—Please communicate full particulars of any difference in the above account direct to Audit Department, Box 67, General Delivery, Toronto, Canada

B.S. LTD. 28424 E. & O. E. THIS ACCOUNT WILL BE CONSIDERED CORRECT IF NO REPORT IS RECEIVED WITHIN TEN DAYS 404

remove the volatility, because gains are not paid out until realized, that is, until or unless the stock on which there are profits are sold by the fund. In any case the reduced volatility was certainly overshadowed by the tremendous leverage and time factors.

When warrants are bought in this scientific manner it is almost impossible for the purchaser to lose, and within two years, although the stock of Investment Company of America had moved up less than 20%, the warrants had jumped to four times their 1954 price, and I was happy to sell many of my warrants between $14 and $15.

JN30 56 DR MORTON P SHULMAN

IN ACCOUNT WITH
EASTMAN, DILLON
15 BROAD STREET, NEW YORK
225 SO 15TH ST
PHILA 2 PA

DATE	BOUGHT RECEIVED OR LONG	SOLD DELIVERED OR SHORT	DESCRIPTION	PRICE OR REFERENCE *	DEBIT
MAY 31			BAL FWD 05 31 56		
JN 01	15		UTS WESTCOAST TRANSM	126¼	192227
JN 01			100DEB3CAP 88 5½ A20		
JN 04		100	WTS INVESTMENT CO AM	14¼	
JN 04		100	WTS INVESTMENT CO AM	14¼	
JN 04		200	WTS INVESTMENT CO AM	14¼	
JN 04		100	WTS INVESTMENT CO AM	14½	

Actually, looking back, I realize that I was very wrong to sell, because even when the warrants were up to $14, the three factors were still very favourable. The time and volatility factors had not changed, of course, and the leverage was still very good. The stock was at $10, so if it doubled to $20 this would put a value of $20 — $10.48 × 11 on the warrant or a value of $104.50 for each warrant. Divide this by $14 and the leverage factor is 7:1 which is much better than can usually be found.

At the time of writing, the stock is $14 and the warrant has jumped to $40. Even at this $40, a figure up tenfold from my original purchase, these warrants are a tremendous buy. The volatility and time factors are still the same, so the leverage is the crucial factor. If the stock doubles to $28 the warrant will be worth $28 — $10.48 × 11 or $192. Divide this by $40 and we get the leverage factor of 5:1 which is higher than can be received on any other long-life warrant.

Thus we have the amazing situation where a stock has gone from $8 to $14 and yet its warrant has jumped from $3.25 to $40 and still remained a bargain. The Investment Company of America warrant truly exemplifies the romance and rewards possible in warrant purchases.

Where do warrants come from? Why do companies issue them? What is the cheapest way to buy them?

Many warrants were legacies of the depression and a few of these are still trading. In the early thirties, when thousands of companies went bankrupt and were reorganized, in many cases not only was there no equity for the shareholders, but in addition many bondholders were left with nothing. In the attempt to give these unfortunate investors something for their lost money, newly reorganized companies often set up warrants which were given to the former stock and bondholders and which at least offered some hope of someday getting some money back. The Investment Company of America warrant was set up in just such a way. The predecessor mutual fund had gone broke, and in the reorganization the shareholders of the predecessor company were thrown a bone in the form of these perpetual warrants. It took thirty years, but if anyone had been able to wait, he woud have got his money back plus interest!

Fortunately warrants issued today are not produced as the result of such unhappy financial situations. Practically all of today's warrants are issued as a "sweetener" with a bond or stock issue. They cost the company nothing and will facilitate the sale of a bond that otherwise might have required much higher interest rates. Most corporations would much rather give away warrants, which cost nothing, than pay the higher interest which comes out of earnings.

A typical example of such an issue was made in 1970 by the Chrysler Corporation. In that year there was a temporary shortage of funds available for bonds and mortgages, and the resulting competition for the available money produced a massive increase in interest rates. At the height of the shortage Chrysler needed to borrow 90 million dollars, and in order to sell this quantity of bonds they were forced to pay the high rate of 7⅜% on a 16-year bond. In addition they gave a bonus of 20 warrants with every $1,000 bond.

These warrants appeared very interesting. They had a six-year life and so were not due to expire until 1976, and each warrant gave its holder the option to purchase one share of Chrysler at a price of $34 until 1976.

The company's stock is a very volatile one, for it is the smallest of the three large automobile manufacturers and a very slight shift in its percentage of car sales can make a tremendous difference to its profit picture. As a result, the warrants appeared very attractive. Thus we had a six-year warrant on a highly volatile company. What was the leverage of this warrant? The company stock was then trading at $30 per share and initial sales of the warrants occurred at $12. If the stock were to double to $60, the warrant would be worth $26, giving a low leverage, but this was offset by the tremendous volatility.

Under these circumstances the warrants were a good buy, as were the Chrysler bonds themselves. However, as so often happens with wonderful issues of this type, the public received it poorly, and the underwriting brokers had difficulty selling their bonds. In less than a week the bonds were actually selling for less than their issue price of $1,000. These sales showed typical lack of investor foresight.

A triple market now developed. First was the selling of these bonds by the ignorant. Second was the purchase of the warrants by speculators who hoped to make a capital gain, and third was the purchase and sale of bonds "ex-warrants", i.e. the purchase of the bonds at issue price of $1,000 and their resale at $700 without the warrants to clever investors who wished to own these high-yield bonds and make a sure capital gain when they moved back up to $1,000.

Everyone who bought in any of these three ways made a great deal of money. Those who bought the original bonds made an almost immediate profit. Within a few days the panic sellers were bought out and the bonds began to move upwards, reaching $1,200 each within a few months.

Those who bought the warrants made a rapid and large capital gain, for they quickly sold up to $17½.

Investors who purchased the bonds ex-warrants did equally well. In addition to drawing an actual interest rate of over 9%, the bonds for which they paid $700 soon moved to $900.

The best brokerage houses find difficulty in putting a value on new warrants. In 1957 the Loblaw Company issued a 6% twenty-year bond carrying a bonus of warrants. Many large institutions were very happy to sell off the warrants so as to get their bonds at a lower price and increase their income yield, but no one was quite sure at what price the warrants should be sold. The underwriting broker thought $4 appeared fair, and this was the price the institutions received. In turn they were resold at $4⅜ to speculators who thought that this price was very cheap.

Within a few days the brokers realized their error and rushed to buy the warrants back at $6.50 (p. 86).

NESBITT, THOMSON AND COMPANY, LIMITED

SALE TO ⌐ Dr. Morton P. Shulman,   ⌐   350 BAY ST.,
378 Roncesvalles Ave.,   **TORONTO 1, ONT.**
TORONTO 3, Ontario.

⌐   August 26 1957
⌐   ⌐ **SETTLEMENT DATE**   August 29 1957

WE HAVE ACTED AS PRINCIPAL IN THIS TRANSACTION

SALESMAN
J.A. McMillan, 5 T 1775

PAR VALUE	SECURITY	PRICE	AMOUNT	INTEREST	TAX	TOTAL	CONTRACT
1,000	Loblaw Companies Limited Stock purchase warrants	4.3/8 net	4,375.00			4,375.00	9482
		INTEREST FROM		TO		DAYS	

DELIVERY
As above, by letter of intent to deliver
as and when available. Street.
REGISTRATION Payment to be made immediately.

Those of us who had bought at $4⅜ and sold right back at $6.50
laughed at those silly stockbrokers, but not for long. The warrants pro-
ceeded to sell up all the way to $30.

NESBITT, THOMSON AND COMPANY, LIMITED

350 BAY ST.,
TORONTO 1, ONT.

PURCHASE FROM ⌐ Dr. Morton P. Shulman & Associates,   September 10 1957
378 Roncesvalles Ave.,
⌐TORONTO, Ontario.   ⌐ **SETTLEMENT DATE**   Septmeber 13 1957

WE HAVE ACTED AS PRINCIPAL IN THIS TRANSACTION

SALESMAN
J.A. McMillan 5 T 1775

PAR VALUE	SECURITY	PRICE	AMOUNT	INTEREST	TAX	TOTAL	CONTRACT
3,000	Loblaw Companies Limited Stock Purchase Warrants if, as & when issued	6.50 net	19,500.00			19,500.00	5774
		INTEREST FROM		TO		DAYS	

Warrants are not always issued with bonds, but sometimes they
are used as a sweetener in takeovers (see Chapter 13). In 1962 Shell Oil
bought out the Canadian Oil Company, giving shareholders of Canadian
Oil their option of two takeover offers. The one that is of importance
here consisted of $52.50 in cash plus a warrant to buy Shell of Canada
stock.

These warrants had a ten-year life at a fixed option price of $20
per share. Thus, unlike the Canadian Chemical warrant, at any time
within ten years the holder of such a warrant had the option to buy one
Class A share of Shell for $20.

Shell was and is a very dynamic, expanding company, so this warrant obviously had both a long life and volatility. What about its leverage? The trouble was that nobody knew what Canadian Shell stock was worth, because up until 1962 it had all been held by the parent companies, Shell U.S. and Shell Investments. These companies now announced that they were going to distribute six million shares of A stock to their shareholders. The first hint of the value of the stock was the issue by Shell of a preferred stock at $20 that was convertible share for share into Shell's A stock. This meant that the Shell was worth something less than $20, and as most of these convertible issues are issued at ten to twenty per cent above the market price of the stock, it meant that the Shell Co. felt the stock was worth about $16 to $18. Actually the first tentative stock trades took place well below this figure, at $11, but then the stock moved up steadily to $14.

Initially the warrants were available free to all takers! This unique situation occurred because thousands of shares of Canadian Oil stock were bought by speculators prior to the Shell offering being made public, and they rushed to take their profits by dumping their stock the morning after the announcement was made. Thus thousands and thousands of shares of Canadian Oil traded between $52 and $52½ that memorable morning. All those who bought were able to hand in the stock to Shell and get back their $52.50 and be left with a free warrant. All that was necessary was the cash or the bank credit to pay for the stock for the few days before Shell reimbursed the holder. For those who did not have this capital or credit available the first warrants were available at $2.

CONFIRMATION   NESBITT, THOMSON AND COMPANY, LIMITED

Licensed with Canada

CONTRACT DATE Oct 23/62	SETTLEMENT DATE Oct 26/62	SALESMANS NAME AND CODE NUMBER B G Burns52-1775-T				CONTRACT NUMBER 2713	
ACTING AS PRINCIPAL WE HAVE TO DAY		BOUGHT FROM YOU	SOLD TO YOU	SECURITY DESCRIPTION		PRICE	AMOUNT
Dr Morton P Shulman 378 Roncesvalles Avenue Toronto, Ontario			200 Wts	Shell Investments Ltd Warrants		200	40000
		ACCRUED INTEREST FROM		TO	DAYS		
					LESS TAX		
					TOTAL		40000

ADDRESSES OF OUR PRINCIPAL OFFICES ARE LISTED ON REVERSE SIDE

NESBITT, THOMSON AND COMPANY LIMITED
PER G. K. McGarland

At this price the leverage factor was 4:1, and this, associated with the very long life of the warrant and the high volatility of the stock, made the warrant an excellent buy. Close to half a million traded below $3.50 over a six-week period. Suddenly toward the end of November, several brokers realized the value of the situation, and they and their clients rushed to buy both the warrants and the stock. The stock moved to $16 and the warrants to $6. At these prices there was absolutely no leverage left in the warrants, and most of the original purchasers sold their holdings.

HECTOR M. CHISHOLM & CO. LIMITED
MEMBERS
TORONTO STOCK EXCHANGE
MONTREAL STOCK EXCHANGE
CANADIAN STOCK EXCHANGE
82 RICHMOND ST. WEST
TORONTO 1. CANADA
TEL. 362—4731

TO Dr. M. Shulman.

			THE TORONTO STOCK EXCHANGE		DATE	Nov 28/6?
WE HAVE THIS DAY **SOLD** FOR YOUR ACCOUNT ON			THE CANADIAN STOCK EXCHANGE			
			X THE UNLISTED MARKET		VALUE	Dec 3/62

BROKER	SHARES	DESCRIPTION	PRICE	AMOUNT	COMMISSION	TAX	TOTAL
Lat.	400	Shell Co. of Can. Wts.	6.00	2400.00	30.00		2370.00

E. & O.E.

HECTOR M CHISHOLM & CO. LIMITED

PURCHASES OR SALES ARE MADE WITH THE DISTINCT UNDERSTANDING THAT ACTUAL DELIVERY IS CONTEMPLATED AND ARE SUBJECT IN ALL RESPECTS TO THE BY LAWS RULES AND CUSTOMS OF THE STOCK EXCHANGE WHERE THE ORDER IS EXECUTED AND TO THE CUSTOMS OF THE BROKERAGE BUSINESS IT IS AGREED THAT ALL SECURITIES CARRIED FROM TIME TO TIME IN THE CUSTOMER'S MARGINAL ACCOUNT OR DEPOSITED TO PROTECT THE SAME MAY BE LOANED BY US OR MAY BE PLEDGED BY US ON OUR GENERAL LOANS EITHER SEPARATELY OR TOGETHER WITH SECURITIES OF OTHERS AND EITHER TO SECURE ADVANCES WITHIN OR IN EXCESS OF THE AMOUNT DUE TO THEREON IT IS ALSO AGREED THAT WE RESERVE THE RIGHT TO CLOSE TRANSACTIONS WITHOUT DEMAND FOR ADDITIONAL MARGIN

The short-term correctness of our trading was proven by subsequent developments. Three years later the Shell A stock had moved up to $20, but the warrants were still trading at $6. By 1972, however, Shell stock had doubled to $40 and the warrants had moved all the way to $25!

Still, the basic rule is: if there is no leverage, the warrant should be sold.

Sometimes warrants are issued as a bonus with a new issue of preferred stock. Preferred stock represents ownership in a corporation just as common stock does, but it is preferred inasmuch as it normally received a fixed dividend annually, even though there may be no dividends paid on the common stock. In any dissolution of the company the preferred stockholders must be paid the face value of their stock before the common shareholders receive anything. Because preferred stocks do not normally participate in increased earnings, they do not have the glamour of common stocks, and when being issued to the public, they often have a warrant attached as a sweetener.

Such an issue was made by the Alberta Gas Trunkline in 1960. They issued a 6¼% preferred at $100 per share carrying a bonus of 2½ warrants per preferred share. The response to this issue was amazing, and within a few few days the preferred sold up to $108 per share.

NESBITT, THOMSON AND COMPANY, LIMITED

350 BAY ST.,

TORONTO 1, ONT.

SALE TO

SETTLEMENT DATE May 2/60
May 17/60

WE HAVE ACTED AS PRINCIPAL IN THIS TRANSACTION

SALESMAN AND CODE NO.

5-T-1775 J. A. McMillan

PAR VALUE	SECURITY	PRICE	AMOUNT	INTEREST	TOTAL	CONTRACT
50 Shs	The Alberta Gas Trunk Line Co.Ltd 6¼% Cum.Red.Pfd Shs Series "A" (of the P.V. of $100 each)(accompanied by Class "A" Common Share Purchase W₁s) I.A.& W.	100.00	5000.00		5000.00	P2577

INTEREST FROM   TO ✓   DAYS

DELIVERY

Bank of Montreal, Adelaide & Spadina Ave., Toronto, Ont.

REGISTRATION
Street

NESBITT, THOMSON AND COMPANY, LIMITED

PER

Delivery Phone:
EMpire 8-7137
EMpire 4-9986

TELEX - LATIMER, TORONTO - 02-2565

TORONTO, ONT.
Confirmation Phone:
EMpire 3-8921

W. D. Latimer Limited
Security Dealers
244 BAY STREET

Date May 2/60

We have this day BOUGHT FROM YOU

Please have cheques made payable at per In Toronto

Broker	Quantity	Security	Price	Amount	Brokerage	Tax Que. Prov.	Total
	200	Alberta Gas Trunk Line 6¼% Pfd. - Cum Wts.	108.10	21620.00		8.00	21,612.00

E.&O.E.

W. D. LATIMER Limited

BY

The owners of the preferred were happy to sell off the warrants at $4.50 each. These warrants had a nine-year life and initially allowed the purchase of common stock at $25 per share while the stock was then trading at $20. Alberta Gas Trunkline was engaged in the piping of natural gas and obviously was a growth stock with great volatility. The leverage factor was over 3:1, which is quite satisfactory, and the warrants were obviously a good buy at $4.50.

NESBITT, THOMSON AND COMPANY, LIMITED
350 BAY ST.

TORONTO 1, ONT.

SALE TO

SETTLEMENT DATE   May 3/60
                   May 17/60

WE HAVE ACTED AS PRINCIPAL IN THIS TRANSACTION

SALESMAN AND CODE NO.
5-T-1775 J.A.McMillan

PAR VALUE	SECURITY	PRICE	AMOUNT	INTEREST	TOTAL	CONTRA
3000 Warrants	The Alberta Gas Trunk Line Co. Ltd. I. A.& W.	4.50	13,500.00		13,500.00	9059

INTEREST FROM   TO   DAYS

REGISTRATION   Street

DELIVERY   Bank of Montreal,
            Adelaide & Spadina Ave.,
            Toronto, Ont.

NESBITT, THOMSON AND COMPANY, LIMITED

PER _____

Within two weeks the warrants had sold up to $5.40. This brought the leverage factor down to less than 3:1. With a long-term warrant of this volatile nature such leverage is still very good, but on this occasion I allowed my better judgment to be overruled by such a rapid profit and I sold by warrants.

ANNETT PARTNERS LIMITED

TELEPHONE
EM. 3-7361

MEMBER TORONTO STOCK EXCHANGE
220 BAY STREET
TORONTO 1

BOUGHT FROM YOU
WE HAVE THIS DAY SOLD

CLIENT	DATE TRADE	DATE VALUE	SHARES	SECURITY	PRICE	AMOUNT	COMMI
Dr. M.P. Shulman, 378 Roncesvalles Ave., Toronto, Ont.	17/5	20/5	100	Alberta Gas Wts.	5 3/8	537.50	
	IF AS AND WHEN ISSUED						

CASH SALES ARE MADE ON THE UNDERSTANDING THAT CERTIFICATED (DULY ENDORSED AND WITNESSED) WILL BE RECEIVED BY PHB
THIS OFFICE BY VALUE DATE, AFTER WHICH PAYMENT WILL BE FORWARDED.

THE NAME OF THE OTHER BROKER IN THIS TRANSACTION WILL BE FORWARDED ON REQUEST.
E. 80 E.

One year later the warrants traded over $17.

There are three pitfalls a warrant purchaser must avoid. These are callability, dilution and the rush of the crowd.

Callability— is a strang provision carried by some warrants that they may be called (cancelled) at the company's option by some minor payment to the warrant holder. Such warrants should never be purchased.

Dilution means increasing the amount of outstanding stock without receiving equivalent value for the stock. For example, if a company were to split its stock two for one, this would automatically halve the stock's value. If the warrant holder were not protected against such dilution, he could easily see his investment wiped out overnight. Never buy a warrant that is not protected against dilution. (The warrant certificate states whether it is protected.)

The "rush of the crowd" refers to the fact that certain types of securities go in and out of fashion. Securities that are out of fashion sell at sensible prices or, if not sensible, prices that are too low. These out-of-fashion securities are the ones that clever speculators seek to buy.

Securities that are in fashion are pursued by the mob and recommended by the customer's men and as a consequence sell at unreasonably high prices. Sad to say, that is the situation in relation to *almost* all warrants today. In the 1960s the public suddenly became aware of the potential profits in warrants and the prices of warrants in general jumped. The result has been that the great advantage in warrant purchasing, leverage, has now all but disappeared and with it the likelihood of making profits.

You will note that in this chapter there are no recent examples of warrant trades. This is because they have become so unattractive I no longer purchase them, and if I receive warrants as a bonus with a bond I sell them off immediately.

In summary, warrants at times are a most important security for the speculator. By carefully choosing warrant purchases, the buyer should on average double his money annually. The risk is, however, greater than with stocks, and warrants are not meant for the investor who cannot afford the occasional loss. The five basic points to seek in buying warrants are:

1. The warrant must have a long life ahead of it.
2. The leverage factor must be a minimum 2:1 and preferably much higher.
3. The warant should be on a stock with high volatility and a prospective expanding future.
4. The warrant should be non-callable and protected against dilution.

When these four features are present, large profits will result, but don't forget —

5. In today's bull market, warrant prices have moved up unreasonably in proportion to other securities. Today is not a good time to buy most warrants.

11
THE FREE RIDERS

Free riding is the purchase and sale of stock without putting up any money. Mentioning the free rider to a stockbroker elicits the same infuriated response as praising term insurance to an insurance executive, and for equally bad reasons. Stockbrokers certainly approve of buying stocks and bonds without putting up any money, but most feel that this practice should be restricted to professionals (themselves) and heartily disapprove of any public participation.

The free rider is an individual who purchases stocks or bonds with no intention of paying for them; he avoids this necessity by selling the security before the day arrives on which payment is due. This cannot often be done with ordinary stocks, because payment must be made within three trading days; except in unusual circumstances, this is not enough time for a stock to go up. However, it can very easily be done on the "if, as, and when" market, where payment commonly is not required for many weeks or months.

The "if, as, and when" market normally begins when a new equity is issued. This can be a true new issue of stock or bonds, which has been announced and sold; it can be a spinoff from an established company; or it can even be a new stock resulting from a stock split.

1. "IF, AS, AND WHEN" WARRANTS   The best opportunities arise when bonds or debentures are issued that carry a bonus of warrants. It is common practice to immediately issue interim bonds; actual physical delivery of the bonus warrants cannot be made until they are printed and delivered with the definitive bonds some three to six months later. These warrants are traded in the interval, however, on an "if, as, and when" issued basis. This means that delivery is not affected and payment is not made until the warrants are available some months later. Before the delivery day arrives, the purchaser can sell the warrants, taking his profit (or loss) without having made any initial investment. Because of the very special circumstances involved here, there is usually a profit to take rather than a loss.

This is because purchasers of such bonds are normally large institutions or investors. The small investor or speculator has usually neither the capital, the knowledge, nor the desire for the small sure profit shown by these bonds. Since these institutions are primarily interested in safety and yield, they are quite happy to sell off at low prices the bonus warrants from their bonds, thus reducing their cost per bond and raising their investment yield. This is well illustrated by an issue in November, 1965. The Traders Finance Corporation issued $10 million worth of 6½% five-year debentures carrying a free bonus of 25 warrants per $1,000 bond. The company is large, well managed, and showed excellent earnings; it had to give such a large yield because of a temporary market shortage of loan money for finance companies. The institutions that purchased the bonds were happy to sell the warrants at $2.50 each, thus reducing their cost per bond to $937.50 (i.e., $1,000 — 25 × $2.50). This meant that they now received a yield of over 8% on their perfectly safe investment, and they were happy to have sold their warrants.

The warrant purchasers received a seven-year warrant (see the preceding chapter), giving an option on Traders Finance A stock at $15, while the market value of the stock was $12.50. Similar warrants from other similar companies listed on various stock exchanges were then trading at prices considerably higher than $2.50. One of Traders Finance's competitors, for example, had a similar warrant outstanding, which was trading at $3.10, even though its terms were less advantageous than those of the Traders warrant.

So here we had a situation in which one could buy a warrant with a probable true value of about $4 for $2.50, and it was not necessary to invest a penny. Reproduced below is a copy of a purchase made at that time. You will note that although the sale took place on November 22, 1965, payment was not required until the settlement date of May 15, 1966.

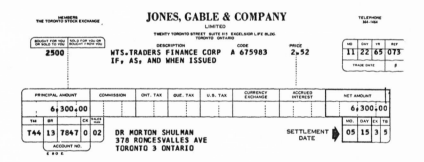

This was truly a free ride, in which almost everyone made money. The insurance companies received 8% on their investment plus a capital gain to be received in 1970 when the debentures would be redeemed. The finance company that borrowed the money did not pay 8% on the money they received, but only 6½%. The issuing stockbroker made a profit of $250,000 for distributing the issue. Other stockbrokers charged a commission or markup for handling the sale of the warrants, varying from two to five cents per warrant. Finally, the warrant purchaser ended up with an item worth much more than the $2.50 purchase price and without having invested a penny.

In the stock market, items do not often remain on the bargain counter for long. Thus, within a very few days, investors began comparing the price of these Traders warrants with other similar issues and began bidding up the price. Within a week, the bid rose to $2.75, and the original free riders were able to sell out a profit of $230 per thousand warrants (see illustration below).

Members of The Investment Dealers' Association of Canada	**WALKER, HARDAKER & COMPANY, LIMITED**		15 KING STREET W. HAMILTON, ONTARIO 527-9217

WE CONFIRM THE FOLLOWING TRANSACTION FOR YOUR ACCOUNT

CONTRACT NO.	SALESMAN	TRANSACTION DATE	SETTLEMENT DATE
6987	Office.	Nov. 29/65.	If As & When Issued

CODE	SOLD TO - BOUGHT FOR	BOUGHT FROM - SOLD FOR	DESCRIPTION	PRICE
2		4,700	TRADERS FINANCE CORPORATION "AA WARRANTS	2.75

PRINCIPAL AMOUNT	COMMISSION	ONTARIO TAX	OTHER TAX	ACCRUED INTEREST	NET AMOUNT
12,925.00					12,925.00

Dr. Morton F. Shulman,
378 Roncesvalles Avenue,
TORONTO, Ontario.

All transactions subject to the rules and regulations of the exchange where executed. At securities carried at any time when indebted to us for your account may be loaned or pledged by us on our general account. Such securities may be bought or sold by us when such transaction is deemed necessary for our protection. All statements of accounts are deemed to be correct unless written notice is given within five days after their receipt. The name of the other broker in any transaction will be provided upon request.

WALKER, HARDAKER & COMPANY, LIMITED

1. OUR SALE TO YOU AS PRINCIPALS.   3. AS AGENTS, OUR SALE FOR YOUR ACCOUNT.
2. OUR PURCHASE FROM YOU AS PRINCIPALS.   4. AS AGENTS, OUR PURCHASE FOR YOUR ACCOUNT.   PER *W.Walker.*

It is interesting to note that even though our original purchaser at $2.50 on November 22 sold his warrants a week later at a profit of $600, he did not receive this profit until the warrants were actually printed and delivered many months later. Until that time it was a book-keeping entry. A minor nuisance indeed in such a lovely situation!

It is obvious that the early bird gets the worm in these "if, as, and when" situations. One does not have weeks or even days to consider one's purchase. When such opportunities arise, they must be quickly taken advantage of. Happily, this specific type of situation becomes available surprisingly often. The three basic factors to be considered when making a purchase are:

1. Is the warrant being offered for a lower price than similar outstanding warrants?
2. Is the free-ride period sufficiently long to allow time for the warrants to receive distribution and rise in price?
3. Is the company that is issuing the debenture sound?

There is one small flaw in this situation. A broker selling warrants on an "if, as, and when" basis obviously must know his customers; he must be sure that they or their estate will be available in six months to complete the transaction. Therefore, in order to protect themselves, such brokers normally require that the purchaser deposit some other stock in their account as security. Inasmuch as most clients normally leave stocks on deposit with their brokers, this produces little difficulty.

2. GOVERNMENT BONDS Without question, this is the area of the "if, as, and when" market which is most lucrative; in addition it has the advantage of having probably the lowest risk of any form of investment anywhere.

Many free riders have been drawn to government bonds because the bonds are freely available and because it is not necessary to scramble with other would-be buyers, as the bonds can be ordered at any bank or brokerage house in almost any quantity.

The free-ride time is much less than in the previous example, usually running around two to three weeks. But this is quite sufficient in this type of ride, and in fact riders here usually sell after three or four days. The size of the profit is usually small, often only $2.50 per $1,000 bond or even less, but inasmuch as large numbers of the bonds are available the overall profit may be substantial.

The reason for the free availability of government bonds is very simple. Unlike corporations, governments must raise vast amounts of money, and so their smallest issues are in the hundreds of millions of dollars. To raise such moneys, they distribute the bonds widely through innumerable banks and brokers. Because printing and distribution of these bonds takes time, there is always a free ride of two or three weeks available to initial purchasers. (These bonds should not be confused with savings bonds available only in limited quantities per individual and which cannot fluctuate in price.)

The reason that free riders almost always make money on government bonds is that, in raising such large amounts of money, the government must price their bonds sufficiently low to attract buyers, and this in effect means putting a slightly higher interest rate on this new issue than is prevalent on outstanding similar bonds. After such an issue has been announced, yields must come into line, and so either the new issue must rise in price or else all similar outstanding issues must fall in price. In actuality both usually occur, and within a very short time the bond prices will come into line with one another.

The free riders have a built-in safety factor in these bonds, because the government will not stop raising money after this issue but must continue to bring out bond issues ad infinitum. Thus they tend to price the bonds sufficiently attractively to ensure their success and, more important, they normally will support the bonds at issue price or slightly below it, at least until distribution has been completed. Thus after a bond has been issued, even if international events should force a fall in general bond prices, new issues normally have sufficient support to allow a free rider to get out with his money. If he is willing to take a small profit and sell after two or three days, the rider can be certain of taking a profit seven times out of ten and of breaking even in two of the remaining times. Because all this is done without investing a penny, patriotism has not been sufficient to slow the pace of free riding in government bonds.

Banks, dealers, and government are extremely loath to see free riders buy these bonds because, when the bonds are unloaded, it puts pressure on the market and in effect they must be sold twice by the dealers, once to the original purchaser and a second time to another person or institution. Therefore, if a free rider is so blatant as to buy and sell his bonds through the same broker or bank, he will soon find that his orders for subsequent issues are either not filled or else are drastically cut. Thus in order to avoid putting any money up (if he does that he is no longer a free rider) he uses the stratagem of "delivery against payment". This means that the rider instructs the broker from whom he purchased the bonds to deliver them to his bank (where he has already sold them) against payment or visa versa. Brokers are quite happy to make such deliveries because they are a normal part of stock business and are usually not associated with free riding.

The free rider's rule for profit in government bonds is to quickly compare new government bond issues with similar outstanding bonds and to buy in large quantities those that compare favourably, selling them three days later regardless of whether or not they have gone up. It means sure profits but no popularity with the brokers or the country's treasury department.

3. NEW STOCK ISSUES This is the ideal place for the free rider to make money, but it must be done with circumspection, because brokers hate free riders in this field and will do anything possible to prevent riding. Basically the same factors apply as with government bonds; new stock issues must be attractively priced in order to pull in buyers, and there is usually a one- to two-week lag between confirmation of purchase and payment date, and the issuers normally support the stock at its issue price for some days or weeks after issue. Normally the underwriter will oversell his stock inventory, so that he will have a short position from which he can support the issue. He is naturally not anxious to buy back the stock he had just gone to such trouble and expense to distribute — and so free riders never sell their stock back directly. Instead they sell through a bank or an over-the-counter broker. Otherwise they would quickly be blackballed from receiving future issues.

There is a very simple rule for the free rider in such issues, and it should be strictly followed, because unlike government bonds there is no government behind these issues, just a broker. If the issue starts to go down, it can go down fast. Also it is much more difficult to evaluate the true demand for and value of these issues before they come out than it is in the bond field. The rule is this: after a new stock issue is released *if it trades at or below its issue price, sell it immediately*. This is because the "hot" issues will go to an immediate premium, and it will be perfectly safe to ride them until payment is demanded, whereas those issues that were overpriced to start, or which were not well sold, or which have not caught the public imagination, will begin trading at their issue price with a so-called "penalty" bid. A penalty bid is one that is made by the underwriting broker at issue price for a few days after the issue, and its purpose is to attempt to stabilize the stock price. The "penalty" involved does not affect the speculator but in effect represents a loss of the original selling commission by the broker. This is why brokers hate free riders.

If the new issue begins selling at is issue price it should be immediately sold but not forgotten, for when the penalty bid is withdrawn these stocks often will trade at ridiculously low prices as the brokers dump their unsold stock. This can be the opportunity for large profits; for example, Playboy "went public" at the end of 1971 issuing its stock at $23 per share. It began trading at $23 "penalty" bid and when this bid was withdrawn it plunged to $16. Purchases made at that time showed an immediate profit.

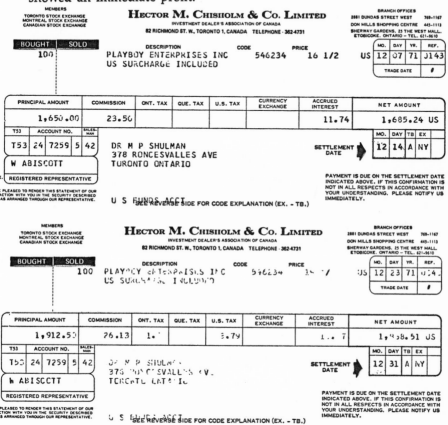

The perfect example of a "hot" new issue was the issue of Comsat in 1965. Coming out at $20, the stock immediately sold at $22, then fell back to 20½ but did not sell at or below issue price. Almost every broker in the United States had blocks of this stock to distribute to its clients, and those who either paid for the stock and kept it or alternatively sold it when payment was demanded made excellent profits, for the stock went up to over $70 per share. There are literally dozens of similarly profitable issues every year where no funds need be invested. An example is shown below:

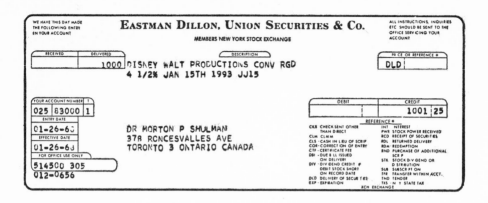

EASTMAN DILLON, UNION SECURITIES & CO.

MEMBERS NEW YORK STOCK EXCHANGE

WE HAVE THIS DAY MADE THE FOLLOWING ENTRY IN YOUR ACCOUNT

ALL INSTRUCTIONS, INQUIRIES ETC SHOULD BE SENT TO THE OFFICE SERVICING YOUR ACCOUNT

RECEIVED	DELIVERED	DESCRIPTION	PRICE OR REFERENCE #
	1000	DISNEY WALT PRODUCTIONS CONV RGD 4 1/2% JAN 15TH 1993 JJ15	DLD

YOUR ACCOUNT NUMBER
025 83000 1

	DEBIT	CREDIT
		1001 25

REFERENCE #

ENTRY DATE
01-26-6J

EFFECTIVE DATE
01-26-6J

DR MORTON P SHULMAN
378 RONCESVALLES AVE
TORONTO 3 ONTARIO CANADA

FOR OFFICE USE ONLY
514500 305
012-0656

CKB CHECK SENT OTHER THAN DIRECT
CLM CLAIM
CLS CASH IN LIEU OF SCRIP
COR CORRECTION OF ENTRY
CTF CERTIFICATE FEE
DBI DUE B LL ISSUED ON DELIVERY
DIV DIV DEND CREDIT #
DEBIT STOCK SHORT ON RECORD DATE
DLD DELIVERY OF SECURITIES
EXP EXPIRATION

INT INTEREST
PWR STOCK POWER RECEIVED
RCD RECEIPT OF SECURITIES
RDL RETURNED DELIVERY
RDM REDEMPTION
RND PURCHASE OF ADDITIONAL SCRIP
STK STOCK DIV DEND OR DISTRIBUTION
SUB SUBSCRIPTION
TFR TRANSFER WITHIN ACCT.
TND TENDER
TXS N Y STATE TAX
XCH EXCHANGE

MEMBERS
TORONTO STOCK EXCHANGE
MONTREAL STOCK EXCHANGE
CANADIAN STOCK EXCHANGE

HECTOR M. CHISHOLM & CO. LIMITED

INVESTMENT DEALERS ASSOCIATION OF CANADA
82 RICHMOND ST. W., TORONTO 1, CANADA   TELEPHONE - 362-4731

BRANCH OFFICES
KING EDWARD SHERATON HOTEL 363-3074
2881 DUNDAS STREET WEST 769-1167
DON MILLS SHOPPING CENTRE 445-1113

BOUGHT	SOLD	DESCRIPTION	CODE	PRICE	MO.	DAY	YR.	REF.
	1000	WALT DISNEY CONV. 4 1/2%JAN 15/93	993709	105.50 US	01	30	68	134
					TRADE DATE			#

PRINCIPAL AMOUNT	COMMISSION	ONT. TAX	QUE. TAX	U.S. TAX	CURRENCY EXCHANGE	ACCRUED INTEREST	NET AMOUNT	
1,055.00	2.50	.30				2.13	1,054.33	US

T53	BR	CK	SMN			MO.	DAY	EX.	TB
T53	24	7259 5	02	DR M P SHULMAN 378 RONCESVALLES AVE TORONTO ONTARIO	SETTLEMENT DATE	02	02	8	1

ACCOUNT NO.
E & O E

WE ARE PLEASED TO RENDER THIS STATEMENT OF OUR TRANSACTION WITH YOU IN THE SECURITY DESCRIBED ABOVE AS ARRANGED THROUGH OUR REPRESENTATIVE.

U S FUNDS ACCT
SEE REVERSE SIDE FOR CODE EXPLANATION (EX.—TB.)

PAYMENT IS DUE ON THE SETTLEMENT DATE INDICATED ABOVE. IF THIS CONFIRMATION IS NOT IN ALL RESPECTS IN ACCORDANCE WITH YOUR UNDERSTANDING, PLEASE NOTIFY US IMMEDIATELY.

Note that the Walt Disney was purchased January 15, 1968 for $1,001.25 and payment presumably should have been made or the stock sold immediately. In actuality, physical delivery was not made until January 30, 1968, by which time the bond had moved up to $1,055.00, where it was sold. This is an interesting and profitable characteristic of of new issues. Because of the delays and red tape attendant upon a new issue, often there is a two or three week delay in actual physical delivery, and this means a longer ride and larger profit for the free rider. It is, of course, essential that at the time of purchase the broker be instructed to deliver the stock against payment to a bank or Canadian broker, for this delay allows the free ride. The broker must be a Canadian one, because U.S. brokers will not cooperate with free riders, but any American citizen can open a U.S. account with a Canadian broker.

The delay in delivery is well illustrated here. The M.G.M. was purchased July 17, but the delivery wasn't made till August 20.

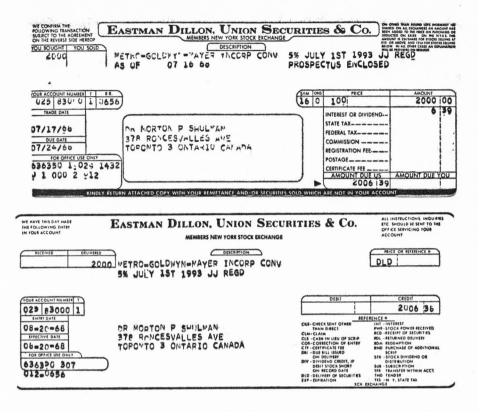

Occasionally a broker will attempt to minimize or prevent free riding by issuing a contract of sale like the one below:

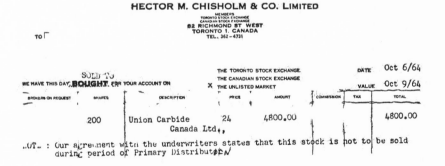

The agreement referred to, however, is between two brokers and does not involve either the purchaser or any third broker with whom he consummates the ultimate sale. Indeed, the broker issuing such a contract often knows perfectly well that the stock will be immediately resold, but prints the contract as illustrated so as to satisfy the original underwriters. There is no problem in making the sale.

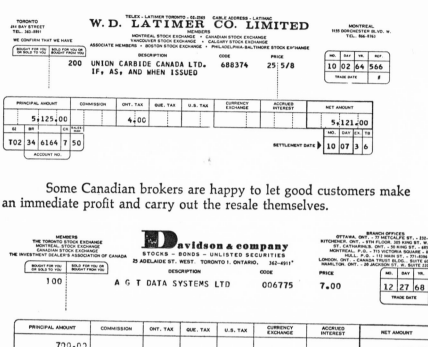

Some Canadian brokers are happy to let good customers make an immediate profit and carry out the resale themselves.

4. SECONDARY ISSUES A secondary stock issue is a distribution of stock in a company that already has outstanding stock, which is usually listed and trading on an exchange. The new stock is either from the treasury of the company and is being issued to raise the money for corporate purposes, or else is a distribution of stock previously held by one or more large shareholders. (Brokers define secondary issues as stocks that have already been sold once to the public and which are being resold in a large block by their current owner.) Possibilities of profit are much more limited here than in new issues, and as a general rule the free rider would be well advised to avoid such issues. There are exceptions, however.

The mechanism of a secondary issue is such that after the market closes the underwriting broker will announce the price of the secondary issue, other details of which have been previously announced, and will then distribute it to his clients at the announced price and with *no* added commission.

If the announced issue price is well below the price at which the stock was trading on the exchange, there is a good opportunity for the rider, because in the days or weeks before physical delivery is made and payment demanded, the stock is very likely to bounce back to its original price. An example of such a trade is given below:

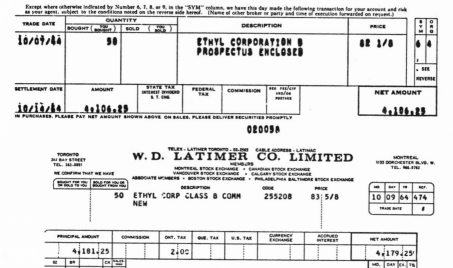

In this case the Ethyl stock moved up within two days to its previous level, giving a very rapid profit. Actually it moved much higher in subsequent days, and the patient rider would have made very much larger profits.

5. OUTSTANDING STOCKS Prolonged free riding in the normal stock purchase is not as easy as in previously described groups, but it is even more important because opportunities arise daily.

At the time of purchase the broker should be instructed to register the stock in his (the broker's) name and then forward it against payment to the client's bank or a Canadian broker. Such registration and delivery instructions are very common.

If an actively traded stock has been purchased, very often within the one to two weeks required for delivery the stock will have fluctuated sufficiently to ensure a profit.

On the American exchange there are large price movements and many such opportunities.

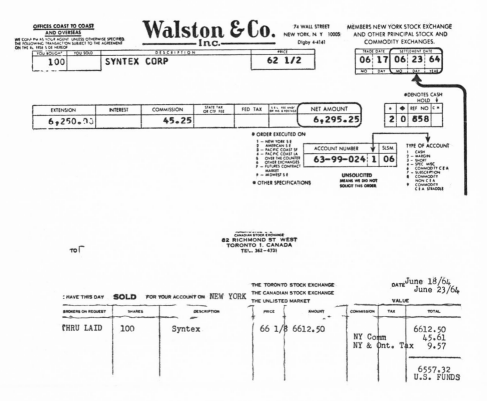

Thus in one day the Syntex moved substantially, giving $260 profit.

Even more striking is the example below:

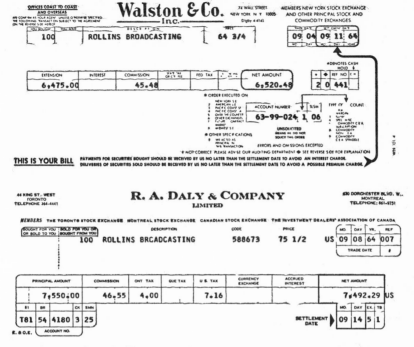

In four days Rollins moved up over $10, giving a profit of almost $1,000 on the purchase of 100 shares — without any investment.

Although these opportunities are not as common on the New York exchange, even the big board does give the occasional free-ride profit. In 1964, for example R.C.A. became very active.

Not a large profit, but after all, there was no investment!

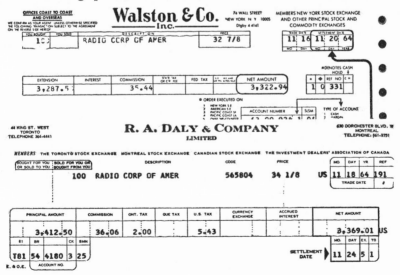

I have an acquaintance who, using the above method, last year traded over one million dollars' worth of listed stocks, never put up any money, and showed a net profit of $28,000. He had 130 trades and showed a profit on 94 of these. He warns that this method is not suitable for a bear market.

In summary, free riding is the purchase of securities for which no payment is required.

In successful free riding:

1. The free period should be as long as possible, preferably at least one month.

2. Other securities must be deposited with your broker to protect him.

3. No security should be purchased just because it involves free riding, but it should present the same value and potential as if cash were being paid.

4. The best place for free riding is in the field of convertible bonds, for they almost all have at least an initial rise. Year in and year out, good market or bad, this system never fails.

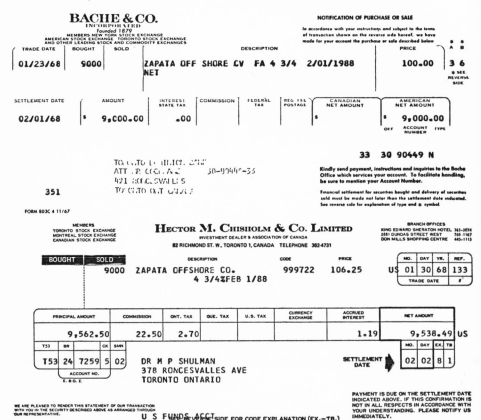

The experienced free rider can proceed to the ultimate in free riding, which is the investing of imaginary money in order to earn real interest from it.

The mechanism is simple. The rider makes an initial deposit of a few thousand U.S. dollars to open a new account, preferably with a Canadian broker. He then proceeds to order new issues of European or U.S. convertible bonds through his regular American or Canadian brokers, with instructions that they be delivered against payment to the broker where the cash deposit has been made. Although he may have only deposited $5,000, he will order $100,000 or more of various convertible bonds. Because of the long distances and delays attendant upon new issues, delivery takes many weeks or months, and the rider draws interest on his bonds even though he has put up no money for them. He instructs his new broker to accept the first five bonds and just deposit them in the account, using the original cash deposit to pay for them. Then, as more bonds arrive for payment, the first are sold to pay for the new ones.

The results are spectacular, for in addition to making the normal free-riding profit, the rider draws amounts of interest on non-existing money. In fact it is possible to earn up to 80% per annum in interest alone by continually ordering more bonds. A typical example is illustrated below.

The Allied Supermarket bonds were ordered on January 1, but as can be seen on the sales slip, delivery was not made until March 6. The $163.82 interest from January 1 until March 6 was earned with no investment and was added to the $650 capital gain.

During the same short period when Allied Supermarkets issued their convertible bonds, J. C. Penny, M.G.M., A.P.L., and American Export made similar issues. Each went up after delivery, and in every case weeks were required for delivery.

To draw real interest on imaginary money is surely the ultimate in free riding.

12
THE WHOLESALE MARKET

Very few members of the investment profession and even fewer members of the public are aware that some stocks are sold at two prices – the regular price charged the ordinary Joe and a special discount price given to large speculators. In order to qualify for the special discount price, theoretically you must be able to purchase individual stocks in huge quantities of $250,000 and more and secondly you must persuade your broker to place you on the "special" list. Actually the second requirement is the most difficult one, for you don't need a penny of cash to buy the stock itself!

In every large underwriting that takes place of a stock listed on the New York Exchange, a group of brokers band together to underwrite the issue and to guarantee that any shares that are not purchased by the public will be purchased by them and distributed through their clients. This type of underwriting is common and takes place many times every year, and because of the mechanism used it provides the easiest and surest way for a speculator to make money in the market.

The way it works is very simple. With every large offering of additional stock to shareholders there is always a substantial number of persons who don't have the cash to purchase the additional shares offered to them and so somebody else gets the chance to purchase their rights and their stock.

My favourite companies for this type of endeavour are American Telephone & Telegraph in the U.S. and Bell Telephone in Canada, both of whom make frequent offers to their shareholders to buy additional stock at a discount. The last gravy train of this type took place in 1971 when A.T.&T. made a new multimillion dollar issue of a 4% convertible preferred stock, all of which was offered to A.T.&T.'s old shareholders, who were given "rights" to buy in proportion to the size of their holdings of A.T.&T. The rights allowed the purchase of the new stock at $50 per share, but because many shareholders did not have the capital to purchase this new stock they sold the free rights which they had received.

In order to keep the price from collapsing and ruining the offering as these thousands of rights were dumped on the market, a group of brokers banded together and purchased hundreds of thousands of rights which they then exercised, ending up with millions of dollars' worth of shares of A.T.&T. convertible preferred. The brokers now began to call their customers, urging them to buy the stock and, as an inducement, offering to sell it to them at the current price of $55.25 "flat", i.e. the purchaser would not have to pay any commission. This was a reasonable deal and many thousands of shares were sold in this way.

If, however, you were lucky enough to be on the wholesale list (which I was) it was very easy to make large sums of money because the brokers offered their "special" customers a special price of $54.63 "flat" on blocks of 10,000 shares or more.

On July 5 my customer's man at Bache & Co. suggested I buy 10,000 shares to start, and I was delighted to do so because within seconds I had sold this stock at a very substantial profit.

What is even better is that in these deals it is not necessary to put up or even have any money. All I did was tell the customer's man at Bache & Co. to deliver the stock to my account at Chisholm and Co. "against payment" while I told Chisholm & Co., the selling broker, to pay Bache for the stock "when delivered" and to forward the balance to me as my profit.

STATEMENT TO: DR M P SHULMAN
                 379 RONCESVALLES AVE
                 TORONTO ONTARIO

24-7259-5   02   08 31 71
ACCOUNT NO.   SMN   MO. DAY YR.

*** U.S. FUNDS ACCOUNT ***

U S FUNDS ACCT

| DATE | | QUANTITY | | DESCRIPTION | PRICE OR TYPE OF ITEM | AMOUNT | | BALANCE |
MO.	DAY	BOUGHT RECEIVED LONG	SOLD DELIVERED SHORT			DEBIT	CREDIT	DEBIT UNLESS MARKED CR.
07	31			BALANCE	BAL		524354.04	
08	04			RE A T & T	JE2671	546250.00		
08	04	10000		AMER TEL & TEL 4.00 CV PR	JE2672			
08	05			BY CHEQUE	CR		9000.00	
08	20		10000	ITEL CORP. 8%1JUN96	DEL			
08	25			INTEREST TO AUG 25TH	INT	67.08		
						BALANCE AS OF AUG 31		$12,963.04
				* SECURITY POSITION *				
		25000		ITEL CORP. 8%1JUN96				
		5000		OKONITE CONV.4.75%1JUNE92	5000	SFK		

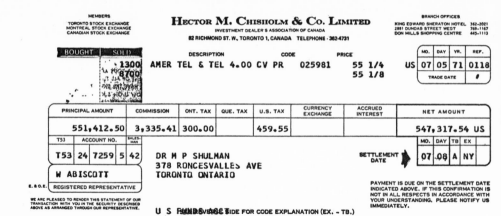

MEMBERS
TORONTO STOCK EXCHANGE
MONTREAL STOCK EXCHANGE
CANADIAN STOCK EXCHANGE

HECTOR M. CHISHOLM & CO. LIMITED
INVESTMENT DEALER'S ASSOCIATION OF CANADA
82 RICHMOND ST. W., TORONTO 1, CANADA   TELEPHONE - 382-4731

BRANCH OFFICES
KING EDWARD SHERATON HOTEL   362-2021
2881 DUNDAS STREET WEST   769-1167
DON MILLS SHOPPING CENTRE   445-1113

	BOUGHT	SOLD	DESCRIPTION	CODE	PRICE	MO.	DAY	YR.	REF.
	1300		AMER TEL & TEL 4.00 CV PR	025981	55 1/4	US 07	05	71	0118
		8700			55 1/8		TRADE DATE		

PRINCIPAL AMOUNT	COMMISSION	ONT. TAX	QUE. TAX	U.S. TAX	CURRENCY EXCHANGE	ACCRUED INTEREST	NET AMOUNT
551,412.50	3,335.41	300.00		459.55			547,317.54 US

T53	ACCOUNT NO.	SALES-MAN		MO.	DAY	TB	EX
T53 24 7259 5	42		DR M P SHULMAN	SETTLEMENT DATE	07 08	A	NY

W ABISCOTT
378 RONCESVALLES AVE
TORONTO ONTARIO

E.&O.E.   REGISTERED REPRESENTATIVE

PAYMENT IS DUE ON THE SETTLEMENT DATE INDICATED ABOVE. IF THIS CONFIRMATION IS NOT IN ALL RESPECTS IN ACCORDANCE WITH YOUR UNDERSTANDING, PLEASE NOTIFY US IMMEDIATELY.

WE ARE PLEASED TO RENDER THIS STATEMENT OF OUR TRANSACTION WITH YOU IN THE SECURITY DESCRIBED ABOVE AS ARRANGED THROUGH OUR REPRESENTATIVE.

U S FUNDS   SEE REVERSE SIDE FOR CODE EXPLANATION (EX. - TB.)

This type of trade is foolproof because both purchase and sale are made simultaneously so as to avoid the danger of the stock's price dropping after the purchase has been made. After all you don't want to be in the position of actually owning a huge block of such a basically unattractive stock as A.T.&T. even for five minutes, even if you have that kind of money!

This type of deal comes up every month, in busy times sometimes every week. Unfortunately only those few persons will be allowed to make this easy money who, the brokers are convinced, are wealthy enough not to need it.

13

THE TAKE OVER

Since the late fifties there has been an increasing number of large companies buying out smaller ones. These "takeovers" often produce very unusual profit opportunities for the speculator. In some cases it means tying up funds for some time, but the returns can be spectacular.

In October, 1955, the Regent Oil Refining Co., a small Canadian and West Indies oil company, "went public", issuing stock in conjunction with a bond issue. The stock began trading at $10¼ and remained in the $10 to $11 range for about a year. This company was headed by an aggressive gentleman, a Mr. Reuben Rosefield, who had in a very few years expanded one single gas station into a twenty-million-dollar company. It was an attractive investment for two reasons. The oil business in Canada is constantly expanding and must continue to expand, because nowhere else in the world is sure, safe oil available to the United States. In addition the Canadian economy is growing more rapidly than those of most other countries in the world. This combination appeared unbeatable, and a considerable number of investors seeking growth stocks were happy to buy shares in Regent Oil Refining. Below are reproduced my purchases for that month.

Larger oil companies were aware of the promise provided by Regent, and just two years later huge McColl Frontenac Oil Company decided to increase their rate of growth by buying out Regent. They offered a share exchange which was equivalent to a price of $20 per Regent share. Practically all the shareholders were delighted to have doubled their money in two years and sold their stock to McColl. I was no exception and considered the price a very fair one.

IN ACCOUNT WITH

DOHERTY ROADHOUSE & CO.

255 BAY STREET
TORONTO

DR. M. SHULMAN
378 RONCESVALLES AVENUE
TORONTO ONTARIO.
109-B.

DATE	No. OF SHARES BOT. OR RECEIVED	No. OF SHARES SOLD OR DELIVERED	S T O C K	PRICE	DEBIT	CREDIT	BALANCE
1955 SEP.			BALANCE				4,653 47
OCT. 3,	100.		REGENT OIL COMMON	10¾	1,095 00		
	100.		DO	11	1,120 00		
	200.		REGENT OIL COMM.	10½	2,090 00		51,497 32
6.	200.		DO	10½	2,100 00		
	300.		DO	10½	3,150 00		
	100.		DO	10½	1,050 00		
	100.		DO	10½	1,050 00		

However, I remembered that Reuben Rosefield had started his first gas station with one thousand dollars earned selling life insurance with my father, and as a sentimental gesture I put aside five shares to give to my son. The five shares gave me quite an education.

Because the oil business is growing so very rapidly in Canada, the huge oil companies were soon coveted by the giants. Just two years later, in 1959, McColl Frontenac disappeared when it was completely taken over by Texaco. McColl had not cared if there was a small minority interest in Regent. Texaco, however, wanted to integrate Regent into the Texaco Company, and so they determined to buy my five shares.

In 1964 their offers began to move upwards — to $75 per share, then $100, and finally $200. My protests that I didn't want to sell were brushed aside with, "How much do you really want?"

In early 1965 my friend and broker, Mr. Bev Burns, pointed out that I was seriously impeding the development of a billion dollar corporation. He said that, although I could probably hold them up for a huge sum, their offers were really very fair, and he suggested that I set a price and get out of their way. I sold my five shares in June, 1965.

After all, $50 to $6,000 is pretty good, even for a ten-year investment.

This fantastic tale is unusual but not unique in the very remunerative takeovers now going on in the United States and Canada. It appears only common sense that, if a large corporation is willing to pay $20 for a share of a small company, the share is probably worth at least $20, for large corporations do not make many mistakes in valuations. On this basis there can be no possible danger in making small purchases of such takeover stocks to be put away for the long pull. Many of these purchases will be futile, but the occasional one will hit the jackpot. Even those that are futile will not produce a financial loss, though they may produce a temporary tie-up of capital with no return. In these cases some jurisdictions have a law which allows a corporation to call in all held-out shares if a minimum of 90% of outstanding stockholders have accepted an offer. For example, Ontario chartered stocks cannot be called in, but if the charter is a Federal Canadian one and 90% accept an offer, the other 10% can be forced to go along.

To give an indication of the huge profits possible, in 1960 I purchased 25 shares of stock in a small company, Canada Foils, that made paper for cigarettes. In 1968 the company was bought out by Imperial Tobacco who offered to pay me $50 a share for my stock. I asked for $400 a share. Gradually their offers rose until finally they stopped at $200 a share. I refused, and to my disappointment they cancelled their offer and announced that they were selling their holdings in Canada Foils to the Aluminum Company of Canada. Then to my great delight this huge firm offered to pay me $650 per share for my stock and I rushed to sell. I had originally bought at $8 per share.

One occasional occurrence is that the corporation taking over the smaller company may get so annoyed with the hold-out shareholders that they will try to punish them. An example was Robin Hood Mills. In 1969 this company bought out the firm of Bick's Pickles and made an offer of $19 a share to all the minority shareholders. Five of the shareholders felt that this was insufficient and held out, but because none of them had more than 25 shares, instead of increasing their offer, Robin Hood Mills pulled a real Robin Hood. They effected the amalgamation of Bick's with several tiny companies and gave out one new share of the new company for every 95 shares previously held. Because none of them had held 95 shares, the five minority shareholders each received a fractional share. These, by law, cannot be registered with the corporation, so all shareholders' rights were in effect wiped-out! The five shareholders found themselves about to lose their voting rights, their ability to attend annual meetings and possibly even the right to receive dividends.

A comedy of errors now ensued, because the directors of Robin Hood called a shareholders' meeting to ratify the change and rather foolishly showed up a half-hour late. Two of the minority shareholders arrived on time and because the bylaws of the company state that any two shareholders constitute a quorum at a meeting called by the board of directors, these two called the meeting to order, voted down the amalgamation and elected themselves president and treasurer.

It looked as though Robin Hood and the Bick's shareholders were going to be tied up in the courts for years, but cooler heads prevailed and the president of Robin Hood personally phoned each of the minority shareholders and offered to pay them $160 a share. Of course they accepted.

The largest profits in takeovers, of course, occur if the takeover stock is purchased before the announcement is made. Selecting the right stock is not just a matter of blind luck and can often be forecast with reasonable accuracy. Some companies are obvious targets for takeovers.

In the first edition of this book, published in 1966, I wrote as follows:

"Certain industries go through periods of widespread takeover, usually due to expansion and strong competition. The Canadian petroleum industry has been going through just such a period for the past fifteen years. One after another, each of the small integrated oil companies has been bought out, until finally only one remains.

In 1962 Shell decided to expand in Canada by taking over the Canadian Oil Company, a medium-size, well-diversified Canadian company. Just prior to Shell's move there were only two independents left in Canada, Canadian Oil and Supertest. Canadian Oil was then trading at around $25, and as is common in such takeovers, the offer was made for a much higher price, an astronomical $55. The shareholders of Canadian Oil were happy to receive this huge sum, and as in the story of the ten little Indians, "Then there was only one".

The one remaining Canadian independent is Supertest. Among oil men, the question is not *whether* one of the U.S. giants will take over Supertest, but rather *when* will it occur? Market- and oil-wise investors have been gradually buying this stock since 1962 ($19 at time of writing). The delightful part of such a speculation is that this is a highly regarded company which meanwhile pays a reasonable dividend. It is another "can't-lose" situation. Such likely takeovers appear periodically and should be included in every investment portfolio."

I couldn't have been more correct. In 1971 British Petroleum bought out Supertest for a cash and stock offer worth $65 per share.

Two Canadian companies that are obvious targets for similar takeovers within the next few years are St. Lawrence Corporation trading at $20 and Ford of Canada trading at $89. Both of these companies have had over 90% of their stock gradually bought up by the parent companies, Domtar and Ford, and there is no question but that an offer much in excess of current prices will be forthcoming to the remaining shareholders.

The only question is when. It has to be a good idea to put a few shares away for the future.

Very rarely a broker will pass on to his clients advance information about a takeover. This should be a once-a-life-time opportunity to make a large amount of money, but sometimes plain bad luck intervenes.

For years my wife's gynecologist has complained of his unbelievably bad luck in the stock market — as soon as he bought a stock its price would begin to sink. Al Capp created a character in Lil Abner called Joe Bflspk who was followed by a black cloud and disaster wherever he went. The gynecologist felt that he was the Joe Bflspk of the market, but I was determined to show him that by scientific stock purchasing, even he could make money. One day I learned that the Hancock Oil Company of California was to receive a $50 takeover offer the next morning. The stock was then only $43. With great excitement I phoned this doctor, explained the situation, and said "Buy." He bought. Two hours later Hancock Oil's major field caught fire and burnt up $17 million worth of oil. The takeover offer was temporarily withdrawn, and the stock opened the next morning at $38. Some people just shouldn't be in the market.

The classic example of making money by refusing a takeover offer is Seven Arts, a company listed on the American Stock Exchange, which is in the business of producing and distributing movie films. Few remember that in 1955 Seven Arts' business was confined to the tanning of leather and the sale of mouton fur.

The company was then called Donnell and Mudge, and for 35 years it had run a moderately successful tannery. After the war, however, competition had increased, and Donnell & Mudge had not kept up. Sales and earnings plummetted, and by the early fifties the company had dropped its dividends and was showing losses of over a quarter of a million dollars annually. The stock fell from a postwar high of $12½ to reach a low of 35¢ in 1955.

At this point bankruptcy appeared imminent, and when a group of apparently foolish financiers appeared on the scene and offered to pay $2 per share for all the outstanding stock, the directors of the company hastened to turn in their stock and advised all the shareholders to follow suit. Practically everyone did, but as I held only 100 shares I hesitated. My hopes of higher prices were confirmed when after only two weeks the new owners raised their offer to the few holdouts to $2.50 per share. The stock remained at this level for only a few days. then began to soar upwards. By March of 1956 it was trading at $23.50. A twenty-for-one stock split was now announced, and an underwriting and sale of debentures was arranged, while the company now declared that it was going into the business of distributing motion pictures to television.

In March, 1958, the company's name was changed to United Telefilm, and in 1960 a reverse split was announced whereby the company's name was again changed, this time to Creative Telefilm. Shareholders received one share of Creative Telefilm for every three shares they had of United Telefilm. The following year the company once again changed its name, to its current Seven Arts, and announced an expansion of its business to include the distribution to television of motion pictures, the production and distribution of motion pictures, the production of plays, the production and distribution of phonograph records, and incongruously, the development of land on Grand Bahama Island. They no longer, however, sell mouton fur, nor do they tan leather.

Seven Arts has done well. My $35 investment would now be worth $21,000, whereas if I had accepted the takeover offer I would have received only $200. Seven Arts once again proves that if you have only a small investment in a company receiving a takeover offer, there is no harm in waiting a while to see what developments may take place.

After all, a $1,000 investment in Donnell & Mudge in 1955 would be worth $600,000 today!

In summary the rules for sure profits in takeovers or potential takeovers are these:

1. Try to buy stock in companies which are likely to receive takeover offers. These should be chosen by the rules given previously.

2. When takeover offers are extended to U.S. or Canadian corporations in which you hold stock, hold back a few shares for good luck.

3. It never does any harm to purchase for speculation a little stock for which a takeover offer has already been made. If the takeover fails, much higher prices may result.

14
GLAMOUR STOCKS

Toronto Star went from $11 to $50 in one year.

Levitz Furniture went from $3.50 to $145 in 6 months.

Velcro went from $3 to $200 in one year.

Robinson Little went from $10 to $80 in less than one year.

A glamour stock is one which has a glamorous new invention or process associated with it and which has moved up many multiples in price as a result.

Every investor and speculator heard of the glamour stocks' fantastic market moves during the sixties. In every case the stocks were legitimate ones which had made a tremendous turnabout in their profit potential often due to a startling new discovery. Most of these companies were listed on the American Stock Exchange, but a few were on the New York exchange.

How can the average speculator make money from these glamour stocks? The answer is that he can't. Unfortunately a glamour stock is about as hard to spot before it has moved up in price as it would be to decide which one of the million babies born this year will some day be president. Theoretically it appears very simple to buy into companies that have new discoveries and watch them grow, but the hidden pitfalls can be crippling. To take two examples, in the early 1960s two companies developed new ideas. One was Syntex, who were pioneering a new pill that they believed women could take to control their fertility cycles; the other was Steadman Industries, who had developed and patented a clever system of directly unloading piggyback from trains to trucks. Both stocks were selling at $8. Any reasonable man could see that Steadman had an immediately usable, revolutionary, money-making invention that must bring a rapid rise in earnings. Syntex's invention, if it worked, would certainly require a long educational campaign to persuade women to use it, and there might very well be dangerous side effects which would prevent it from ever going into practical use. Of the two there appeared little doubt that Steadman was the better buy.

Today Syntex is around $100 and Steadman is $5.

In the first edition of this book in 1966 I wrote:

"Unfortunately it is only clear a glamour stock is a glamour stock after it has become one. That is, unless you are an insider in a company, it will probably be too late to buy its stock once the glamour label is attached. Today the acknowledged glamour stocks are trading at ridiculous multiples of their current earnings — as high as 100 times earnings. These prices discount future earnings for many, many years and render these stocks very vulnerable to any stock market reaction. In fact it is likely that today's leading glamour stocks, which are now being widely distributed to the public, may very well lose half or more of their value in the next two or three years."

I was "right on" in that prediction, for it took exactly three years for the glamour stocks of 1966 to plunge to fractions of their 1966 prices. Stocks like TWA and L.T.V. lost 80% of their value.

There is little doubt that the same fate awaits today's glamour stock purchasers. Many of these stocks cannot justify their current price on any basis, and this bubble too must finally burst.

An interesting side effect of the current glamour stock boom is the emergence of "hot" customer's men. These are salesmen who were fortunate enough to have good inside information on one or more glamour stocks at an early stage in their rise. They recommended purchase of the stocks at relatively low prices and were able to go back and say, "If you had followed my advice and bought and held on, you would have quintupled your money in six months." Some of these salesmen cashed in on their enhanced reputation by recommending other potential glamour stocks. Sooner or later disaster struck their clients.

One very "hot" customer's man was well connected with directors of three New York Exchange listed companies and always knew of their earnings and announcements one or two days before the public were informed. He used this information to very good advantage, and his clients did very well. Unfortunately he did not restrict himself to these companies and soon involved his customers in a variety of potential glamour stocks in such diversified fields as computers and clothing. Within a few weeks several of these stocks lost up to 50% of their value, and another hot customer's man cooled off very rapidly.

In summary, for the average investor to seek or buy so-called glamour stocks is foolishness of the highest degree. The glamour can wear off very quickly and this type of speculation is more likely to yield headaches than profits. To buy these stocks is truly idiotic when there are so many other opportunities for large capital gains with no risks.

15
GOLD

When a businessman spends more than he earns, when he has impoverished distant relatives whom he supports, and when in addition he keeps a very expensive mistress, his impending financial downfall is obvious to all. However, when a country spends more than it earns, when it gives millions away to other countries and destroys more millions by keeping an army stationed around the world or by fighting a chronic war, its financial downfall, though not so obvious, is just as inevitable. In such circumstances the only financial cure is to cut expenses and/or raise revenue. The only way the United States can cut its expenses in a meaningful way is to bring its soldiers home from Europe, cut defense costs, forbid out-of-the-country tourism, or stop foreign aid. It has not done any of these things, but it has imposed an interest equalization tax, it has cut the tourist's limit on duty free imports, and President Nixon has brought home the army based in Indochina.

This is equivalent to the businessman's refusing to give up the mistress and the relatives but agreeing to take the subway to work instead of a taxi. The measures are equally ineffective. The United States can meaningfully raise its revenue in only one way, and that is by drastically raising taxes. This the government finds politically impossible, and so the annual deficit is made up by borrowing more funds.

In 1971 there were hopes that the president would attempt to balance the budget, and economists were stunned when in January 1972 and 1973 he produced budgets with record deficits.

When the improvident businessman carries on like this, his associates soon lose faith in his business. When a country does it, other countries lose faith in its money. The United States have now passed the point of no return. They have found it impossible to take the drastic measures necessary to maintain their solvency, and the rest of the world now is unhappy about holding U.S. dollars. Because of this lack of faith in the dollar, other countries and individuals began selling dollars and buying gold, which the U.S. sold to them at the artifically pegged price of $35 per ounce.

This drain on U.S. gold began immediately after the Second World War, and it has continued and steadily accelerated since then. Because the United States is the most powerful nation in the world, she has from time to time been able to temporarily interfere with and slow down the gold drain by pressure on other countries plus international banking agreements. But each time, after a few weeks, the countries involved quietly began to sell their dollars again. Finally the gold supply at Fort Knox reached a critical level, and something had to be done.

Every American president since Franklin Roosevelt had followed the advice of his treasury officials and proclaimed the soundness of the dollar and his determination to maintain the price of gold. Unfortunately, despite the brave pronouncements, the countries of Western Europe, the oil sheiks of the middle east, and the moguls of the far east continued to sell dollars and buy gold. In 1971 the situation finally deteriorated to the point where U.S. importers were hurrying to pay foreign currency bills and exporters were delaying payment in U.S. funds, in the belief that devaluation was near. This in itself tended to aggravate the dollar drain and brought the moment of reckoning closer.

In 1972 all logic pointed to the fact that the U.S. was rapidly heading toward financial ruin and that in order to avert disaster she had to pull in her belt. This could have been accomplished by doubling or tripling the price of gold and simultaneously cutting expenditures and raising taxes. This would, of course, have meant a drop in the standard of living in the U.S. (as it must in any family or business which has overspent itself) and the U.S. government refused to face this politically unpalatable truth. Instead it has done exactly the opposite; it has *raised* expenditures without increasing taxes, and so as to avoid foreigners buying all its gold, it has removed all relationship between gold and the dollar. In other words, the U.S. government now refuses to sell gold for dollars at any price!! Truly Alice in Wonderland.

How can the individual protect himself against an improvident government which has become caught in such a financial mess? If the dollar is to gradually become worthless, one must own "things" other than dollars, whether they be real estate (but not mortgages), antiques, "wealth in the ground" (oil, copper, or base metal stocks), jewels, or gold.

In 1933, when the United States went off the gold standard, it became illegal for an American citizen to own gold inside the country. In 1960, when the gold drain was being accelerated by Americans purchasing gold and storing it in Canada, a law was passed making it illegal for American citizens to own gold anywhere. A surprising number are breaking U.S. laws by continuing to purchase and store gold in Toronto, but there are preferable ways of protecting one's investment without breaking the law.

The simplest way to own gold is by buying stock in a producing gold mine; the three favourites are Homestake Mines on the New York Exchange and Dome Mines and Campbell Red Lake on the New York and Toronto exchanges. Unfortunately so many investors want to buy the small amount of stock available that the price of these stocks has moved up drastically. Dome has gone from $11 ten years ago to over $80 today, while the others have acted equally well. Thus even if the price of gold were to be raised tomorrow, much of the increased profits which would be shown by gold mines have already been discounted, and so it is now probably too late to buy these stocks.

For many years the best way for investors to protect themselves was by owning the gold itself. This is perfectly legal for any non-American and the method is quite simple.

The Bank of Nova Scotia is the largest trader in gold in North America, and it is prepared to handle purchases and sales of any size. Until recently, the amount of money that had to be put up in a down payment was only 3% of the purchase price plus interest for three months at the rate of 7% per year, and this produced the possibility of huge capital gains. For example:

Cost of 400 ounces of gold at $35 per ounce was $14,000.
Down payment of 3% was $420.
Three months interest at 7% was $245.
Therefore the total down payment was $665 plus a small storage charge.

Fortunes were made in this way until finally the U.S. government exerted so much pressure on the Canadian government that it succumbed and passed a law forbidding the sale of gold on margin.

American citizens cannot own gold. However, they could participate in this type of speculation by buying gold options from a Canadian broker. An option holder does not own any gold; he merely has the right to buy the gold at some future date. Provided he does not exercise that right, he has broken no U.S. law. Before the price of gold rose to its present level, Americans buying gold options paid about 8½% for a one-year-option to buy gold bars at $38 per ounce. An option on a 400-ounce bar cost $1,100 for one year. Thus the possible loss was $275 for 90 days or $1,100 for one year if the price of gold did not go up. When the price rose, the U.S. citizens could not exercise their options but they sold them to the broker and took their profit in cash without ever taking ownership of the gold.

I personally know of dozens of U.S. citizens who made large profits in gold options in 1968. Canadian brokers were happy to supply the demand.

TELEX - LATIMER TORONTO - 02-2565

TORONTO
199 BAY STREET
TEL. 363-5631

W. D. LATIMER CO. LIMITED

MEMBERS
MONTREAL STOCK EXCHANGE • CANADIAN STOCK EXCHANGE
VANCOUVER STOCK EXCHANGE • CALGARY STOCK EXCHANGE
ASSOCIATE MEMBERS • BOSTON STOCK EXCHANGE • PHILADELPHIA BALTIMORE STOCK EXCHANGE

MONTREAL
STOCK EXCHANGE TOWER
TEL. 866-8763

STATEMENT TO:

DR M P SHULMAN
378 RONCESVALLES AVENUE
TORONTO ONTARIO

34-6163-9 · ACCOUNT NO.

34 · SMN

06 | 30 | 68
MO. | DAY | YR.

| DATE | | QUANTITY | | DESCRIPTION | PRICE OR TYPE OF ITEM | AMOUNT | | BALANCE |
MO.	DAY	BOUGHT RECEIVED LONG	SOLD DELIVERED SHORT			DEBIT	CREDIT	DEBIT UNLESS MARKED CR
06	10	1		CALL-GOLD	REC			
06	17		200	OZS OF GOLD BULLION	36.50		7856.63	
06	17	200		OZS OF GOLD BULLION	35.36	7611.24		
06	27	1		CALL-GOLD	REC			
					BALANCE AS OF JUN 30			$245.39C
			13	* SECURITY POSITION *				
				CALL-GOLD				

Unfortunately this gravy train is now finished because the price of gold has risen in the free market to over $80 per oz. and it is no longer profitable to sell gold options.

The basic situation, however, has not changed — U.S. dollars are only paper and are backed by less true value every year. One should attempt to get rid of them as quickly as possible and buy "real wealth" in their place. The best form of real wealth is the rare metals — their supply is limited and they will remain stable in terms of buying power; in other words their value will rise in direct proportion as the value of the dollar falls.

Today the best investment of this type lies in silver because of its low price due to speculators' dumping of the metal. At time of writing it is available at $1.40 per oz. and although it could go slightly lower (to $1.25) I predict that this price will multiply many times over the next few years. (The same applies to platinum.)

If you don't want to own silver bullion, buy your wife a tea service.

16
COMMODITY FUTURES — THE IDEAL GAMBLE

"Mrs. Jordan, your husband bought 30,000 pounds of sugar futures six months ago. Apparently he went on his vacation without arranging its sale. Where do you want it delivered?"

Everyone has heard this old chestnut, and it still frightens the novice "future" buyer. Actually it is just a myth, and no one has ever had 30,000 pounds of anything dumped in his backyard. Like everything else in future trading, even the stories are magnified tenfold.

Commodity futures represent the quickest possible way to get rich or go bankrupt amongst all forms of market trading. They are exceeded only by puts and calls in their volatility and are exceeded by nothing in their low margin requirements. Comparatively few speculators participate in this form of gambling because of a mistaken belief in the complications of commodity trading and because the books available read with such great difficulty. This is a pity, because here is probably the only completely honest form of pure gambling in the market. Commodity futures are neither investments nor speculations and should not be purchased for either purpose. But as an exciting form of gambling from which small amounts of money can turn into huge fortunes, futures can be recommended for risk capital. Only moneys which can afford to be lost should be used in such ventures for the entire capital can disappear with disquieting rapidity.

What are commodity futures?

Commodities are articles produced for trade. They include things that are grown, such as wheat and animals, and things that are dug up, such as copper and silver. All commodities are bought and sold or traded.

Futures are titles of ownership of specified commodities at some future date. For example, one contract of December cocoa represents title to 30,000 pounds of cocoa that will be ready for delivery in December. All commodities do not have future trading, for in order to be so traded they must be storable, have a fluctuating price, and be widely traded. Practically speaking, the commodities that are traded in futures are copper, tin, lead, zinc, platinum, silver, and aluminum; plus cottonseed oil, silk, wool, potatoes, rice, eggs, cotton, cattle, pork, hides, and wool; and also rubber, cocoa, coffee, and sugar. For the speculator's purposes, this list can be drastically shortened.

There are two groups who trade in futures: those who produce and use the commodities and who are future trading to avoid risks; and speculators who seek the risks because of the great rewards possible. Originally commodity future trading served two purposes:

1. To enable producers of commodities to be certain of receiving a fair price for their commodity. For example, if a planter is producing

sugar there are many months between the time of planting and the time that actual physical delivery of the sugar can be made. If during this interval the wholesale price of sugar were to fall from say 4¢ a pound down to 2¢, the planter might discover that all his labour produced no profit. On the other hand, sugar might have climbed to 6¢, but planters cannot afford to gamble with their crops, and so they seek some way to ensure a fair profit for themselves. They accomplish this by selling their crop, or at least a portion of it, through a future trade. Thus, if the sugar were trading at 4¢ a pound for immediate delivery, there should be little difficulty in selling futures on sugar at 4¢ a pound (possibly a little more or less; this will be explained later) for delivery six months hence. In this way the planter has ensured a successful sale of his crop at a good price.

2. To enable users of commodities to be certain of obtaining supplies of their needed commodities at a reasonable price. For example, a manufacturer of candy bars must contract in advance to deliver the candy to his wholesalers. If while his contract is still in force he finds that the price of sugar has considerably increased, he may be put in the difficult position of having to produce his candy and sell it at a loss. It is not possible for him to store his sugar supplies very far in advance because of the costs and capital involved, so he protects himself by purchasing a sugar future at 4¢ a pound. Regardless of any price fluctuations, the manufacturer is now sure that he can manufacture and sell his candy bars at a profit.

Who runs the risks that these producers and consumers are seeking to avoid? Unfortunately the times when producers wish to sell futures rarely coincide with those when consumers wish to buy, and so a third party is welcomed to commodity trading — the speculator. Because producers and consumers *must* buy and sell at certain times (or *hedge*, which is the technical term) there are tremendous profit opportunities for the speculator who can buy or sell when and if he chooses.

Because the speculator has become essential to the smooth running of the futures markets, a huge industry has developed to service and inform him. Numerous firms specialize in handling speculators' accounts and in rushing information about commodities to them. Newspapers carry crop and weather reports, and even the United States government cooperates by simultaneously releasing crop forecasts to all interested parties. Because weather changes or large sales or purchases can rapidly affect commodity prices, the brokerage firm with whom each speculator deals will send him a daily letter, reporting all such changes and giving that firm's opinion as to future changes. Thus it is very easy for the speculator to keep well informed about the current national and world factors which may affect any commodity in which he is interested. In fact it is not uncommon for a speculator in a certain commodity to be far better informed about that commodity's current and prospective market than are the actual producers of the commodity. Certainly it is easier for a sugar speculator in New York City who is reading Merrill Lynch's daily sugar bulletin to be more up to date on the world sugar situation than can be any sugar beet grower in Louisiana or Haiti.

How are these futures traded? The mechanism is very simple.

Each commodity has a specific trading unit which represents the quantity of the commodity covered by one future contract. For cocoa, for example, the trading unit is 30,000 pounds. (Although it is possible to trade in fractions of a contract, it is unwise because it may be difficult to dispose of such a purchase). When one buys or sells one cocoa contract, one is automatically buying or selling 30,000 pounds of cocoa. The orders to buy or sell these contracts can be placed with any member of the various commodity exchanges who are listed in every city's telephone book. Many of them are also prominent stockbrokers.

Primarily because it is essential that there be a large volume of trading if futures are to be easily bought and sold, each commodity is normally traded for delivery in certain specified months. Cocoa, for example, is traded for delivery in March, May, July, September, and December. This increases the number of contracts for these months to a level where individual large buy or sell orders do not unduly raise or depress the market.

```
 COPPER -
    CLOSED 50 TO 55 HIGHER WITH VOLUME FALLING
 FROM RECENT HIGH LEVELS TO ONLY 977 LOTS INCLUDING
    30 STRADDLES.

    MARKET MOVED IN RELATIVELY NARROW RANGE FOLLOWING
 SLIGHTLY BETTER OPENING AND EARLY SELLOFF.

    PRICES STABILIZED ABOUT 20 UP ON DAY EARLY
 IN SESSION THEN SLOWLY BUT STEADILY TRADED HIGHER
 ON CONTINUED COMMISSION HOUSE BUYING ALONG WITH
 SOME LIGHT COVERING. PRICES ENDED AT OR NEAR HIGHS
 OF THE DAY.

    THE LONDON MARKET PERFORMED SIMILARLY ENDING
 JUST OFF ITS BEST LEVELS. AGAIN THERE WAS
 NO FRESH NEWS INFLUENCES THE MARKET APPEARING
 TO TRADE ON TECHNICAL BASIS.

    TRADE SELLING WICH HAD BEEN EVIDENT IN MARKET
 OVER LAST FEW WEEKS APPEARED TO BE AVAILABLE
 ONLY ON A SCALE UP. THE TRADE IS APPARENTLY
 WILLING TO LET SPECULATORS ADVANCE THE MARKET
 SINCE WITH LITTLE FRESH PHYSICAL DEMAND THE BOARD
 IS ALLOWING FOR ATTRACTIVE SELLING HEDGES IN
 THESE RALLIES.

    COMEX STOCKS WERE UNCHANGED AT 23671.

    OPEN INTEREST WAS UP 89 AT 12916.
```

SILVER -
- CLOSED VERY STRONG 340 TO 350 HIGHER ON 3559 LOTS WITH 423 STRADDLES.

- THE HEAVIEST TRADING VOLUME WAS COMPACTED INTO THE LAST HOUR OF TRADING.

- THE MARKET HAD BEEN TRADING STEADILY ABOUT 150 HIGHER THROUGH MOST OF SESSION WHEN LITE COVERING APPEARED TO TOUCH OFF TECHNICAL BUY POINTS WITH
- COMMISSION HOUSE BUYING SURGING INTO THE MARKET PLACE. LATE PROFIT TAKING SEEMED TO STOP ADVANCES NEARLY 400 POINTS UP ON THE DAY PRICES THEN
- DIPPING SHARPLY BUT AGAIN TAKEN UP BY CONTINUED COMMISSON HOUSE BUYING THEN ENDING SLIGHTLY OFF THE BEST OF THE DAY.

- THERE WAS NO FRESH NEWS GERMAIN TO SILVER THOUGH SOME OF THE BUYING WAS LIKELY MOTIVATED
- BY EXTREME WEAKNESS IN DOLLAR AND FACT THAT GOLD TRADED TO NEW HIGHS OF 46 DOLLARS AN OUNCE IN LONDON TODAY.

- COMEX STOCKS WERE DOWN 139739 AT 115.6 MILLION.

- OPEN INTEREST WAS DOWN 159 AT 46541.

This is very important, because if a trader wishes to sell 10 contracts of December cocoa and the total daily trades in December cocoa number only 20, it is obvious that such a sale will seriously depress the market and restrict trading. If, on the other hand, the total daily volume is 200 contracts, then a sale of 10 or 20 contracts can easily take place.

Once a future contract has been purchased, it can just as easily be sold. It is different from a put or call, which has little liquidity; it can be compared with a common stock, except that it has a limited life. A future contract is neither a warrant nor a call, which represent only options to buy; a future represents actual ownership, even though only a small amount of the purchase price has been paid as a downpayment.

Before proceeding further, one should understand certain terms used in commodity trading.

Hedge: The sale of a future in a commodity by a producer of the commodity or the purchase of a future in a commodity by a consumer of that commodity.

Last trading day: The last day on which a commodity may be sold before actual physical delivery occurs (physical delivery means delivery to a warehouse).

Limit: The maximum daily price move permitted in a commodity by the exchange on which it is traded.

Long: The owner of a future.

Short: The seller of a future in a commodity that he has sold

Commodities

• • •   • • •

Price Trends of Tomorrow's Meals and Manufactures

Consumer demand perked up for copper in the U.S. and abroad yesterday and the development prompted speculators and trade interests to buy futures.

The price for immediate-delivery copper on the London Metal Exchange improved ¼ cent a pound to 52¾ cents. The New York futures market posted a gain of almost ½ cent a pound.

Brokers in London • said demand was stronger from European consumers, notably West Germany. U.S. producing sources said there was active interest from users for their copper for delivery next month. One large producer already had sold anticipated April production, and active bookings were described by other large producers.

Consumers bought producer copper because it was the cheapest available. Producers quote it at 52½ to 52¾ cents a pound. Dealers offered refined copper for delivery this month at 53 cents a pound and for shipment next month at 53¼ cents. Their price for May delivery copper was 53½ cents. Because these prices were above producer levels, business in the dealer market was slow.

Sugar Market Calms Down

The hectic trading in New York and London world sugar futures markets of the past several months dissipated yesterday as speculators and other dealers awaited developments. Price changes also were the smallest in some time.

Prices for world sugar contracts dipped at the opening as speculators who started taking profits Tuesday had more contracts to sell. When this selling was completed, trading slowed.

Business in the world sugar export market also was quiet yesterday, but there was some alteration of reports on previous transactions. Exporters heard reports that purchases by China of raw sugar on Tuesday that had been placed at 50,000 tons were closer to 100,000 tons. It also was indicated that a London company had an option to sell another 100,000 tons, or any part, of refined sugar to China if that country was interested. The option, according to London sugar brokers, is due to expire next Wednesday. Market sources suggested that the appearance of these supplies in the export market after recent large sales damped buying enthusiasm of some speculators. Talk was heard that Japan was ready to buy more sugar for delivery this year. A figure of 150,000 tons

Commodity Indexes

Dow Jones Futures—147.01, up 0.03; last year, 141.94.

Dow Jones Spot—151.38, up 0.41; last year, 141.59.

Reuter United Kingdom—563.2, up 0.2; last year, 532.8.

was mentioned. This would follow purchases made last month of 1.8 million tons and would round out Japan's needs for 1972.

Slack Grain Business

Business in grains, soybeans and soybean products on the Chicago Board of Trade also slackened, as traders awaited the outcome of a vote by dock workers at Atlantic and Gulf ports on new wage contracts. The men currently are working under a 30-day extension of a Taft-Hartley injunction. It expires Tuesday.

Exporters believe approval of new labor contracts will expand sales of U.S. soybeans, soybean products and grains. A large volume of flour also is expected to be exported with the "coast clear" and no possibility that movement of the supplies will be held up at the ports.

Late in the day speculators bought soybeans and grain futures. The soybean market ended with a six-cent-a-bushel gain, and some wheat contracts advanced ⅞ cent. Deferred soybean positions rose to contract highs. Activity was attributed to optimism over the dock situation.

Japan in regular weekly tender bought 3.5 million bushels of U.S. hard and soft wheat as well as 1.7 million bushels of Canadian wheat and 639,000 bushels of Australian wheat. It was the first time in a month or more that the Japanese bought more wheat in the U.S. than in other areas.

Prices for live hogs rose 50 cents a 100 pounds at Indianapolis and 25 cents at other leading markets. Farmers shipped 42,300 hogs to the 11 major terminals, 20% more than a week earlier, when wintry weather curtailed the movement. It was the second straight day of firming hog prices.

Pork belly futures in Chicago rose more than one cent a pound before profit taking erased part of the gain.

Demand was good for cattle, and prices advanced 25 cents a 100 pounds. Farmers shipped 19,700 cattle to the 11 major centers, up from 18,200 a week earlier, but packers were ready buyers. It was thought the packers wanted to replenish low slaughter supplies in their yards.

without any offsetting ownership of production in that commodity.

Margin: Money put up by the speculator when purchasing (or selling short) a futures contract. It will vary between 5% and 15% of the value of the contract.

Margin call: A request for more margin from a broker if a loss is occurring on a futures contract.

Stop loss order: An order to automatically sell a contract if the price of that contract falls to a predesignated figure.

Option, call, spread, straddle: It is not necessary for the speculator to understand these terms, but he *should* understand that their meanings are quite different from the same terms when applied to puts and calls as described in Chapter 9.

Pyramid: To automatically increase one's holdings in a specific future as its price rises. This is without a doubt the most important tool that a speculator in futures can use to increase his profits. It is based on the fact that trends often develop in certain futures, and a price movement in a future is often sustained for long periods of time. It will be fully explained later in this chapter.

Now, what are the financial advantages to the speculator in buying commodity futures?

1. The commission is very low — only a fraction of that compared to stock purchases. This is very important to the trader who is doing a lot of buying and selling. When, for example, world sugar is trading at 3¢ a pound, one contract is worth $3,360, and the commission on such a purchase is only $12.50. The commission on a stock purchase of equal value on the stock exchange may be up to five times as high.

2. Margin requirements are very low. In the stock exchange these requirements are never under 50%, but in the purchase of commodity futures they may be as low as 5%. This can produce tremendous percentage profits on the small amount of money put up. Very important is the fact that no interest is payable on the balance, unlike stocks purchased on margin, where interest payments can materially raise the cost of the stocks purchased. As an example of how this low margin requirement can produce spectacular profits, examine the situation if one had bought sugar futures at the beginning of 1971. At that time sugar was selling at a little over 3¢ a pound but by the end of the year it had moved up to 8¢ a pound. Each contract which had been bought at $3,000 moved up to $8,000. If $300 had been deposited as initial margin it would have grown to be worth $5,500 — an increase of over 1,500%. Furthermore, if pyramiding of the original investment had been fully followed, the $300 would have grown to almost a million dollars! That is why this type of gambling speculation should be carefully examined. An example of a single trade is shown below. One September silver contract was purchased in August; the deposit required was $750.

Although silver moved up only 13% during this time, the profit was about 150%. The $750 investment grew to $1,970 in three weeks.

What are the disadvantages and dangers in commodity trading? There are two.

1. Because of the small amount of margin which is deposited in purchase of a future contract, a very small fluctuation can completely wipe out an investment. For example, if a world sugar future contract is purchased when sugar is trading at 3¢ a pound, the deposit may be $500 on the $3,300 contract. A decline of only ½¢ in the price of sugar would produce a total loss of the $500 put down as margin. One must be prepared to lose his initial margin time and time again in order to await and follow a trend.

2. In order to protect commodity prices from very severe price fluctuations on the receipt of good or bad news, every commodity has a daily price limit beyond which it may not move. For example, sugar may not move more than ½¢ per pound per day. There is no more unnerving experience in the whole financial world than to be attempting to sell a position held in some commodity, and to be unable to do so at any price because there are no bids at the price level within which the commodity may legally be sold that day. When a situation of this type is prolonged for several days and the speculator sees his profits or capital melting away without his being able to do anything about it, even the most strong-minded may have difficulty sleeping. Fortunately this type of situation is not common, although when it does occur it may persist for several consecutive days.

In commodity trading one must have strong nerves!

Now what should the speculator do to make money in commodity trading? First he must understand volume, open interest, short sales, and charting. Volume refers to the amount of trading taking place in each commodity daily and is broken up into the various trading months. It is unwise to speculate in commodities or in months in which the volume is small. This is because it may be difficult to liquidate a commodity at a fair price if there is little interest. The daily future volumes are listed in the *Wall Street Journal* and other newspapers. Two such lists are reproduced on pp. 121-122.

Note that some of the commodities had very few sales; some, none at all. Aluminum, for example, declined 50¢ per pound on only one sale. Commodities that are inactive should not be purchased.

Open interest refers to the number of contracts currently outstanding in each commodity, divided up into the various delivery months. These are also listed every day in the press, and the same rule applies here as in volume: Don't buy commodities for delivery at a time when there is a small open interest. The larger the open interest, the easier to liquidate your purchases.

Short selling is the sale of a commodity which the seller does not own, but which he believes will decline in price so that he will be able to repurchase his commodity more cheaply and thus make a profit. This stratagem is mentally difficult for the average speculator, who is never quite comfortable making such a sale. In the stock market it is very inadvisable for non-professionals to participate in short selling, because certain unpleasant circumstances occasionally develop, such as a "short squeeze", in which the promoter of the stock buys up all the floating supply of the stock, temporarily forces the stock price up, then demands delivery of his stock. In the commodity market, however, such a corner of the market cannot occur, because there is a regulating body for commodities which strictly limits the amount of any commodity that may be held by any single speculator.

In addition the seller of a commodity cannot be requested to make delivery "on demand" but only when his futures contract has expired. For these reasons short selling in commodities is not so dangerous as short selling in stocks. Because there will be circumstances when certain commodities are obviously overpriced, speculators should overcome their prejudices against short selling. Short sales represent 50% of all profit possibilities in the commodity market and can be made as easily as a purchase.

An essential for the speculator in a commodity is to understand his commodity. He may never see the actual product, but he should know everything about it. No one can hope to keep track of all the commodities, and at least initially it is wise to restrict oneself to one or at the most two commodities. The daily market letter from a firm such as Merrill Lynch should be carefully read for some weeks before an initial trade is made. This diligence will take only ten minutes a day and will be amply repaid. It will not be long before the reader thinks that a commodity shows a possibility of price improvement. At that time he should buy one contract.

In order to make large profits, the speculator must determine to ride with the market but never to fight it. In purchasing a stock at a certain price, the intelligent speculator or investor will have carefully analyzed the company's value and prospects. If after such a purchase the price of the stock declines, it is often wise to buy more and average down the overall cost. After all, if Newconex stock appeared a good buy at $5.25, it was an even better one at $4.75. This logic definitely does not apply to commodity futures, and the smart speculator *never* averages down. The reason is that it is impossible to analyze the value of a commodity as one can do with many stocks, and sugar that appears cheap at 3½¢ a pound may sell at only half of that figure in a few weeks. If a

Futures Prices

Tuesday, March 7, 1972

	Open	High	Low	Close	Change	Season's High	Low
CHICAGO—WHEAT							
Mar	159½	161¾	159½	159⅝-160	—⅜to unch	175¼	143⅛
May	153¾	155	153¾	154-154¼	+¼to½	174½	142¼
July	147	147⅝	146¾	146⅞-147	+½to¼	152½	135⅝
Sept	149¼	150	149¼	149¼	—¼	153¾	138⅞
Dec	153¾	154	153	153¾	—¼	155¾	145¼
CORN							
Mar	119¼	119¾	119	119⅛-⅛	—⅛to uhch	167¼	116⅞
May	123¼	123¼	122¾	123		167⅞	120¼
July	126¼	126⅝	126	126⅝-⅛	+⅛to unch	145½	122¼
Sept	127⅞	128¼	127⅝	127¾		131¼	122¾
Dec	125⅞	126¼	125½	125¾	—⅛	130	120⅞
Mar'73	130⅜	130½	130¼	130¼	—⅛	134½	124½
OATS							
Mar	79	79½	78½	78½	....	80'	64⅝
May	74½	74⅞	74½	74¾	+⅜	80¼	64¾
July	71	71	70⅞	71	+⅜	71⅞	63½
Sept	68¼	68¼	68¼	68¼	+¼	70	64½
SOYBEANS							
Mar	336¼	336⅞	334¾	335⅝-¾	—¾to⅝	348⅞	288½
May	340⅝	341½	338¾	339⅝-⅞	—1½to⅞	351¼	299¼
July	343½	344½	341½	342¾-343	—1½to1¼	350	313
Aug	341½	342½	339¾	340¾	—1½	343¾	310½
Sept	324½	325¼	323¾	324-324¼	—¾to½	326½	291½
Nov	309¾	311¼	309½	310½	+½	313¼	295¼
Jan'73	314	315½	313¼	314½	+⅜	316¾	295¼
SOYBEAN OIL							
Mar	11.73	11.73	11.55	11.59-.57	—.12to.14	13.75	10.03
May	11.85	11.88	11.68	11.69-.71	—.17to.15	13.65	10.25
July	11.98	11.98	11.78	11.82-.84	—.14to.12	13.50	10.82
Aug	11.96	11.96	11.79	11.80-.82	—.13to.11	12.65	10.88
Sept	11.78	11.78	11.61	11.64	—.11	12.40	10.80
Oct	11.40	11.40	11.25	11.28-.29	—.12to.11	12.10	10.55
Nov	11.08	11.15	11.06	11.10	—.09	11.60	10.46
Dec	11.08	11.12	11.03	11.06	—.08to.06	11.50	10.45
Jan'73	11.14	11.15	11.03	11.07-.09	—.07to.05	11.45	10.36
SOYBEAN MEAL							
Mar	92.15	92.15	91.15	91.40	—.60	92.35	74.50
May	92.90	93.00	92.30	92.60-.65	—.50to.45	93.50	77.50
July	93.60	93.95	93.30	93.60-.65	—.40to.35	94.30	81.90
Aug	92.50	92.80	92.40	92.50	—.20	93.15	81.70
Sept	90.00	90.50	90.00	90.40	—.55	92.75	77.50
Oct	86.60	86.70	86.15	86.60-.70unch to+.10		87.00	78.50
Nov	85.25	85.25	85.25	85.25		85.25	78.00
Dec	84.40	84.75	84.40	84.75	—.15	85.60	78.00
Jan'73	85.00	85.15	84.75	84.75b	—.25	85.40	78.50
ICED BROILERS							
Mar	28.45	28.55	28.42	28.50	+.10	29.25	25.12
Apr	27.70	27.70	27.65	27.65	—.05	28.70	27.05
May	28.55	28.70	28.55	28.55		29.55	27.9?
July	29.35	29.45	29.27	29.27	—.10	29.45	28.7?
Nov	26.05	26.05	26.05	26.05	+.05	26.45	26.0?
PLYWOOD							
Mar	102.50	102.80	101.70	102.00-.20unch to+.2		105.90	82
May	103.90	104.00	103.00	103.30-.40	—.20to.10	107.00	83
July	103.00	105.10	104.00	104.40	—.20	107.30	8?
Sept	103.80	104.30	103.90	103.60	—.20	107.40	9?
Nov	103.50	103.90	103.20	103.40	—.20	107.10	9?
Jan73	104.00	104.40	103.70	103.80	—.20	107.70	10?
CHICAGO—SILVER							
Apr	154.60	156.00	153.40	153.80-.90	—.50to.40	191.30	1?
June	156.40	157.70	155.10	155.70	—.10	192.60	?
Aug	157.90	159.30	156.70	157.90	—.10	187.30	?
Oct	160.00	160.80	158.80	159.10b	—.20	178.80	?
Dec	161.40	162.50	159.80	161.10	+.10	166.8?	?
Feb73	163.00	164.00	161.80	163.00	+.10	165.6?	?
Apr	164.80	165.60	164.00	164.80	+.40	167.3?	?
June	167.20	167.20	165.80	166.30b	no comp	167.2?	?
KANSAS CITY—WHEAT							
Mar	151¾	152½	151¾	152	+¼	163	141
May	147¾	147⅞	147¼	147⅜-½	+⅛to unch	161⅝	139
July	144¼	145	144½	144½	....	149	134½
Sept	146½	146½	146½	146½		146¼	142¼
MINNEAPOLIS—WHEAT							
Mar	156¼	156⅞	156½	156⅜	—⅞	168	154
May	160¼	161	160½	160⅜	—¾	165⅜	158½
July	162¼	162¾	162¼	162¼	—¾	163	160¼
WINNIPEG—RAPESEED (VANCOUVER)							
Mar	259	260	256½	256½	—7½	298	233¾
June	257½	258	255½	255½-½	—2to1½	280	236
Sept	257¾	258	256½	256½	—1¼	259½	242

	Open	High	Low	Close	Change	Season's High	Low
FROZEN PORK BELLIES							
Mar	38.65	38.95	38.50	38.80-.85	—.02to+.03	42.95	26.70
May	38.85	39.10	38.60	38.95-39.05unch to+.10		42.97	27.25
July	37.90	38.20	37.70	38.20-.07+	.19to.02	42.12	27.75
Aug	35.90	36.32	35.87	36.20-.25+	.20to.25	40.15	26.82
Feb'73	33.50	33.82	33.40	33.77	+ .15	38.90	32.00
May	33.85	34.35	33.85	34.35	+ .55	34.35	33.00

Sales estimated at: 5,902 contracts.

	Open	High	Low	Close	Change	Season's High	Low
HOGS							
Apr	24		24.45	24.62-.65+	.20to.23	27.90	19.20
June	26		24.43		+ .05	28.95	21.00
July	26					28.95	21.27
Oct	24						21.00
Dec	2?						
Feb'73	2?						
LUMBER							
Mar	11						
May	1?						
July	1?						
Sept	1?						
Nov							

Sales...

NEW

Volume and Open Interest

The Commodity Exchange Authority reported grain futures trading on the Chicago Board of Trade as of the close of business Monday, March 6, 1972 (in thousands of bushels):

	Mar. '72	May	July	Sept.	Dec.	Total
Wheat	915	3,270	3,005	420	375	7,985
Corn	2,730	7,020		555	2,695	x21,885
Oats	105	70	65	20		260

x-Includes 300 for March '73.

Soybeans: March, 5,240; May, 38,825; July, 29,495; August, 5,240; September, 2,870; November, 11,375; January '73, 2,060; Total, 95,105.

Soybean oil trading totaled 4,672; soybean meal trading totaled 1,808.

Open Interest (in thousands of bushels):

	Wheat	Corn	Oats	Soybeans	r-Meal	s-Oil
March	11,830	5,740	1,510	12,330	1,654	1,570
May	21,305	90,445	3,355	109,265	3,805	9,195
July	20,535	80,445	2,220	84,935	1,791	7,987
August				23,365		3,288
September	5,040	14,560	1,360	22,365	14,200	2,296
October						1,895
November				59,065	717	1,200
December	3,510	28,330	130			1,853
January '73			9,610			655
Total	62,220	224,155	8,575	312,770	12,521	29,949

r-In hundreds of tons. s-In tank cars of 60,000 pounds.

Frozen Pork Bellies for March 6 and changes from Friday:
May 7,190, off 406. Cattle (40,000 pounds each), Feb. 2,451, No. 11 17,076, off 406. June 7,143, Aug. 1,570, Feb. 491, March 10, 358. Total 25,723, off 307. Total 12,357, up 186. Maine Po-March 1,006, April 4,010, Oct. 1,721, Dec. 1,106, Feb. 9, Sept. 244, Oct. 9, Dec. 33, Total 1,003, March 145, April tatoes 50,000 pounds each, May 2,558, off 186. World Sugar No. 11 (112,000 pounds each), May 7, Total 145, April 659, May 2,668, Oct. 2,744, Jan. 1, March 1,003, June 36, July 32, Aug. Total 16,187, up 42, Cocoa (30,000 pounds each), May 137, July 119. May 590, July 2,459, Sept. 2,985, Dec. 914, March 85, S up 65, Sept. Dec. 1,005, Jan. 4,708, July 2,588, Sept. 1, Copper (25,000 703, Oct. 438, Dec. 494, May 143, March 574, 9, May 7,031, July 8,449, Sept. 143, March 777, April 1, Silver (10,000 troy ounces each), March 11,227, S ton (500-pound bales), March 1,906, July 308, Aug. 8,262, Dec. March 5,083, J 308,800, Oct. 432,200, Dec. 34,700, May 43,170, off Juice (15,000 pounds each), May 533,900, March 182,400, July 754, May 1,117, Nov. 399, March 828, May 1,259, July July 14. Total 5,748, up 59. Jan. 1,209, March 12, May 53,

	Mar						46.30
Mar	53.85						46.65
May	53.00	54.00	52.9?				48.25
July	53.10	53.75	52.90	53.70b			50.85
Sept	49.85	51.10	49.85	50.95	+1.15		47.80
Jan'73	44.95	45.40	44.75	45.45b	+.65	56.25	42.90
Mar	44.75	44.75	44.45	44.50b	+.55	55.75	42.80
May	44.70	44.70	44.70	44.90b	+.55	50.25	43.10

Sales estimated at: 600 contracts.

	Open	High	Low	Close	Change	Season's High	Low
COTTON							
Mar	38.32	38.50	38.00	38.00	—.30	38.50	28.10
May	37.58	37.65	37.01	37.01-.07	—.65to.59	37.95	28.11

downward price trend develops in a commodity, it may go a very long way further than logic would suggest, and the speculator who continues to buy as it falls will soon have his capital wiped out.

Thus the primary rule for making money in futures is to sell if there is a small price decline after purchase, but hold on and buy more if the price goes up. An example is shown below.

NORTON P SHULMAN
378 RONCESVALLES AV
TORONTO 3 ONTARIO   1962 606 10186

c

MERRILL LYNCH,
PIERCE, FENNER & SMITH

4-14-58

DATE			QUANTITY PURCHASED	QUANTITY SOLD	DESCRIPTION		MKT	PRICE	COST OR PROCEEDS	DIFFERENCE	FEE AND OR TAX	COMMISSION
MO	DAY	YR										
4	8	58	1		CAK JUL 58 SUGAR	4	14	343	384160			
4	14	58		1	CAK JUL 58 SUGAR	4	14	339	379680			
										4480DR		3000

This way the speculator ends up with many small losses and a few huge profits. He need only detect and buy with one trend in order to make a fortune from a small investment.

Understanding charts and chartists is essential to the speculator in commodity futures. I have briefly discussed charts in an earlier chapter. Everything that has been said about them in reference to stocks applies twice as strongly in the commodity field, because chart followers are so very much more numerous here. Chart followers comprise the vast majority of speculators dealing in commodity futures. This produces tremendous opportunities for more sensible speculators.

The chartist pays little or no attention to news regarding supply and demand in his commodity; he ignores weather data and world crises but makes his sales and purchases according to records of the daily price range and volume fluctuations of each commodity. He believes that future price fluctuations can be predicted by studying recent, past, and current market action. The chartist explains his theories by saying that all news and facts are subject to different interpretations and that it is impossible for any individual to forecast price changes, because in addition to misinterpreting the significance of some facts, he is unaware of others. Furthermore, he believes that by the time pertinent events reach the newspapers, many individuals who have had prior knowledge have already made their own purchases or sales. The market, however, cannot be fooled (he believes), because all events and news are reflected in buying and selling in the market, and so by carefully studying market action one can predict future prices. The market action is studied by producing pictures or charts of daily price volumes and ranges in individual commodities. He believes that certain pictures forecast higher prices and other pictures lower prices.

To add to the confusion, chartists produce their charts in several different ways. Some use the daily price range and close; some also study the volume at each individual price; while others use price averages over longer periods of time.

Perhaps the market cannot be fooled, but unfortunately most chartists have a little problem in that they cannot understand their own charts. There is not a commodity salesman who has not heard the plaintive complaint. "My chart was right, but I read it wrong." Another important factor is that even when the chartist makes a correct guess of what he believes the charts says, he is often buying well after a trend has been established.

Despite all this scoffing, there is no question that when there are many chartists trading in commodities (or anything else), and when certain well-recognized "signals" appear in trading charts, indicating an upward or downward move in prices, usually such a move immediately follows. The reason is obvious. When thousands of chart followers expect an upward move in price, they buy — and of course there then occurs an upward price movement. Similarly, when thousands of chart followers expect a price fall, they sell, and prices must fall. Fantastic as this sounds, it is undoubtedly true; the chartists are producing their own price changes — and thus proving the merit of charting!

Because of the large number of chartists in the future market and because of the tremendous impact they can have on commodity prices, there will develop irrational price moves from time to time, based purely on widespread buying and selling by chart followers.

Because of the combination on the one hand of hedgers who must buy and sell regardless of price and on the other hand of chartists who follow present and past price and volume performance, an intelligent speculator has a greater chance of making huge profits in commodity futures than in any other gambling activity.

Briefly the pictures which chartists look for as guides are trend lines, double bottoms, double tops, head and shoulders tops, head and shoulders bottoms, congestion areas, triangles, flags, round tops and bottoms and gaps. These are illustrated on the following pages (pp. 130-131).

There does not appear to be any point in the speculator preparing his own charts. They are of value only to keep him informed of whether the thousands of chartists are buying or selling. His broker will be glad to inform him when the charts are clear cut, or he can subscribe to an excellent, reasonable service supplied by the Commodity Research Bureau, Inc., 82 Beaver St., New York.

In what commodity or commodities should a speculator seek to make his fortune?

Of the many that were listed earlier, the vast majority are unsuitable because of low volume or minimal price changes. For example, the low volume of aluminum rules it out; the protected market in domes-

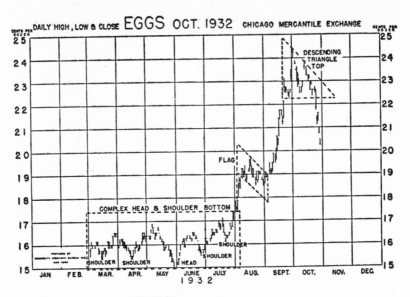

DAILY HIGH, LOW & CLOSE EGGS OCT. 1932 CHICAGO MERCANTILE EXCHANGE

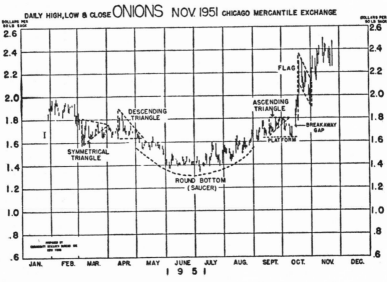

DAILY HIGH, LOW & CLOSE ONIONS NOV. 1951 CHICAGO MERCANTILE EXCHANGE

tic sugar makes a price rise rare and a price fall impossible. Out of the entire list, the six with the best possibilities of large price fluctuations are world sugar, coffee, cocoa, soybeans, silver, and copper. This list will

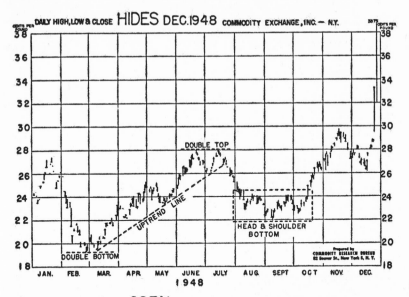

DAILY HIGH,LOW & CLOSE HIDES DEC.1948 COMMODITY EXCHANGE, INC. — N.Y.

DOUBLE TOP

UPTREND LINE

HEAD & SHOULDER BOTTOM

DOUBLE BOTTOM

Prepared by
COMMODITY RESEARCH BUREAU
82 Beaver St., New York 5, N.Y.

JAN. FEB. MAR. APR. MAY JUNE JULY AUG. SEPT OCT NOV. DEC.

1948

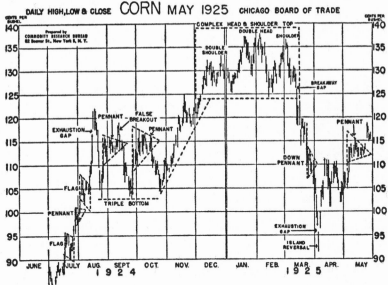

DAILY HIGH,LOW & CLOSE CORN MAY 1925 CHICAGO BOARD OF TRADE

Prepared by
COMMODITY RESEARCH BUREAU
82 Beaver St., New York 5, N.Y.

COMPLEX HEAD & SHOULDER TOP

DOUBLE HEAD   SHOULDER

DOUBLE SHOULDER

BREAKAWAY GAP

PENNANT   FALSE BREAKOUT

EXHAUSTION GAP

PENNANT

PENNANT

DOWN PENNANT

FLAG

TRIPLE BOTTOM

PENNANT

EXHAUSTION GAP

FLAG

ISLAND REVERSAL

JUNE   JULY   AUG.   SEPT   OCT.   NOV.   DEC.   JAN.   FEB.   MAR.   APR.   MAY

1924   1925

vary from time to time depending on world news and market conditions; when war threatens, for example, rubber futures soar. But four commodities that are always volatile are world sugar, cocoa, soybeans, and copper.

The single factor that produces volatility in the price of a commodity is a varying supply and/or demand. Inasmuch as demand usually remains fairly constant, showing a steady growth or decline, supply is the big factor. In some commodities, such as nickel or aluminum, supply is usually closely attuned to the demand, but in others, such as copper, supply is often outstripped by demand, resulting in much higher prices. This in turn stimulates more production, which finally results in prices falling. This is the ideal situation for a commodity speculator. Commodities that show the widest price swings invariably are produced in many countries and consumed in many other countries. The constant competition prevents price stabilization.

Occasionally a special situation develops in a normally stable commodity due to static supply but suddenly or gradually increased demand. This occurred in the silver market in 1968. For four years the price of silver had been stabilized at $1.29 by the U.S. government's freely selling silver at that price. A price rise had been forecast for years by numerous authorities, because consumption was greater than production and the United States would certainly not be willing to sell their whole stockpile just to maintain silver's price at an artificially low level. Sure enough, the U.S. government stopped selling their silver, and the priced soared to $2.50. Six-month and one-year futures had been available at prices ranging between $1.29 and $1.30 with only 7½¢ deposit. Thus speculators who had run practically no risk turned every $750 put up into $12,000 within a very few weeks. These advertised special situations appear every few years in the commodity market and the speculator should take advantage of them.

When making his initial investment the speculator should pick a "hot" commodity, one that is receiving a heavy trading volume and has a large open interest. It should show a large price range over the previous year and should be currently the subject of newspaper comment either as to its large price fall or its current short supply associated with a price rise.

The speculator must then decide whether he thinks this commodity will increase or fall in price in coming weeks. Strangely enough, it doesn't really matter what conclusion is arrived at, because half the time the "guess" will be right and half the time wrong. The speculator who pyramids his right guesses can afford to be wrong nine times out of ten and still end up a winner. The reason is that the wrong guesses should each end up with a small loss, whereas the right guesses should produce very large profits. This is where the stop loss comes in.

In an earlier chapter about stop-loss selling, I condemned it as a practically useless tool in the stock market. The situation is quite different in the commodity market, because much more often trends will develop, producing a steady upward or downward price swing which goes far past true value levels. Because of this, it is essential that a speculator not attempt to fight a trend. Once a purchase has been made of a commodity future, a stop-loss sell order should be entered at a level 5% below the purchase price. If there has been a short sale, a stop-loss buy order should be entered 5% above the sale price. This 5% will actually represent 50% or more of your initial margin, and no loss on any contract should ever exceed 50% of the original margin. As an alternative to entering a stop-loss order, one can follow the blanket rule of never putting up more margin.

Once a futures commodity has moved in price sufficiently to lose 25% of an initial margin deposit, the commodity broker will phone his client requesting more margin. On such occasions the astute speculator will not put up more money but will sell out his contract and take his loss.

This rule is basic to commodity trading — the man who becomes stubborn and sticks with a commodity that is going against him will soon be bankrupt. If a person cannot admit making a mistake, he should not buy commodities. The speculator who makes money in commodities is willing to accept loss after loss until he finds a commodity future that goes as he had expected. Such a future will quickly make up his losses.

The numerous losses are all quickly forgotten when one has a winner. The essential with a winner is to take full advantage of it and to make the largest possible profits. This is done by pyramiding. Pyramiding can be carried out in two ways.

The first is by simply instructing the broker to keep you within 10% of being fully margined. That is, if a commodity future which has been purchased goes up, the broker will buy another contract on the same future as soon as he can do so without any further investment of capital. If a November sugar contract has been purchased at a price of 3¢ per pound with a $500 down payment, once the sugar price climbs to 3½¢ and there has been a $500 paper profit, the broker uses the paper profit as margin to purchase a second contract in November sugar. Each contract represents 112,000 pounds of sugar, and so now the speculator owns 224,000 pounds of sugar. Now if sugar goes to 3¾¢, the broker buys another contract, using the additional $500 paper profit from the first two contracts as margin. Now the speculator owns 3 contracts, and sugar has only to go up one-sixth of a cent to 3.91¢ per pound to produce another $500 paper profit, allowing the purchase of still another contract. Following along on the same system, by the time sugar reaches 5¢ a pound, the speculator would own 33 contracts and would show a profit of $16,500 on his original $500 investment.

The reason that the broker is not instructed to keep you fully margined, but only 90% so, is to act as a protection in case of minor dips in the upward movement, which otherwise would result in a call for more margin.

The second type of pyramiding is usually the more profitable one, but it requires more margin and thus more risk. This involves purchasing more contracts at stated intervals as the price goes up. Thus the initial contract is purchased at a price of 3¢ per pound, and instructions are given to purchase additional contracts as quickly as they can be purchased at intervals of no more than one-tenth of a cent. Thus when the sugar price reaches 3.1¢, a second contract will be purchased. At this point the profit is only $100, so an additional $400 margin must be deposited. At 3.2¢ a third contract is purchased which requires another $300 margin. At 3.3¢ a fourth contract is purchased which requires $200 margin, and at 3.4¢ a fifth contract, which will require $100 margin. From this point on no further margin is required and the total margin remains at $1,500.

If this procedure is continued and sugar continues to rise in price, by the time it reaches only 4½¢ a pound the speculator will own 38 contracts and will have made a profit of $38,000.

Admittedly this type of fantastic run is unusual without intermediate corrections, but it illustrates in a dramatic way the large profits possible in commodities, if one pyramids one's winning purchases and cuts losses to a minimum. It is very important that, if an upward move should be broken and more margin called for, the account be sold out and profits taken. There is always another commodity that can be purchased.

Exactly the same rules should be followed in selling a commodity short. If it then goes up, buy it back and take a small loss. If it goes down, sell more and pyramid the profits.

Below is an example of pyramiding in which more lead was purchased with the profits from earlier buys.

FRIEDBERG & CO. LTD.

34 ADELAIDE ST. WEST
TORONTO 1, ONTARIO
Tel. (416) 864-1195
Cable Address: FRIEDCO Toronto

CONFIRMATION

DATE ·28/1/72   ACCOUNT NO.

TO   Dr. Morton Shulman

WE HAVE THIS DAY MADE THE FOLLOWING TRADES FOR YOUR ACCOUNT AND RISK   as agents on LME

BOUGHT			SOLD		
QUANTITY	COMMODITY	PRICE	QUANTITY	COMMODITY	PRICE
50 tons	April 28/1972 Lead	£104.25			

NOTICE— It is understood and agreed that all futures transactions made by us for your account are either hedges or contemplate actual delivery and receipt of the property and payment therefor; and that all property sold for your account is sold upon the representation that you have the same in your possession actually or potentially. These transactions are made in accordance with and subject to the rules, regulations and customs of the exchange where made and also in accordance with and subject to Federal and State laws. It is understood and agreed that we reserve the right to close out transactions without notice when the margins on deposit with us (1) are exhausted or (2) are inadequate in our judgment to protect us against price fluctuations, or (3) are below the minimum margin requirements under the rules and regulations of the exchange relating thereto.

N.B.— Any apparent error should be immediately reported by telegraph or telephone, otherwise this account will be considered approved by you. Name of other party to contract furnished on request.   E. & O.E.

FRIEDBERG & CO. LTD.

34 ADELAIDE ST. WEST
TORONTO 1, ONTARIO
Tel. (416) 864-1195
Cable Address: FRIEDCO Toronto

CONFIRMATION

DATE 2/2/72   ACCOUNT NO.

TO   Dr. Horton Shulman

WE HAVE THIS DAY MADE THE FOLLOWING TRADES FOR YOUR ACCOUNT AND RISK   as agents on LME

BOUGHT			SOLD		
QUANTITY	COMMODITY	PRICE	QUANTITY	COMMODITY	PRICE
25 tons	May 2/72 Lead	£107.50			

NOTICE— It is understood and agreed that all futures transactions made by us for your account are either hedges or contemplate actual delivery and receipt of the property and payment therefor; and that all property sold for your account is sold upon the representation that you have the same in your possession actually or potentially. These transactions are made in accordance with and subject to the rules, regulations and customs of the exchange where made and also in accordance with and subject to Federal and State laws. It is understood and agreed that we reserve the right to close out transactions without notice when the margins on deposit with us (1) are exhausted. or (2) are inadequate in our judgment to protect us against price fluctuations, or (3) are below the minimum margin requirements under the rules and regulations of the exchange relating thereto.

N.B.— Any apparent error should be immediately reported by telegraph or telephone, otherwise this account will be considered approved by you. Name of other party to contract furnished on request.   E. & O.E.

FRIEDBERG & CO. LTD.

34 ADELAIDE ST. WEST
TORONTO 1, ONTARIO
Tel. (416) 864-1195
Cable Address: FRIEDCO Toronto

CONFIRMATION

DATE 4/2/72   ACCOUNT NO.

TO   Dr. Horton Shulman

WE HAVE THIS DAY MADE THE FOLLOWING TRADES FOR YOUR ACCOUNT AND RISK   as agents on LME

BOUGHT			SOLD		
QUANTITY	COMMODITY	PRICE	QUANTITY	COMMODITY	PRICE
25 tons	May 4/72 Lead	£108.75			

NOTICE— It is understood and agreed that all futures transactions made by us for your account are either hedges or contemplate actual delivery and receipt of the property and payment therefor; and that all property sold for your account is sold upon the representation that you have the same in your possession actually or potentially. These transactions are made in accordance with and subject to the rules, regulations and customs of the exchange where made and also in accordance with and subject to Federal and State laws. It is understood and agreed that we reserve the right to close out transactions without notice when the margins on deposit with us (1) are exhausted or (2) are inadequate in our judgment to protect us against price fluctuations. or (3) are below the minimum margin requirements under the rules and regulations of the exchange relating thereto

N.B.— Any apparent error should be immediately reported by telegraph or telephone, otherwise this account will be considered approved by you. Name of other party to contract furnished on request.   E. & O.E.

FRIEDBERG & CO. LTD.

34 ADELAIDE ST. WEST
TORONTO 1, ONTARIO
Tel. (416) 864-1195
Cable Address: FRIEDCO Toronto

CONFIRMATION

	DATE	ACCOUNT NO.
	9/2/72	

TO   Dr. Morton Shulman

WE HAVE THIS DAY MADE THE FOLLOWING TRADES FOR YOUR ACCOUNT AND RISK   as agents   on LME

BOUGHT				SOLD		
QUANTITY	COMMODITY		PRICE	QUANTITY	COMMODITY	PRICE
25 tons	Lead 8 May '72		£111.50			

NOTICE— It is understood and agreed that all futures transactions made by us for your account are either hedges or contemplate actual delivery and receipt of the property and payment therefor; and that all property sold for your account is sold upon the representation that you have the same in your possession actually or potentially. These transactions are made in accordance with and subject to the rules, regulations and customs of the exchange where made and also in accordance with and subject to Federal and State laws. It is understood and agreed that we reserve the right to close out transactions without notice when the margins on deposit with us (1) are exhausted or (2) are inadequate in our judgment to protect us against price fluctuations or (3) are below the minimum margin requirements under the rules and regulations of the exchange relating thereto

N.B.— Any apparent error should be immediately reported by telegraph or telephone, otherwise this account will be considered approved by you. Name of other party to contract furnished on request.   E. & O.E.

I was content to have doubled my money in two weeks and happily sold my lead.

Tel. (416)864-1195   34 Adelaide St. West
                                                               Toronto 1, Ontario

Dr. Morton Shulman   ....February..9,...........19..72.........

IN ACCOUNT WITH

FRIEDBERG & CO. LTD.

Settlement Account

		Tons	Due		Debit	Credit
Bought	28/1/72	50 Lead	28/4/72	£104.25		
	2/2/72	25	2/5/72	107.50		
	4/2/72	25	4/5/72	108.75		
	8/2/72	25	8/5/72	111.50		
Sold	9/2/72	50	28/4/72	112.75		
	9/2/72	25	2/5/72	112.75		
	9/2/72	25	4/5/72	112.75		
	9/2/72	25	8/5/72	113.00		
		Balance -----------------------------				£693.75/U.S.$1,803.75
		Round turn commissions			U.S $250.00	
		Special commissions for prompt settlement U.S. $7.50 per 25 tons			37.50	
		Enclosed our cheque --------------			$3307.32	

In all commodity trading there is one basic rule, which is exactly opposite to that in stock market trading: cut your losses and let your profits ride. Never average down.

One point which has not been discussed is which trading month should be bought or sold. Commodity brokers will usually recommend the earlier months and the shorter contracts, which automatically produce more frequent commissions, rationalizing this by saying that these months show the widest price swings and one can always trade the position for a later month if the contract becomes due. This is bad advice. It is wisest to purchase contracts for the most distant months except when there is a very wide price differential between the near and far months. (The price differential between near and far months should never exceed storage charges, because a commodity can always be purchased and stored for later delivery.) Buying distant contracts avoids the necessity of trading of contracts, thus reducing commissions.

In summary the rules for commodity trading are:

1. Pick an active commodity with a large open interest that is vulnerable to wide price swings. Soybeans, cocoa, world sugar, and copper are four perennial favourites.

2. Restrict your trades to one or, at the most, two different commodities.

3. Take an initial small position of one or two contracts in a distant month. Put in a stop-loss order 5% below the market price in purchases and 5% above the market price in short sales.

4. Never put up additional margin.

5. Pyramid profits to within 90% of the maximum possible.

17
THE MONEY MARKET

This is also a future market — only instead of buying and selling commodities it involves the buying and selling of currency. This can be a very profitable undertaking and carries very little risk. Even more remarkable is the fact that no margin need be put up and this past year hundreds of millions of dollars have been made with absolutely no investment.

The buying and selling of foreign currency is done constantly by importers. If an importer has ordered from another country a shipment of goods that he will have to pay for in some months, he may purchase a future for that amount of foreign currency, thus protecting himself against any price fluctuations. He wants to be sure to get his goods at the prearranged price and does not wish to gamble on the chance that the foreign currency might cost him more some months hence. It could, of course, also cost him less, but an importer knows that he can make money sticking to importing, and few of them wish to gamble in other matters. An exporter, on the other hand, may have sold to another country manufactured goods that are to be paid for in that country's currency. He cannot afford to take the chance that the foreign currency may have been devalued by the time he is paid, so he sells the equivalent amount of foreign currency in a future.

The mechanism of such a sale is very simple. The person wishing to buy or sell the future goes to his local bank and tells the accountant that he wishes to buy or sell the amount of the foreign currency for delivery on a predesignated date. For example, he may say, "I wish to sell 10,000 English pounds for delivery next July." The accountant will then say, "The rate is $2.99 15/16 per pound for next July delivery." The bank will require a form to be signed, a copy of which is given to the seller.

FORM 505 (Rev. 4-50) **THE TORONTO-DOMINION BANK**

June 10,1966
DATE

We confirm having bought from/ ~~sold to~~ you today exchange
as detailed below:

TO ⌐ ⌐

L ⌐

RATE — 2.99 15/16

AMOUNT AND KIND OF CURRENCY —

DELIVERY spot 30 days
Your Option — July 10th, 1966 £10,000.

REMARKS —

_____ _____
Accountant Manager
NOTE — Please sign duplicate officially
and return promptly.

The exporter or importer has now protected himself completely and can forget all about the foreign currency. When the goods are ready, they will be paid for and delivered and the matter is finished.

The speculator has a different interest but his transactions are handled in the same way. When the speculator believes that a currency is about to be revalued, he will go to his bank and purchase or sell a future in that currency. When the future's time is up, or before if he wishes, he liquidates the transaction by buying or selling back the foreign currency.

This type of speculation is a relatively safe one, in that the risk is very small while the potential profit can be very large, because currency changes are rarely deep, dark secrets but are almost always predicted in the public press. The reason for this is that in the past thirty years most currency changes have been devaluations (with the exception of the recent *de facto* devaluation of the U.S. dollar which was done by changing *upward* the value of other currencies), and devaluations only occur as a result of pressure upon a country's finances; these pressures build up gradually until the affected country finds it easier to devalue than to continue to fight. For months before each devaluation, rumours and hints of the coming event are discussed in the financial pages.

In every such case the speculator cannot go very wrong by selling the threatened currency via a future. Even if the suggested devaluation does not ensue, the speculator loses very little. For example, in the fall of 1965 there were widespread rumours of a devaluation of the English pound. The English government was able to stave off this change and succeeded in maintaining the price of the pound at $2.73 U.S. Even at the height of the pressures against the pound, futures never sold at more than a few pennies below its spot conversion price, and so speculators who were proven wrong had very limited losses. On the other hand, those who sold the pound short after the war, when it was last devalued, made huge fortunes. At that time the value of the pound was lowered from $5 to $2.75, and a speculator selling 100,000 pounds short would have made a profit of almost a quarter of a million dollars.

Sometimes governments publicly proclaim their intention to devalue. In 1962 Donald Fleming, the Canadian Minister of Finance, announced in a public speech that he felt the Canadian dollar was at too high a level and that it was his government's intention to force it lower. On that date the Canadian dollar was at par with the U.S. dollar. Any Canadian who wished to make money merely had to go to his bank and buy a future on the U.S. dollar. Any American who wished to make money sold a future in Canadian dollars. The banks asked for no down payment or margin as long as they knew you and your credit rating was satisfactory. The $500,000 purchase shown below was made without putting up a penny.

Six months after Mr. Fleming's speech, the Canadian dollar was reduced to 92½ U.S. cents, giving a clear profit on such a trade of $37,000.

Such devaluations are not always predicted as definitely as Mr. Fleming announced the Canadian one, but they are almost all announced in one way or another. Since the war one country after another has solved its balance of payments problem by devaluation. Some countries, like Canada, have done this twice.

THE TORONTO-DOMINION BANK

July 19/63
DATE

We confirm having bought from/ ~~sold to~~ you today exchange
as detailed below:

TO ┌   ┐

   └   ┘

RATE   — 8 1/8%

AMOUNT AND KIND OF CURRENCY —	
$500,000	U.S. Currency

DELIVERY
Your Option —

REMARKS —

_____   _____
           Accountant   Manager
NOTE — Please sign duplicate officially
and return promptly.

Up till 1972, the U.S. had been the only country never to devalue its currency. However, the reason was not that its money was holding its value; instead it was simply a matter of pride. How could the most powerful country in the world, the country that had never lost a war, admit that it had overspent its income and tailor its coat accordingly?

Instead, as the economic forces on the U.S. dollar rose in the late sixties, the U.S. government responded by exerting pressure on its allies and client states to raise the value of their currencies in relation to the dollar so as to prevent the necessity of the U.S. devaluing! It was just as though Lewis Carroll had written the script. Because it was obvious to the foreign ministers of finance that this was economic madness, these revaluations did not take place without considerable publicity and frequent protestations from the foreign governments involved that they would never revalue. This produced incredible and frequent opportunities to make fortunes for anyone who read the newspapers. The tip-off that it was time to buy the foreign currency always came in the front page statements by the finance minister involved that he would "never" revalue. This meant that revaluation was to take place the following weekend and anyone who wanted to make money had to phone his bank and purchase foreign currency for future delivery — no money was put up and the bank would automatically send you your profit.

FOR..i 565 (REV. 4-59)

THE TORONTO-DOMINION BANK

421 Roncesvalles Avenue
& Howard Park Avenue   **1752**
TORONTO, ONTARIO
BRANCH

May 2/69
DATE

We confirm having ~~bought~~ from/   sold to   you today exchange
as detailed below:

TO ⌐

     Dr. Morton Shulman,
     66 Russell Hill Rd.,
     Toronto, Ontario.

   ⌐

RATE   —   7-9/16
     25 40 DM

	AMOUNT AND KIND OF CURRENCY —	

DELIVERY   5 months
Your Option — 121 days to 150 days   150,000 DM

REMARKS —

_____
Accountant

_____
Manager

NOTE — Please sign duplicate officially
      and return promptly.

TELEPHONE: (416) 366-4461
TELEX: 02-21308

Cable address: DEAKNICK
Codes: PETERSON 3rd & 4th

Please address all mail to:
DEAK & CO. (ONTARIO) LIMITED
P.O. BOX 850, STATION "A"
TORONTO 1, ONT., CANADA

DEAK & CO. (ONTARIO) LIMITED
FOREIGN EXCHANGE
100 KING STREET WEST   TORONTO 1, ONT., CANADA

October 6   19 69

⌐ DM amount payable to:
   Bayerische Gemeindebank
   Munich, Germany
     for our account.

⌐ Dr. Morton P. Shulman
    378 Roncesvalles Avenue
    Toronto 3, Ontario

Please be informed that the following entries have been made in your account:

DEBIT	Re: Our telephone conversation today	CREDIT
	We confirm our purchase from you of:	
	DM 150,000.00 @ .2650 T.T. Munich, value Oct. 8, 1969	US$39,750.00
US$39,750.00	In settlement we are remitting to The Toronto-Dominion Bank, Roncesvalles & Howard Park Branch, Toronto, for your account.	
	Very truly yours,	
	DEAK & CO. (ONTARIO) LIMITED per:	

As time went along and it always worked, observers of the U.S. mania for face-saving became bolder and took bigger slices of the pie. After all, there was no risk — certainly the U.S. government was strong enough to convince its European allies that black was white and vice versa. The banks too were convinced and didn't even ask for a penny of security.

FORM 565 (REV. 4-59)

THE TORONTO-DOMINION BANK

421 Roncesvalles Avenue
& Howard Park Avenue **1752**
TORONTO 3, ONTARIO BRANCH

May 4, 1971
DATE

We confirm having ~~bought from~~ sold to you today exchange as detailed below:

TO

Dr. Morton S. Shulman
66 Russell Hill Road
Toronto, Ont.

RATE — US$ 27.69/100DM

DELIVERY
Your Option —
On or about August 3rd 1971

REMARKS —

Kindly sign yellow copy and return promptly.

K. Inokon
Accountant

NOTE — Please sign duplicate officially and return promptly.

AMOUNT AND KIND OF CURRENCY —	
German Marks	1,000,000.00

Manager

DEAK & CO. (ONTARIO) LIMITED

FOREIGN EXCHANGE

Please address all mail to:
DEAK & CO. (ONTARIO) LIMITED
P.O. BOX 850, STATION "A"
TORONTO 1, ONT., CANADA

10 KING STREET EAST • TORONTO 1, ONTARIO • CANADA

May 21, 1971

Dr. Morton P. Shulman
378 Roncesvalles Avenue
Toronto 154, Ontario

Dear Sir:

We confirm the following future exchange contract entered into with
you today:

BOUGHT FROM YOU

Deutsche Mark 500,000.00 at the rate of US$ .2856
equivalent to US$142,800.00
delivery August 3, 1971.

Please sign and return to us the enclosed copy signifying your
agreement.

Very truly yours,

DEAK & CO. (ONTARIO) LIMITED

Fred Hirschler

FH:ld
Encl.

Fred Hirschler
Vice-President & Treasurer

_____
Morton P. Shulman

signed on _____ 1971

AFFILIATES: HONG KONG   HONOLULU   LOS ANGELES   MIAMI   NEW YORK   SAN FRANCISCO   VIENNA   WASHINGTON   ZURICH

CABLES: DEAKNICK
TELEX: 02-21308

AREA CODE: 416
863-1611

DEAK & CO. (ONTARIO) LIMITED

FOREIGN EXCHANGE

Please address all mail to:
DEAK & CO. (ONTARIO) LIMITED
P.O. BOX 354, STATION "A"
TORONTO 1, ONT., CANADA

10 KING STREET EAST • TORONTO 1, ONTARIO • CANADA

July 13, 1971

Dr. Morton P. Shulman
378 Roncesvalles Avenue
Toronto 154, Ontario

Dear Sir:

We confirm the following future exchange contract entered into with
you today:

<u>BOUGHT FROM YOU</u>

    Deutsche Mark 500,000.00 at the rate of US$ .2856
    equivalent to US$142,800.00
    delivery August 3, 1971.

Please <u>sign and return</u> to us the enclosed copy signifying your
agreement.

Very truly yours,

DEAK & CO. (ONTARIO) LIMITED

Fred Hirschler

FH:ld
Encl.

Fred Hirschler
Vice-President & Treasurer

_____
      Morton P. Shulman

signed on _____ 1971

AFFILIATES: HONG KONG HONOLULU LOS ANGELES MIAMI NEW YORK SAN FRANCISCO VIENNA WASHINGTON ZURICH

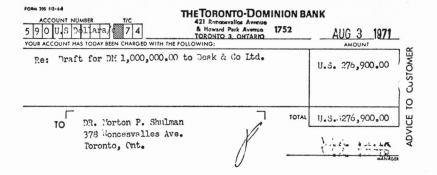

FORM 205 (12-64)

THE TORONTO-DOMINION BANK
421 Roncesvalles Avenue
& Howard Park Avenue
TORONTO 3, ONTARIO   1752

ACCOUNT NUMBER	T/C
5 9 0 U.S Dollars / 7 4	

AUG 3 1971

YOUR ACCOUNT HAS TODAY BEEN CHARGED WITH THE FOLLOWING: AMOUNT

Re: Draft for DM 1,000,000.00 to Deak & Co Ltd.

U.S. 276,900.00

TO   DR. Morton P. Shulman
     378 Roncesvalles Ave.
     Toronto, Ont.

TOTAL   U.S. 276,900.00

MANAGER

ADVICE TO CUSTOMER

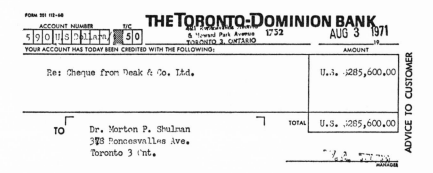

FORM 201 (12-64)

THE TORONTO-DOMINION BANK
421 Roncesvalles Avenue
& Howard Park Avenue
TORONTO 3, ONTARIO   1752

ACCOUNT NUMBER	T/C
5 9 0 U.S Dollars / 5 0	

AUG 3 1971
19

YOUR ACCOUNT HAS TODAY BEEN CREDITED WITH THE FOLLOWING: AMOUNT

Re: Cheque from Deak & Co. Ltd.

U.S. 285,600.00

TO   Dr. Morton P. Shulman
     378 Roncesvalles Ave.
     Toronto 3 Ont.

TOTAL   U.S. 285,600.00

MANAGER

ADVICE TO CUSTOMER

Finally the temporary culmination came at the end of 1971 when Richard Nixon reluctantly devalued the U.S. dollar. He gave the world weeks of notice so that there was plenty of time for the speculators to take Uncle Sam for a few more hundreds of millions of dollars. Incredibly the U.S. only devalued by an ineffective 10%, so that Nixon was forced to repeat the whole procedure in February 1973.

Unquestionably this is the area where the largest and easiest sums of money will be made in the 1970s. In buying currency futures through a bank, you do not have to put up any deposit but, unfortunately, only major banks handle this type of transaction. Speculators who do not deal with such a bank may also make this type of investment through the International Monetary Market of the Chicago Mercantile Exchange. A deposit is required but it is very low; for example, to purchase $200,000 (Canadian) requires only $2,000 deposit. Any commodity broker will be happy to handle the trade for you.

18
INVESTMENT
CLUBS

An investment club consists of a group of people who have joined together to pool funds, which are then invested in securities.

In the 1950s there was a rapid proliferation of these clubs, and many thousands were formed in the United States and Canada. In the boom markets which have since generally prevailed, many of these clubs have done fairly well, a few have foundered disastrously, and the vast majority have bumbled along with their investments doing slightly worse than the stock market averages. The reasons for this are not difficult to find.

Most clubs have anywhere from 6 to 20 members who make a monthly contribution to the general kitty. At the regular meetings (usually monthly) the portfolio of the club is discussed and sales or new purchases are voted upon. Various members will discuss stocks they have heard about or read about and they will recommend these stocks for purchase by the group. Occasionally one member is assigned to study a specific stock and report back at the next meeting. Sometimes individual stockbrokers are invited to the meetings to give advice on the current portfolio. It has been my experience that impatience, inconsistency, a desire to take profits, and plain greed are the basic causes of the problems of investment clubs.

When a group forms an investment club, presumably it should be for the purpose of making their dollars grow while at the same time having the pleasure of monthly get-togethers. Capital gains should be the primary interest, and dividends should be of little account. Thus every stock purchase should be made with growth in mind, and each security should be analyzed as to its growth possibilities and its safety. Once a stock has been bought for these reasons, it should be held indefinitely.

Unfortunately impatience is the keynote of too many investment clubs. All too often I have heard, "We've held it for a year, and it's done nothing. Let's sell it and switch the money into something that's moving." Six years ago those words persuaded one group to sell Simpson's stock at $23 and Bank of Montreal stock at $40. Both more than doubled during the following months.

An investment club is constantly hearing new suggestions of stocks in which to invest. The temptation to sell part of their holdings in order to buy something new succeeds only in giving commissions to the brokers. This urge to buy every stock suggested leads some groups to trade the market so as to catch the price swings. It is absolutely impossible to be successful in such a venture, and it invariably leads to a serious loss of capital.

Inconsistency is a very serious problem in some investment clubs. Because of the number of people involved in the investing, some of whom will present their arguments more forcefully from time to time, and some of whom may not be present at subsequent meetings, the club may change its investment policy many times in a year. One club swung from buying convertible bonds, to selling calls, to buying mining stocks, and finally to buying American exchange glamour stocks. Every time they changed their policy, they lost money because of the switch in securities with consequent necessity to pay extra commissions. There does not appear to be any way to prevent these inconsistencies. One club had written into its constitution the rule that it must not buy on margin, and yet within a year it was persuaded to do just that.

The desire to realize profits often is overwhelming: "All right, this has gone up from $50 to $55. That's a pretty good profit for a three-month hold; let's sell it and switch into something that's still down." Two years ago I persuaded an investment club, of which I am a member, to buy several hundred shares of Federal Pacific Pioneer Electric convertible preferred at $53 a share. It has moved up steadily since that time to its current $70, but there has not been a meeting since when some well-meaning soul has not suggested selling "at least half" before it goes back down again.

The club has one member who has a new "hot tip" for every meeting: "My customer's man says Fairchild (or Syntex or Moly) is going to $200 a share this year. Let's sell everything and buy it. It earned 20¢ last year and next year he says earnings will be over $10." The fact that the stock may be selling at 100 times its current earnings does not faze this gullible investor, and he is quite willing to accept fantastic estimates of future earnings as definite fact. I missed one meeting and he triumphantly persuaded the members of the investment group to sell part of their Federal Pacific Electric and buy Sharon Steel at $25 a share. "It'll earn $3 a share next year." The group sold the Sharon at $22 one month later.

Greed is the final drawback to investment clubs. We are all greedy in that we want to make money either for its own sake (a very common illness today) or else for the material comforts and ease that the money can buy, or perhaps for the good that we think we will be able to perform with money. Unfortunately greed in a group often will cause the group to toss aside prudent restraints as no individual in that group would on his own.

Thus we find investment groups purchasing wild promotional stock which may very easily lose its entire value before the investment group's next meeting. They find it hard to resist the lure of, "It could easily go from $2 to $200. They have a patent on a new invention that will revolutionize the industry." It is amazing how much worthless stock is sold in this way.

Despite the foregoing, investment clubs are not all bad. They have two great virtues.

1. They enable the novice investor to learn many of the market rules at very little cost to himself. If a stock costs $1,000 to buy and it goes down to $100, each individual member of an average size club will have lost only $50, which is a pretty cheap lesson of this sort. Membership in a club gives a beginner the chance to participate in discussions leading to purchase of many securities. In this way an investment club is better than a mutual fund, in which the investor may make money but will learn nothing. Besides which it is much more fun.

2. I am afraid that the major advantage of investment clubs is social. Many of these organizations have a brief half-hour meeting, which is followed by a poker game. In many clubs the card game has become the major attraction, to the point where it attracts many ex-members or non-members of the club. And it's a lot easier to tell your wife that you are going to an investment meeting than to a poker game.

In summary, investment clubs can be a lot of fun for social and educational reasons. Individual investments should be kept to a very small sum, and under these circumstances the fun cannot be seriously marred by financial loss. Large investments should not be made in this way.

19
LIFE INSURANCE

The single most common investment for the individual in North America today is life insurance. In addition to being the most common investment it is also the least productive, in fact, insurance should not be considered an investment at all.

Life insurance is bought for two reasons — protection and savings. As pure survivor protection there can be no quarrel with insurance. By paying small premiums each individual helps alleviate the risk of untimely death of many other individuals. This is term insurance; its cost is very low, and it allows the family's breadwinner to be sure that his wife and children will have an adequate income should he die unexpectedly. The man who buys term insurance is proving his love for his family.

Unfortunately most insurance that is sold is not term insurance. All other insurance plans contain a combination of protection and savings and cost much more than term insurance plans. The names of the various policies may be ordinary life, 20-year pay or endowment, or whole life, but these terms refer only to the varying percentages of protection and savings in each policy.

Millions of dollars have been spent in advertising the merits of ordinary insurance and the virtues of investing in life insurance. The protection aspect of insurance is often played down and the excellent investment aspect is emphasized. Who has not seen an ad in which the happy 65-year-old has completely paid up his policy and now begins to draw monthly annuity cheques? Unfortunately when we consider the three basics of any investment — yield, safety, and possible capital appreciation — it soon becomes clear that insurance is probably the worst investment of any described in this book.

Most insurance companies sell term insurance only when requested. They strongly advise their agents to recommend the other types of insurance, and as a financial inducement to the agents, have made the commission on term insurance only a small fraction of that paid when other life insurance is sold. The companies even go so far as to accuse an agent of "twisting" if he advises any insured person, whether or not he is that company's client, to change from higher cost insurance to term. A twister will be quickly fired by many insurance companies and, in Ontario, the government, responding to pressure from the insurance lobby, has actually made it a criminal offence for *anyone* (including authors) to advise an insured person to cash in his expensive policy and take out term insurance with another company. When an individual has purchased term insurance, the company will periodically go to great efforts in an attempt to persuade him to convert his policy to a more expensive insurance.

Why do insurance companies prefer not to sell term insurance? Their salesmen give 6 reasons:

1. Regular insurance gives permanent protection. Term insurance runs out at age 65.

True: but if the purpose of insurance is to protect one's family from financial loss in case of death of the breadwinner, this reason is foolish. How many men of 65 have children still going to school? How many dying with insurance at that age do not already have adequate investments elsewhere to look after their widows?

2. The cost of term insurance rises yearly until it becomes prohibitively expensive in one's late fifties.

This is only true if the term insurance is so-called one-year renewable term, which is usually purchased by the man investing elsewhere who wants temporary protection. He buys this insurance because it is very cheap and he has no intention of keeping it for more than a few years. The individual wanting permanent protection should buy flat-rate term insurance. The premium on this type of policy remains constant and does not rise as the owner gets older.

3. Regular insurance compels people to save who would otherwise spend their money on frivolities.

I have wondered for some years whether this might not be the only valid reason to recommend ordinary insurance. However, I have concluded that any individual who has the will power to meet the regular insurance payments would also have enough will power to save in any other scheme. In any case if there are a few persons to whom this forced saving would be of value, they are unlikely to be among those who have invested several dollars to buy this book.

    4. With regular insurance there is always a backlog of savings which can be borrowed if necessary. This is not possible with term insurance.

Very true, but what the insurance companies do not point out is that the amount that can be borrowed is equivalent to the overpayments that have been made on the policy in excess of the cost of term insurance. What is much worse is the fact that the insurance company will charge you 5% for the privilege of borrowing your own money! Furthermore if there should be such a loan outstanding at the time of your death, the amount of the loan will be deducted from the face value of the policy, even though it represented an earlier overpayment premium.

    5. Ordinary insurance has a cash surrender value in case of emergency. The policy can be turned in, and the policy holder will receive a sum of money equal to the size of the savings portion of the policy.

Also very true, but the flaw is that in order to get his cash surrender value, the policy holder must give up his insurance protection. If the savings had been in some other form than insurance and the same emergency arose, the policy holder could have used his savings without losing his insurance.

    6. The lapse rate of term insurance is much higher than that of ordinary insurance.

This is very true, and the reason is very obvious. Term insurance is like fire insurance in that it is purchased for a specific purpose, in this case to insure a specific life. Once that need for protection is gone — if, for example, children have grown up and gone to work or the owner of the insurance has made a great deal of money — then the insurance will often be deliberately cancelled. Ordinary insurance, on the other hand, has involved the owner in a long-term savings program which will be lost if the insurance is lapsed.

    What is wrong with ordinary insurance as an investment? Let us consider the three basies — yield, safety, and possibilities of capital appreciation.

    First it must be understood that the premium in an ordinary insurance policy consists of two parts; one for protection, which is the term insurance part, and one for savings. When considering the yield, one must disregard the part of the premium that goes for protection, because this money would have to be spent for protection anyway and so no yield should be expected upon it. Let us suppose that the owner of an ordinary policy has the good fortune to live out his policy term, say twenty years, and receives a capital sum. He will find that he will have received back his complete overpayment plus interest at the rate of about 6% compounded annually. Not bad, except for one flaw. If he makes the mistake of dying before the twenty years is up, the entire "savings" portion of the policy is forfeited to the insurance company. Therefore, in order to make certain that his capital is safe and that he will get his 6%, the policy holder must be sure to outlive his policy. If he does not do so, both capital and interest are completely lost to his surviving family.

But won't they get the insurance? Certainly it will be paid, but the total overpayment of premiums which went into the savings part of the policy is lost.

The third factor is appreciation of capital. There is no argument on this point. There is no possibility of capital appreciation in the savings portion of a life insurance policy. The best than can be hoped for is a return of capital plus interest.

Now we find a seventh reason why insurance companies prefer to sell ordinary insurance, but their salesmen don't tell you this one: They must make money from such sales. When they sell term insurance, the insurance company ends up making less than 10% of the total premiums as a profit after paying all claims and expenses. The percentage is arrived at by continually adjusting insurance premiums downwards as human longevity increases so as to maintain a reasonable profit margin.

In ordinary insurance, even if the same profit percentage were to be maintained, the company would make much larger profits because it would be making the same percentage on double or triple the premiums. In fact, their actual percentage profit is much higher because a little thought will show that the customer cannot win.

Everyone who buys a policy must either live for the lifetime of that policy or die before it has come due. If he dies before the policy has come due, the protection portion of the policy is paid to the family, but the savings portion is forfeited to the company. If, on the other hand, the policy holder outlives his policy, then he receives back his savings plus interest, but he has obliged the insurance company by not forcing them to pay a death claim, so that they gained all his premiums at no cost to themselves.

In other words, heads the policy holder loses, tails the insurance company wins! Small wonder that insurance company stocks have soared by thousands per cent in the past decade.

What then is the proper course for the individual to follow? It is a very simple one. He should buy the insurance necessary to protect his family in case of an untimely death. He should buy the cheapest form of insurance, which is term, and he should drop it just as soon as the need for protection has passed. This point will come either when the family are independently on their own or when the policy holder's assets have reached the point that they are sufficiently large to look after his family in case of his death. The extra money that is left over, and which can represent as much as 90% of the premiums on certain endowment policies, should be invested in convertible bonds, mutual funds, or certain of the other investment suggestions described in this book.

These facts are not new. Thousands of insurance men know their truth, and a book was first published 'way back in 1936 exposing the truth. Yet every time some brave insurance agent attempts to show these facts to the public, he is fired, there is an outraged cry of heresy from the insurance companies, and long, learned treatises are published pointing out the virtues of buying insurance.

I can't blame the insurance companies very much or their agents at all. After all, it is a multibillion dollar industry upon which now depend thousands of jobs. However, it is not necessary for the life insurance industry to survive by using these methods. The fire insurance companies make money every year by selling fire insurance protection, and they don't insist on their policy holders making a savings deposit with every fire insurance premium; nor should the life insurance companies.

What should the investor do who has been carrying insurance for some years and now finds that due to his over payments his policies now have a large cash surrender value? Regardless of his age he will find that he is better off to cash in these policies and purchase whatever insurance protection is needed in the form of term insurance. Caution must be followed here, however. The policy holder was physically fit when he originally bought his insurance, but today it may not be possible for him to pass the physical examination. Therefore, he should buy whatever term insurance he needs first before surrendering his other life insurance. The capital received back should be carefully invested.

Many holders of insurance have not given real consideration to their true insurance protection needs for many years. They have just automatically paid their annual premiums. A lot of these people will discover that they no longer need any protection at all and can cash in their policies without buying any term insurance. After all, the purpose of insurance is to leave sufficient money to allow the surviving family to continue to maintain the same standard of living. There is no need to leave survivors moneys beyond this necessity. The premiums going for unnecessary insurance would be better used to give more leisure from work, to travel, to enjoy, or for charity.

What kind of term insurance should the individual purchase? There are 3 basic types:
1. Renewable term
2. Flat-rate term
3. Decreasing term

Renewable term should be purchased by the individual seeking temporary protection. This is initially the cheapest possible type of insurance, but the premium gradually rises over the life of the policy. A professional man just starting his practice could buy this type of insurance with the intention of dropping it after he has built up a reasonable estate.

Flat-rate term is the cheapest long-term form of life insurance. It is recommended for the person who is probably always going to need protection insurance. Initially it will cost more than double the price of renewable term, but the premium remains constant at about one-half or less that of regular insurance.

Decreasing term is a special type of term insurance in which the premium remains constant but the face value of the policy gradually decreases. This is the best type of insurance for the person who is building up an estate and whose requirements for insurance are gradually decreasing.

In summary:

1. Life insurance is the worst possible form of investment. A young man in his twenties can buy $100,000 worth of term insurance for as little as $350 a year. He is foolish indeed if he pays $1,000 or $3,000 for the same protection, the savings feature of which disappears on death.

2. Buy enough term insurance necessary to protect your family.

3. When the need for protection ceases drop the insurance.

4. Invest the extra funds in convertible bonds or preferreds or in a mutual fund.

5. Do not continue to maintain ordinary insurance policies just because they have been held for some years. It is better to buy term insurance and cash the older policies.

6. When buying any insurance get the advice of a lawyer or trust company. It is very difficult for an insurance agent to give unbiased advice when one firm's term insurance policy pays him a commission of $12.50 while by selling an endowment policy with the same face value he will receive $190.00. It is asking too much of human nature for him to be unbiased.

7. Buy one year renewable term or flat rate term or reducing term, depending on your individual needs as described earlier.

8. Never convert term insurance to regular insurance.

9. Finally, don't buy insurance as an investment. It is an excellent protection; buy it for that reason only.

20
REAL ESTATE

Real estate is second only to life insurance in the numbers of those who invest in it. Every worker in every factory in the country has the ambition to own his own home. Today more than ever he is succeeding in his ambition. For most North Americans, purchase of a home will be the largest investment they will ever make. How good is real estate as an investment? How does it compare with the stock market, with mutual funds, or with convertible bonds?

First, real estate must be defined. It includes raw land, homes, apartments, and commercial properties. It does not include mortgages. Mortgages are loans given to individuals by lenders at a fixed rate of interest with real estate deposited as security for the loan. If the value of the real estate is many times that of the loan, the risk is very small. The interest rate will then be lower than if the loan is very close to the value of the real estate, in which case the risk is much larger. A first mortgage represents a primary debt; in the event of default of the loan, the real estate must be sold to pay this debt. A second mortgage in such a case will be paid only if there are funds available after the first mortgage has been paid. Interest rates are, therefore, much higher on second mortgages. On a first mortgage rates vary between 6 and 9 per cent, depending on current money costs. On a second mortgage the rate may go as high as 15% per year.

Most homes that are bought today are largely paid for by placing a mortgage on the home. This will normally supply three-quarters of the cost of acquiring the home. If the new homeowner does not have enough money to pay the remaining portion, he must place a second mortgage on his house, greatly increasing the interest and payment burden he must meet.

Mortgages are, therefore, loans. They are directly comparable with bonds, which were discussed previously, and most mortgages are given out by large corporations, trust and insurance companies, etc., who make their profits by collecting the interest. Some individuals also give mortgages in real estate, often at the suggestion of their lawyer, who will also have clients buying homes who need such mortgages. These individuals are making a serious error. Some investments are excellent in good times and dangerous in bad, while others flourish in bad times and are not so good in inflationary days. Mortgages, on the other hand, can be bad in bad times and bad in good times. It is best to leave them to the insurance companies.

The problem of the mortgage in times of inflation such as we are now experiencing is that the dollar can lose its buying value faster than it earns interest. Thus a ten-year mortgage paying 6% interest may very well have a buying power of only 60% of its face value when it comes due ten years hence. This is the same problem that bondholders face — no possibility of capital appreciation and no protection against inflation. In the real rip-roaring inflation some European countries suffered in the late twenties and early thirties, mortgage holders lost everything, for their mortgages were finally paid off with worthless money.

The problems of the mortgage holder in periods of severe deflation or depression can be just as bad. In the 1930s in the United States and Canada, thousands of homeowners could not meet their mortgage payments, and in many cases the homes were not worth in 1930 dollars anywhere near the face value of the mortgage. Not only the homeowner, but in many cases the mortgage owner as well, lost everything. To add to the woes of mortgage owners, many governments declared a "moratorium" which removed any requirements for payments on mortgages during the years that the moratorium was in force.

On top of everything else, there is one further serious disadvantage to ownership of mortgages even in normal times, and this is the complete lack of liquidity. Most of the disadvantages of mortgages apply to bonds, but at least a bond can always be sold even though sometimes at a loss. A mortgage, however, can only be sold by finding an individual buyer, and there is no exchange where buyers are always waiting. Practically speaking, because of the difficulty and expense involved, mortgages are rarely resold but must be held until maturity.

In brief, mortgages are poor investments for individuals. They should be avoided.

Now back to real estate. This can be arbitrarily divided between land and structures built upon the land. If there are structures on the land, a purchase can give income in the form of rent or it can give shelter if the owner lives in the building — or it can give both, as with a duplex. The purchaser of bare land, on the other hand, can usually get neither income nor security; if he is astute and lucky, however, he may make sizable capital gains.

Since purchase of a home is the American's commonest and largest investment, let us discuss it first. What should be paid, what should one look for, should one buy or rent, how does a home purchase compare with other investments?

On a purely financial basis, purchase of a home by the average person is bad economics. It is cheaper to live in an apartment close to the centre of the city both as to actual cost of living and time and expense saved in commuting. However, psychological and other factors are perhaps more important than finance in this particular investment. Wives want " a house of their own with a patch of grass", while there is no doubt that a husband gets more satisfaction and sheer pleasure from a home than he will get from any pile of stock and bond certificates. So on this particular subject I will plead "Nolo Contendere" and confine my remarks to what should be paid for a house.

The maximum total price should be three times the husband's annual income. Couples who use their combined incomes in calculating this figure may come to regret it, for all too often the wife's income soon ceases. In addition, the couple should be able to make a cash down payment of 25% of the purchase price, while the balance should be financed with one long-term mortgage, and provision should be made for unexpected house expenses.

Purchase of a house or houses for the purpose of renting is economically unproductive when compared with other investments. This is not true in reference to apartment houses. A fully rented apartment house today (and in most areas they are fully rented) can easily give an annual return of 15 to 20% after all expenses and mortgage payments are met. This high return has allowed a number of individuals to make very profitable investments in this field in recent years. The disadvantages are two. Lack of liquidity is one, although this is probably not so bad as with mortgages. The more serious one is the very grave financial setbacks that can occur in times of recession. That 20% return will rapidly diminish with a few vacant apartments. If a situation ensues as it did thirty years ago where apartments are half or more empty, financial disaster can supervene. The great disadvantage of this type of investment as compared with stocks or bonds is that while all of them will go down in price in depression times, the stocks and bonds may stop bringing an income, but they do not produce a drain. Apartment owners, however, may find that their steady income has turned into a steady outlay, because the apartment must still be serviced; it must be heated and tax and mortgage payments must continue.

Despite the return possible on this investment, it should be reserved strictly for the wealthy businessman or investor with large assets who can afford the potential risks involved. Apartment owning is not for the investor with limited means and is definitely not for the widow or orphan.

Now we come to land. This is the primary and ultimate wealth. All other assets and valuables can be increased or more can be found. Not so with land; there is only so much and it is all highly coveted. As our population continues to increase, the amount of land available per person must fall and its value must rise. Over the long-term picture, land is an investment that must increase in value. Unfortunately, long term is not too important to us, because we humans are short term. It really doesn't matter much to the individual if land goes up ten times in value over a fifty-year period. The original owner will not be there to enjoy his investment, and practically speaking no investment should be bought whose prospective rewards may take longer than five years to come to fruition.

Short-term land holding may be profitable, but it can be exactly the opposite. When we consider the three basics, income, safety, and capital gain, plus the problem of liquidity, it becomes clear that land speculation is very chancy indeed.

Raw land usually brings no income. In fact there is a constant outlay, because all potentially valuable land requires the annual payment of a land tax to the local municipality. This can range up to $200 an acre or much higher in highly developed areas. Occasionally the land can be rented for farming, but this brings very little income.

Raw land is much more liquid than other forms of real estate, with the exception of the single family home. It can always be sold. There is always someone willing to buy land, but the price may be disappointing.

There is certainly no safety of capital in owning raw land. In fact prices can fluctuate downwards by 50% or more in a few weeks. During the tremendous building boom in the fifties, raw land around Toronto surged from $20 an acre up as high as $10,000 an acre in a few areas. There was then a tightening of moneys available for mortgages and building, and this undeveloped land in many cases was dumped for whatever it would bring. In one case I know of, a 40-

acre site was bought for $55,000 and the $10,000 down payment was completely abandoned in only ten weeks when the initial mortgage payment came due.

Capital gains are certainly possible in the purchase of land. In fact this is the only one of the three requirements for an investment that applies to the purchase of land (unless it is intended to develop it). Since the war huge fortunes have been made around every city in North America by land speculators. The technique that is used often will see $1,000 turn into $100,000 or even $1,000,000, even though the land only goes up perhaps two or three times in price. This is done through options or else through the small down payment-huge mortgage system.

Ideally a land speculator will attempt to buy a tract of land near a city by offering the farmer or original holder perhaps 20% more than the land is worth. After dazzling him with this relatively high figure, however, he then gives him perhaps 1% of the named price for a one-year option on the land. If the boom continues the speculator can make a huge capital gain. If it does not, he just drops his option. For example, a large farm twelve miles from Toronto might be worth on an immediate sale perhaps $500,000. The speculator will offer to pay the farmer $600,000 on an option basis. If the farmer bites, he will actually be given $7,500 cash for a one-year option on his land at the $600,000 price.

One year later, if the boom has continued, that same land might be worth $1,000,000. The speculator now exercises his option and resells the land, receiving $400,000 for a one-year $7,500 speculation. If, on the other hand, the land boom falters, the speculator will drop his option and lose his $7,500.

The alternative method of land speculation is the actual purchase of the land but with a small down payment and no sizable payments for some time. For example, the speculator might offer $550,000 for that same farm that was worth $500,000, but the down payment will only be $10,000 with no further payments for one year. The actual purchaser will be a limited company, and if land prices falter no second payment will be made and the mortgage will be defaulted.

Although land speculators can make huge profits, there is one additional overriding drawback to this type of speculation. Presumably most speculators and investors have their own jobs or businesses to which they devote most of their working hours. They find it quite possible to intelligently invest in convertible bonds or even in stocks or warrants by giving up only a few minutes per day. This is not true of land speculation or indeed of any aspect of real estate investment. This type of speculation is extremely demanding of time if it is to be successful, because each individual transaction requires days to properly investigate and consummate. Land speculation, therefore, cannot be successfully carried on by the dabbler. All drawbacks considered, it is best left to the full-time expert in this field.

One word of warning — do not ever purchase land that you

have not seen. In recent years a special breed of Canadian and U.S. crooks have developed a new technique of selling raw land, lavishly described in glowing terms "for your retirement". These lands are advertised in pulp magazines and are largely sold by mail. They are vastly overpriced and in no sense of the word can be considered an investment. If you see an ad suggesting you buy "beautiful Florida ocean-front lots" or "wonderful northern Ontario vacation land", you can be reasonably sure someone is attempting to swindle you. All too often the ocean-front lot turns out to be visible only at low tide and the Ontario vacation land to be inaccessible bush inhabited only by our delightful black flies and mosquitoes. The type of land that is sold by this type of advertising is usually not worth purchasing and is never a good investment.

In summary, although the rewards in real estate can be staggering in size, the costs, the time, the dangers and the lack of liquidity completely offset them. With the exception of purchase of a home, the ordinary investor or speculator is well advised to keep away from real estate.

21
CASH IN THE BANK—AND OTHER ODDS AND ENDS

How much money should be kept as a cash reserve? Most financial advisors recommend that 25% of one's capital should be kept liquid in case of emergency. I do not agree with this, and in fact I have never had more than two or three hundred dollars in the bank for longer than a few days. It is my belief that investment money should be kept working all the time, and when it is in a bank earning 5% interest per year it is working for only a very small part of the day. Far better to invest your money in a mutual fund or convertible bond and draw 5% or 6% interest with the excellent possibility of large capital gains.

The bogie of financial emergencies has been greatly overdone. Mutual funds or bonds can be sold and the cash received within three days. It is hard to imagine an emergency in which the money must be produced in less than that time. If such a disaster should occur, it should be remembered that brokers will be happy to margin securities, lending 50% of the value on stocks and up to 90% on bonds. This cash loan can be arranged and picked up within minutes.

There is, therefore, no need for the average investor to have large sums of cash lying idle in bank accounts. However, for those investing largely in common stock, funds are necessary in case the stock moves down in price so that the investor can average down. Those persons buying stock on margin also must have a cash reserve; otherwise they may be forcibly sold out if their stocks move down in value and they are unable to put up more margin.

With these two exceptions there are better places for money than in bank accounts. This is not to suggest that investors should rush to buy securities just for the sake of having all their money invested. There will be occasions when securities have been sold and there does not appear to be a good buying opportunity currently available. It is far better to wait for a good investment rather than rush to buy one which may be only so-so. What should be done with the cash in the meantime?

Guaranteed trust certificates are now available whereby cash can be deposited with a trust company for periods varying anywhere from thirty days to five years, with a guaranteed return of anywhere from 5% to 7%, depending on the length of the deposit. For the speculator or investor with temporary cash, the thirty-days deposit is perfect. At the present time such deposits will give a yield of $6\frac{1}{8}$%, and the money is soon available if during the thirty days a good investment opportunity arises. If at the end of that time there is no need for the cash, it can be redeposited for another thirty days. Furthermore, the risk to the invested capital is practically nil.

Long-term trust certificates should not be purchased. They are equivalent to bonds in all of their characteristics, except that they are less liquid. They are quite safe and the yield is very reasonable, but there is no possibility of capital appreciation and there is no protection against inflation.

Some speculators hold on to their cash in an effort to buy stocks in market depressions with the intention of selling when the market moves back up.

How well can the market action be predicted? Everyone wants to buy low and sell high. But the trouble is that no one agrees on when the market is low or high. It is useless to try and follow the experts' advice, for they seem to be consistently wrong. The Securities Exchange Commission made a detailed study of the 900 pieces of advice sent out by 166 investment advisers and brokers before the 1946 market break. Only 4% of these forecast the market fall. Going back to 1929, Alfred Cowles III made a study of some 7,500 specific recommendations. He found out that, over all, the recommendations behaved slightly worse than the average behaviour of all common stocks.

Since the experts are consistently wrong, how can the ordinary investor hope to predict the market's moves. Of course he can't. The point was well answered by Bernard Baruch who replied to the question of whether the market was too high, "I have never answered that question, because I do not think anyone is smart enough to know and I certainly would not want to put myself in that class of demigod." Baruch's must be the final word in forecasting the market, and anyone who is foolish enough to attempt to trade the market swings must end up losing his capital. The market does not follow patterns of the past, and its future cannot be predicted.

As a final note on the difficult art of predicting the future, the experience of a friend corroborated my belief. The man is a psychologist and statistics expert who has done very well in numerous financial enterprises. He has rented from I.B.M. a complicated computer into which he has fed thousands of facts about the market's past performances. He is convinced that this mighty machine, which is wiser and more knowledgable than any human mind, has now solved the prediction problem. As proof some months ago he handed me the computer's prediction of an immediate rise in market prices. Since then stocks have moved steadily downwards to reach a two-year low . . . and there goes another theory.

Although market action cannot be predicted, the action of individual securities often can. If they are purchased for reasons of basic value, as previously explained, the investment must be a profitable one. If the investor has erred in his analysis, he will at least be protected against large loss if he has been sufficiently prudent to purchase one of the convertible securities.

Dollar averaging is a very popular method of investment. It involves buying one stock on a regular basis, putting in the same amount of money every month. If the stock goes up in price your dollars buy fewer shares, but you are making a profit. If, on the other hand, the stock falls in price you are able to buy more shares with the same monthly investment and therefore are further ahead when (or if) the stock ultimately rises in value.

This is an excellent method of investment *provided* (1) it is carried out over a period of a least two or three years and (2) the stock chosen is a high-grade growth company, preferably a wealth-in-the-ground company, e.g. one of our bigger oil companies or a company mining and refining base metals, or a nationwide merchandiser such as Standard Oil or Noranda or Simpsons.

The subject of margin has not been discussed earlier. Whether to margin or not cannot be answered with a straight yes or no. Margin involves only putting up a portion of the purchase price of a security and borrowing the balance from the broker and paying interest on it. Buying on margin greatly increases both the profit possibilities and the risks. For that reason widows and orphans or anyone who cannot afford to lose should never use margin. For the speculating businessman there are occasions when he would be foolish not to margin.

To take an example, when Federal Pacific Electric issued their 5½% convertible preferred at $50 a share, it was the perfect time to margin. It was obvious to anyone examining the company and the stock that there was no risk of the stock's collapsing, and so there was no increased danger through margining. Also the 5½% yield of this preferred stock would more than cover the interest charges payable to the broker for the borrowed money. If the investor had $5,000 to invest, he could have either bought 100 shares of F.P.E. preferred outright or 200 shares on margin. When the stock rose the next year to $80, he would have made $3,000 without the margin, or $6,000 if he had margined — in either case there was the same $5,000 investment. Thus here was an example of how margining could double profits without either risk or cost.

In cases of convertible bonds the difference in profit through margining can range up to 1,000 per cent. For example, when Canadian Utilities issued their convertible bond, the downside risk was nil due to the high interest rate of 5½% on the bond plus the convertible factor. These bonds could be margined by putting up only 10% of the purchase price, (today it would be 20%) so that an investor with $1,000 could buy one bond outright or 10 bonds on margin. Two years later when the bonds reached $1,600, the outright purchaser had made $600 while the man who margined made $6,000.

Margin properly used will greatly increase profits without undue risk. Improperly used it will increase risks beyond the potential profits. Each case must be decided on its individual merits. If the downside risk, as in a convertible security with a good yield, is minimal it is smart to margin.

At the end of October 1967, in response to the greatly increased volume of trading in and margining of convertible bonds, the Securities Exchange Commission passed new regulations which increased the margin requirements on convertible bonds to 70 per cent of their face value.

This has resulted in what is certainly a greater opportunity for capital gains in the convertible bond field than has ever been seen before. Because many convertible bonds were held on low margin down payments, prices of many of these issues dropped and companies issuing new convertible bonds were now forced to give attractive terms, with high interest rates and excellent conversion features.

For example, West Coast Transmission in 1970 issued a new convertible bond with a 7½% coupon convertible into common stock at a price just above the then current market. The bond today sells at $1,350. This was not an unusual example, as dozens of other attractive convertibles quickly followed.

The interesting side result of the S.E.C.'s ruling was that clever investors were not affected by it because it is still perfectly legal for any U.S. citizen to open a U.S. dollar account with a Canadian broker and still purchase his U.S. convertible bonds with the 20% down payment that prevailed before the S.E.C. ruling. Thus these speculators are better off than before the ruling.

Today, with the combination of low margin requirements and attractive new bonds, it is easier than ever to make money in convertibles.

RIGHTS, SPLITS, AND SHORTS Often a corporation will decide to raise fresh capital through the issue of more common stock. In order to successfully sell this stock, the corporation must offer it at a price below the current market price of the stock. In order (a) not to force down the market for the company's stock and (b) to be fair to the stockholders, the corporation will usually issue transferable options to its shareholders to purchase the new shares. These options differ from warrants in that they have a much shorter life, usually running for only three or four weeks. This is because the corporation wishes to have the money immediately, and issuance of a long-term option or warrant would not bring in any cash for some time.

These options are called rights. Because of their short life, they also differ from warrants in that they usually carry no premium over their true value. Thus if Newconex is trading at $6 and has a warrant outstanding good to buy stock at $5 for two years, it will trade at about $2. However, a right to buy Newconex at $5 which is good for one month will trade at only $1. Because these rights do not trade at a premium, they often will have tremendous leverage (explained in chapter on warrants), and sometimes in a few days they can move up or down spectacularly. For example, the Bell Telephone Company issues very few bonds and instead every year or so will give its shareholders rights to buy more stock at a price below the market. A typical issue might see Bell stock trading at $55 and rights issued to buy more stock at $50, with 20 rights required to buy one share. Each right is therefore worth 25¢ and would trade at 25¢. The leverage factor is very high; the actual figure is 12:1, and in order for the rights to double in value the Bell stock need only move up 10%. Unfortunately Bell stock is very stable, and price moves tend to be very slow.

Thus in order for the speculator to make money in rights, leverage is not enough, and because of the short time available, the stock involved must be a very volatile one. An example of such an issue was made in March, 1963, by the Trans Canada Pipeline Company. At this time the company needed further capital to complete its expansion pro-

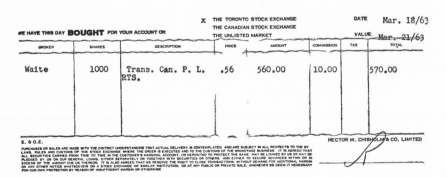

gram and issued free rights to its shareholders at the rate of one right per share. For every 23 rights held, the bearer was entitled to buy one $100 convertible bond which was convertible into stock of the company at a price of $26 per share. The rights were good only until April 4. The common stock was then trading at $22 per share and the rights were freely available between 50¢ and 56¢.

Within a very few days the Trans Canada stock had moved up 10% to $24.50. This produced a much higher percentage move in the rights, for they jumped up to 77¢.

This right illustrates how the liability of a short life can be an advantage in disguise, because it results in the right's trading at its true value with no premium, and thus with a very high leverage. If the stock is volatile, large, rapid profits may result. The danger, however, is equally large, and for that reason rights should only be purchased on stocks that are trading at a low price in relation to assets or earnings. If this precaution is taken and if the rights do not move up in price, there will be no great disadvantage in exercising them.

Incidentally, this Trans Canada Pipeline issue once again illustrates an underpriced situation in which everyone made money. Speculators in the rights made 50% on their money in two weeks; sellers of the rights received 50¢ per share for something which they had received free; those who exercised the rights saw the convertible bond go up by 75%; and finally the shareholders made huge profits as their stock boomed up over $40. Truly a dream issue!

Another great advantage of a right to the stockholder is that it allows an increase of holdings in the company at a very favourable price and without the necessity of paying any commission. Therefore, a shareholder receiving rights and who has free money available is well advised to exercise his rights rather than sell them.

In summary, rights are a form of dividend which should be exercised when received free. For the speculator they represent the opportunity for rapid capital gains, but the risk is high. The rules in purchasing a right are:

1. Do not pay any premium over the right's true value.
2. Make sure that the leverage factor is high and the stock potentially volatile.
3. Do not buy any right if you have no cash available to exercise the right if necessary.

One other subject which should be considered is the stock split. This is the practice of subdividing a company's shares so as to keep each share at a relatively low price. That is, rather than have 1 million shares worth $100 each, after a 5 for 1 split there will be 5 million shares worth $20 each. A shareholder who held one hundred shares before, worth $10,000, will now have 500 shares worth $10,000.

The worth of a share, however, does not always decide the price at which it will trade. Its price depends on supply and demand — on the number of persons wishing to buy a stock in comparison with those wishing to sell. This factor will often temporarily make a stock sell too low or too high in relation to its true value. One of the phenomena of recent years has been that announcement of a stock split almost always produces an immediate substantial increase in the price of that stock.

The theory behind this activity is that when a stock sells at a lower price more individuals are likely to buy it, and this in itself will give at a higher value. Also it is felt that owners of stock in a company are more likely to use that company's products, which help sales and earnings. That this theory is just an explanation for stock market sentiment becomes clear when we look at some of the companies which have split their stock. For example, pipelines obviously will not have more customers regardless of how many shareholders they have, and many of these companies find that the number of their shareholders continues to increase at the same rate as before the split.

Anyway this is not too important. What does matter is that stock splits produce higher prices for the stock, even though there may be no commensurate increase in stock value. After all, one is purchasing a stock because of its earnings or its potential, not because of the number of shares outstanding or their unit price. It is therefore a good basic rule that if one owns a stock in which a split is announced, and the stock then moves up in price, *sell it immediately*. It is not wise to wait for the actual split to occur. All too many of these split stocks have subsequently lost all of their recent gains and more. One example was Pembina Pipeline. This company's stock moved from $55 all the way to $72 on news of a four-for-one split. The new stock briefly traded at $18, and then slid all the way back to $6.

Ultimately earnings and assets must determine the price of a stock. The number of shares outstanding is immaterial.

On occasion a speculator will see a stock selling at much higher prices than its earnings or assets warrant. In these circumstances there is a temptation to sell the stock "short" in the expectation that the price will decline and it will be possible to buy it back cheaply and make a profit. Short selling is the most dangerous type of speculation in the stock market and should be left strictly to the professional. This is because in the purchase of a stock, the total possible loss is the amount of money invested; but in a short sale there is no limit to the possible loss. Every few years a short "squeeze" develops, in which even the professionals are taken — the Chatco Steel swindle was a classic.

In 1955 Chatco was a small manufacturer of metal products with total assets of less than 5 million dollars, annual net profit of only $20,000, and with only 60,000 common shares authorized and outstanding. These were listed on the Toronto Stock Exchange and traded infrequently around the $4.00 level. By June 4, 1956, the company suffered from a shortage of working capital, and the stock had slipped to $3.30. At that time the shareholders approved an increase in the amount of authorized common stock to 600,000 shares. The somewhat naive directors of the company searched for a way to sell some of this stock, and when a Montreal lawyer offered to arrange an underwriting of 100,000 shares at $4.50 per share, they jumped at it. What the directors did not realize was that the group buying the stock consisted of a number of Americans associated with a master stock swindler, Alexander Guterma, who by 1961 was convicted and/or pleaded guilty to fraud involving five different companies. Four of these individuals now joined the board of Chatco, and one of them became the chairman, although the old president was allowed to continue as a figurehead.

In August, 1956, Chatco's shareholders were informed that this new underwriting had brought the company into association with "a group of financially strong, well informed and broadly connected director personnel through whom your company's scope of operations will undoubtedly broaden". Chatco stock now began to climb, reaching a level of $12.00 by September. This climb was accompanied by a huge increase in volume of stock traded and by a high-pressure sales campaign led by three U.S. investment brokers.

It was obvious to the brokers and professional traders at the Toronto Stock Exchange that Chatco stock was not worth anything near its $12.00 price level, and many of them began to sell the stock short. Very soon the short stock amounted to over 25,000 shares. The brokers felt that, when the underwriters had sold their 100,000 shares and the high pressure sales campaign ended, the stock would then collapse.

In September, 1956, the new chairman of Chatco issued a statement through a New York public relations firm in which he deplored the "distrust caused by stock swindlers" between Canadians and Americans. "So many Canadians and Americans have been shabbily treated by the neighbour country's high pressure stock promoters in the past few years that there is a certain amount of tarnish on the mutual respect and confidence that has existed between the two nations' businessmen." The statement went on to advocate "a stepped-up flow of investment money in both directions across the border".

On November 2, 1956, Chatco stock reached 16⅝ on increasing volume. The Toronto brokers who had been selling the stock short in increasing amounts were disturbed. In all previous cases where they had sold stock short in volume sooner or later their adversary had run out of money or determination and the stock had collapsed, giving the brokers large profits. Now they found that they were short over 100,000 shares and showed a potential loss of half a million dollars.

At a meeting of the Board of Governors of the Toronto Stock Exchange, the decision was made to suspend trading of Chatco stock on the exchange. This was done on Monday, November 5, and the president of the exchange made the following statement. It has been "found that a high pressure stock selling campaign, operated from New York City, was carried on over the long-distance telephone to American investors. The Board of Governors will not permit the facilities of the exchange to be used in stock selling campaigns of this nature. In this particular case the entire campaign originated in the U.S. and all recent sales were made to residents of the U.S. and not to Canadians. The suspension was, therefore, made to protect the interest of American investors."

In all previous cases in which a stock had been suspended, it would immediately collapse, and the brokers who had sold short now expected to make large profits. Sure enough, the next morning, Chatco began trading over the counter at $10.00 with the only bids showing being those of the brokers who were short. They had not counted, however, on the determination of the U.S. wolves to skin these Canadian professionals, and within hours a flood of buying poured into Toronto brokerage offices from New York City. By noon the stock was $12.50 bid, and by the close of trading at 5 p.m. it had moved all the way back up to $16.00. The distraught Toronto brokers attempted to force it down by further heavy short selling the following morning, but the American buyers absorbed all offerings, and that night (November 7) Chatco closed at $17.00.

Suddenly the short sellers realized that they had been beaten. In the following few days they decided to take their loss and buy back their short sales — but now to their horror they found that there was no stock available for sale, because the U.S. swindlers were not willing to settle for a modest profit. Two weeks later the stock was quoted $22.00 bid with no offerings, and there was still a short position of over 100,000 shares.

On the morning of December 1 the Toronto brokers who had sold stock short received a registered letter demanding delivery. That afternoon they each received a phone call from the broker who represented the U.S. sharks, offering to sell them the amount of stock they were short at $25.00 per share cash. They bought it, as they really had no choice. The next day the stock opened at $1.00 and declined to 25¢

within a week. Ten months later Chatco Steel declared bankruptcy "due to lack of working capital," and the stock became absolutely worthless.

Here was a case where the short sellers were 100% right in believing that the stock was overpriced, but they lost over a million dollars in spite of being right. And these men were almost all brokers or professional traders. The moral is quite clear: Do not sell short. The possible gain is not commensurate with the dangers. Short selling is essential to the proper maintaining of regular markets but should be left strictly to professionals.

OTHER INVESTMENTS

The purpose of any investment should not be just to make more money, for accumulating dollars per se appears a barren labour. There are unfortunately a considerable number of individuals in our society for whom both work and investing are just for the purpose of having x more dollars. They are not satisfied to have surplus assets of $100,-000 or 1 million dollars or 10 million dollars, or for that matter any amount. They will work out their lives scrambling for more and more money and will die dissatisfied because they can never have it all.

There are some others who invest and play the market for the fun and thrills involved. They are very like bridge players or poker players or some sportsmen to whom the game is the thing. A great deal of their satisfaction comes in correctly analyzing a situation. The profit that is made from the analysis is a secondary factor.

Many investors are seeking the illusion of security through their profits in investments. Unfortunately security is the one thing that a human being can never have, and no investment or huge sum of money will provide the security illusion for very long.

Fortunately most investors seek profits from securities for more fulfilling purposes. They want to make life a little easier for their children, they want the pleasures of travel, the pleasures of being able to surround themselves with beautiful things, the satisfaction of being able to help others.

For those in this latter group it is possible to arrive at many of the goals without waiting out the years of successful investing. For there is one investment field which gives continual and constant pleasure in the act of investment, which can have the security of the best bond, and yet which can rise in value like the most volatile warrant. That is investing in art and antiques. It is a field which should be carefully considered by more middle-income investors. Those who have done so have been repaid in dollars many times over and in pleasure and satisfaction have been given a daily dividend. This can truly be a case of eating your cake and having it still, for where else can one have continued pleasure and be paid for doing so. A single example of my own at once comes to mind. In 1954 my wife fell in love with a beautiful oil painting of a fountain in Nice by Raoul Dufy which we purchased for $6,000 from the Laing Galleries. This picture hung in our living room for seven years, giving us a repeated pleasure every time we entered that room. In 1961 we finally purchased a home, and in order to pay for it, sold the Dufy among other things. It reached $17,500 at Parke Bernet Galleries in New York. Few stock or bond investments did better.

Investing in antiques has three disadvantages, however, which should be noted.

1. There are rarely any dividends from this type of investment, although occasionally an advertising firm or greeting card company will pay 10% of the value of an object for permission to reproduce its photograph on a card or in an advertisement.

2. There is an actual financial outlay necessary for purposes of insurance. This should amount to only ⅓ of one per cent per year or less.

3. Art investments are not so liquid as stocks or bonds in that they usually cannot be converted into cash as rapidly as other securities. However, with the rise in recent decades of the large international auction galleries, antiques can now be changed into money within two or three months at the outside, and these galleries are usually quite willing to give a large immediate cash advance.

The art field for purposes of investment can be subdivided into eleven different groups, in one of which every person should be able to find something of personal appeal. These are:

Pictures and drawings
Jewellery
Silver
Objects of art and vertu
Antiquities
Porcelain
Books and manuscripts
Furniture
Arms and armour
Stamps and coins
Wine

Space available does not allow for detailed writeups in all of these groups, for this would take the entire book and more. But because in North America the vast majority of art investments fall in the fields of pictures, objects of art, antiquities, and stamps and coins, I shall specially describe these four fields. However, it should be noted that those persons who invested ten years ago in the specialties of antique jewellery, silver, porcelain, or furniture have done very well financially, for prices in these fields have multiplied many times. Armour has not done so well, but even here prices have doubled.

PAINTINGS AND DRAWINGS   Of paintings and drawings there is such a large variety that every taste can be satisfied. Most paintings have no commercial value as art but are purchased because they are appealing or in order to fill a specific spot on a wall. Paintings that can be considered as investments will fall into four categories.

1. The old masters
2. The more recently accepted schools e.g. the impressionists
3. Nineteenth century North American artists
4. Modern art, op art, pop art

The old masters are the convertible bonds of the painting world. These are paintings produced some hundreds of years ago by great masters like Rembrandt or minor masters like Hobbema. In recent years these works have tended to be gradually brought up by museums, but even today less important works of the old masters are available to the public at reasonable prices, and there is no question that their value will continue to rise at the same steady pace as in the past. Here are two examples from different price ranges. The etching below is by Rembrandt and is entitled *Death of the Virgin*. I purchased it in 1956 for $35.00. A similar etching sold in 1966 for $1,200.00.

The various owners of one painting by Meindert Hobbema have been recorded all the way back to 1752. In 1955 it sold for $19,000.00. Today it would bring at least five times that figure.

Much larger price moves have occurred in recent years amongst the impressionist and post-impressionist schools of art. Paintings by Renoir, Boudin, Matisse, Monet, Cézanne, Van Gogh and many others have gone from a few dollars to hundreds of thousands. This last decade has seen a further price multiplication of this type of art, until today a painting Renoir completed in 1914 may very easily sell at double the price of an old master of similar size completed 300 years ago by Van Goyen or Ruisdael. I think that at this point as an investment one should sell his impressionist art and buy old masters. Unfortunately sentiment often precludes such a sale. I purchased this little painting by Renoir in 1956 for $15,000. Since then I have received huge offers, and business sense says that it should be sold, but my family and I have become far too attached to it.

In any case impressionist art is now like blue chip stocks — at tip-top prices — and its purchase cannot be recommended.

American and Canadian primitive art is probably the best buy now available in the painting world. These paintings, by men like Remington or Krieghoff, show America as it was one hundred to two hundred years ago. There were no photographers about at that time, and so these paintings carry a double value—both as art and as history. Most of them are far better history than art, but this in a way enhances their value; a certain type of newly rich businessman who wants to collect

American or Canadian art will automatically seek them out, for he is ill at ease with modern art and has a deep suspicion that today's artists are making a fool of him. This type of primitive art, although it has shown some price appreciation, has not gone up in value by nearly the same amount as other accepted art forms because it does not sell outside of this continent. The American buyer of old masters or impressionist paintings must compete with the industrialists of Berlin and the oil sheiks of Kuwait, whereas American primitive art presents no interest to these worthies. Despite this, in the past decade American primitive art has begun to move up in price as museums and the public have begun to compete more vigorously. As a result U.S. primitives have shown good price increases, but Canadian primitives like Paul Kane and Cornelius Krieghoff have lagged because of their more limited market. Today the finest and largest habitant scene Krieghoff ever painted would probably bring less than $25,000 at auction. In years to come these prices will undoubtedly appear as ridiculous as when the same situation applied to the impressionists twenty-five years ago.

Modern art presents quite a different problem. This is the warrant of the painting world — luckily chosen, a painting from this group may zoom in value from $100 to $20,000 within two or three years, as did the paintings of Bernard Buffet. But unfortunately most modern work is trash that will have no value to succeeding generations.

The perfection of colour photography has made the work of today's artist immeasurably more difficult than that of preceding generations, because in earlier centuries a good artist merely attempted to duplicate nature. Today the best artist cannot do this as well as an average photographer and so the artist has reached further and further away from reality in an effort to produce something "different". From painting impressions he has moved to painting colour and form and space and finally to just smearing paint. The other great problem affecting modern art as an investment is the huge number of painters and galleries now turning out work. It has reached the point where a city of one million like Toronto has twenty-odd galleries, each supporting about a dozen artists. Obviously from the many thousands of artists now painting in North America today, only a very, very few will have their works live after them. This makes investing in modern art a very chancy affair, and only one piece of advice can be given — don't. If a modern painting appeals, buy it for its appeal and pay only what that appeal is worth to you. There will probably be no resale value.

There are two pitfalls which the investor in paintings must avoid. These are name collecting and forgery.

Name collecting is the practice of buying a painting only because it was painted by a specific artist and irrespective of its appeal. Thus we find foolish individuals spending thousands of dollars to buy a poor Cézanne just because Cézanne put his name on the canvas. It must be remembered that good artists can produce bad paintings; if a painting is being purchased partially or wholly as an investment, it should be one of the artists' better paintings. The good works will probably go up in price. The poor ones likely will not. There is nothing more pitiful than the collector with a dozen paintings by various artists, each of which represents that artist at his worst. This is not only bad investing, but it must inevitably produce feelings of embarrassment rather than pleasure.

Forgery is a far more serious problem. Right at this moment in New York there are a dozen artists busily turning out excellent pictures "by" Goya, "by" Picasso, "by" Gainsborough, and indeed by every selling artist. In today's seller's art market there is a ready sale for these forgeries, and there are galleries in every large city carefully feeding them out to the gullible. The extent to which this racket has grown is truly remarkable, and some of the largest private collections now contain more forgeries than originals. In order to avoid this trap, several rules should be followed:

1. Get an independent opinion before purchasing any expensive painting. Many public galleries will be glad to assist.
2. Never buy an expensive painting at a bargain price from a small gallery or private source. Ten to one it is a fake.
3. When buying a painting as an investment, insist on a complete pedigree. Newly discovered works of great artists of the past are usually only a few days old.
4. Buy your investment paintings either from one of the great established galleries like Knoedler; from a gallery that specializes in an artist as Laing does with Krieghoff; from one of the international auction houses — Sothebys or Christies of London, or Parke Bernet of New York; or in France, where the government stands behind all paintings sold at international auction.

By following these four rules the prospective investor in paintings will not only avoid buying forgeries, he will also find that he has succeeded in buying his paintings at the best possible prices.

In summary, buy paintings as an investment only when they appeal as paintings, when they represent the artists' best work, and when the price is reasonable in relation to that of the old masters. This method must produce both pleasure and profit.

OBJECTS OF ART AND VERTU Objects of art and vertu comprise the interconnected fields of the goldsmith, the enameller, the engraver, the mechanic, and the painter. Here we find the beautiful works of Fabergé, the exciting enamelled automata watches of the French court, and the golden goblets and cups of the middle ages. Truly this is the one investment field which contains a maximum of beauty and value in a minimum of space.

Because objects in this field represent an international form of value and beauty and have the added virtue of easy portability, they are much sought after by uneasy wealthy men, by holders of shaky crowns, and by owners of hot money. If sudden flight is necessary, there may be no time to sell bonds or stocks or there may be no room for large paintings or bullion, but in this form of wealth a fortune can slip into a pocket. Because of this there has been a steady growth in the prices of these objects, and some have multiplied ten or twenty times since the late 'forties. It is an interesting sidelight of the portability factor that in direct contrast to paintings, the smaller the object, the higher the value. Thus the small automata watch bearing five moving figures illustrated below sold for $6,000 in 1965, while simultaneously the clock illustrated, which is of equally fine workmanship with a much more complicated mechanism and a far more valuable case, sold for only $1,600. The watch would be of greater value not only to the monarch considering flight but also to the rich American apartment dweller with no room to place the clock.

As an example of how these objects have jumped in value in recent years, consider this pair of matched musical watches with moving musician figures which I purchased in Hong Kong in 1959 for $250. Prices jumped so rapidly that in 1965 a dealer offered $5,000 for the pair. Today they would bring between $10,000 and $15,000 at auction.

It is interesting that the finest objets d'art of this type all were produced for the French and Russian courts in the last years preceding their collapse. The most valuable pieces from these periods were worked in precious stones and metals, particularly gold, pearls, and jade. In the French period there were dozens or perhaps hundreds of outstanding craftsmen and workshops, but in the Russian period there was only one who stood out — Carl Fabergé.

The workshops of Fabergé in St. Petersburg between the years 1870 and 1918 undoubtedly turned out the most beautiful works of art that human ingenuity has ever produced. They varied all the way from highly elaborate and complicated Easter eggs to simple jade figurines, from priceless presents for a Czar to inexpensive charms for a bracelet, from useful things like cigarette cases and watches to the extreme in pure ornament; but regardless of the object's price or size, Carl Fabergé insisted that it be the ultimate in beauty of its kind, and so one knows that to own anything by Fabergé is to own the best. Because of this, all Fabergé has shown a steady price rise since the workshops closed in 1918, accelerating in recent years and showing no sign of tapering off. Fabergé today represents excellent value. There can never be more produced and it is rapidly disappearing into museums. If you have the opportunity to acquire such a piece, do not let it pass by — you may not have a second chance. The little charm illustrated below was purchased by my wife for $175 in 1960. It could easily bring $500 today. What better investment than to enjoy beauty and watch it increase in value simultaneously?

Where should these pieces of beauty be purchased, and how much should be paid for each object? Although there are shops in New York and London selling these art objects to wealthy collectors, this is not where the investor should buy. He should make his purchases at auction, and there are only three auction houses he should consider; they are Sotheby & Co. and Christie Manson and Woods, both in London, England, and Parke Bernet in New York. When a fine collection of Fabergé, automata, or watches comes to the market, it is practically certain to be sold through these three firms, whose clientele includes every great dealer and almost every large collector in the world. Because of this the prices realized at their sales tend to run about midway between dealer wholesale prices and collector retail prices, although occasionally very high prices will result from two collectors wanting the same object; more rarely a very low price will eventuate.

Catalogues are prepared some months prior to each sale, and the more valuable objects are illustrated and fully described. These catalogues are sent airmail to subscribers on payment of a small annual fee which works out to only pennies per catalogue. The catalogues themselves are a delight to the eye, and many are purchased for their own sake with no intention of bidding at the sale.

Those who do wish to bid, however, can do so without attending the sale and at no charge to themselves. After one determines the maximum price one is willing to pay for an object, this bid is sent to the auction house by registered airmail, and an employee of the auction house will bid on the collector's behalf just as though he were there himself. Unlike certain other auction houses, Sotheby, Parke Bernet and

Christies are scrupulously honest and will never pay a penny more for an art object than is absolutely necessary. (In some other firms a "shill" will bid up the price to just under the maximum price sent in by the mail bidders.) I have often found occasions where I made purchase at a fraction of my maximum bid. For example, in 1965 I authorized Sothebys to bid up to £2,000 for the magician box illustrated below. They purchased it for me for only £900.

If something is bought at such a sale, a bill will be forwarded for the net price with no added commission, and after payment is made the art object will be sent by insured air post.

How much should be the maximum bid for each object? After all, the private collector is bidding against dealers who are far more knowledgeable of value in their fields than the collector can be, and so he would appear to be at a serious disadvantage. In actuality the exact opposite holds true, for the collector is able to economically pay one-third or more higher than the dealer, who must resell at a profit. There are several ways to get a true valuation of art objects appearing at these auctions. The simplest, most reliable, and cheapest is just to write the auction house, who are glad to send out a free current valuation. I have found that these valuations are a very good guide to true value, and auction prices tend to run within 10% of these estimates. When bidding it is wise to bid about 15% to 20% above the auction house's estimate, for this will neatly cut out competition from the dealers. If the object should sell cheaper, nothing will have been lost by entering the higher bid.

As an example of how these auction purchases can increase in value, the watch below sold for £50 at auction in 1950. In 1965 I purchased it in the same auction house for £1,200. In early 1972 I was offered £3,800 for it.

This type of investment can easily give the highest profits as well as the greatest pleasures.

ANTIQUITIES To purchase an elaborately decorated Greek pot made 2,400 years ago, or an iridescent glass made in Syria 3,000 years ago, or even a necklace made for an Egyptian princess 4,000 years ago, represents beauty, investment, and a link with the past all rolled into one. Yet the cost of such a purchase is less than that of the cheapest bond. This pot would cost $350.00 today, this glass $100.00 and this necklace $250.00.

There is no question that antiquities today represent the greatest value possible of any form of art investment. Although prices have moved up slightly in recent years, there has been nothing yet like the price movements seen in paintings and objets d'art. This is undoubtedly yet to come and can be easily participated in by the reader.

Antiquities include all remnants of ancient worlds, including Greek, Egyptian, Roman, Syrian, Pre-Columbian, and so forth, and here value depends on the three factors of rarity, beauty, and demand. Thus a very, very rare ancient Nepalese figure may bring only a few dollars because of the few collectors seeking such works, its large size, and its lack of twentieth-century beauty, whereas the Mesopotamian armilla illustrated below will bring thousands of dollars because of its small size and the fact that Mrs. Collector can wear it to her next cocktail party.

There is one steady buyer for antiquities of all types, the local museum. Yet somehow museums are not given the large budgets to purchase antiquities that art galleries receive for paintings. Thus a leading public art gallery might spend $100,000 or more on a single picture, a figure which would represent a ten-year budget for purchase of antiquities by most museums. A museum is far more likely to spend its budget in seeking out "new" antiquities through archaeological digs, rather than step into the market and buy. This fortunate factor has helped to maintain the current, relatively low prices for antiquities.

For a collector of antiquities there are two ways in which I would recommend purchases. For the new collector the best possible introduction is through the firm of Messrs. Spink & Son Ltd. in London. The five-storey building off Picadilly is worth a trip to England in itself, for on the various floors is an almost complete cross-section of the art world, all at very reasonable prices. To step down into the basement is to enter the ancient worlds of Caesar and Cyrus. Here are cases full of Egyptian amulets, dozens of beautiful Greek amphorae, jewellery from ancient China — truly something for everyone and to fit every pocket-book from the initial $25 purchaser of an amulet to the sophisticated museum director seeking a mummy. A visit to Spinks can be a day-long, or a week-long, exercise in self-control.

However, Spinks is not the cheapest place to buy antiquities, and after the prospective investor has increased his knowledge through one or two small purchases, he should then again look to the auction houses of Christie, Sotheby and Parke Bernet. Several times a year these firms run auctions of collections of antiquities from various cultures. All are well illustrated, and the prices received are invariably at the current low museum level. (Many dealers do a lot of buying here.) The arrangements for bidding and purchase are exactly the same as described under objets d'art, and I strongly recommend their consideration. This is truly the current bargain basement of the art world.

One word of caution. There are dozens of small stores in the United States and Europe selling antiquities. Many forgeries are sold by them unknowingly. A pedigree means little to an antiquity, unlike a painting, for even if ownership can be traced back three hundred years, it proves nothing. Ancient Rome was plagued with forgeries of Greek amphorae. So restrict your purchases of antiquities to those bought from experts. You are then sure to make money.

COINS—THE SOUTH SEA BUBBLE MADE IN THE U.S.A. In 1965 I wrote the following paragraphs for the first edition of this book:

"As an offshoot from the hobby of coin collecting, there has developed in the past decade a strange speculation in modern coins, specifically the coins of the United States and Canada. This speculation has produced large profits for its originators and is certain to produce equally large losses for its current blinded devotees, because this gamble is based on constantly rising prices which allow waves of speculators to continually sell out to new speculators. Like pyramid clubs, somewhere along the line the whole edifice must collapse.

Today's hoarders do not seek individual examples of each coin as did the old-time collector. Rather they will collect rolls or even bags of the same coin. Thus a bag containing one thousand 1964 dollars was originally purchased from a bank by a well-connected dealer for $1,000. This bag was probably immediately sold to a speculator for $1,040, and he took it back to the bank for storage. Within a month he had probably sold his bag of dollars for $1,100, and in the ensuing two years it was quite possible for such a bag to be resold five or six times, currently reaching a price of $1,600 or more. Similarly, 50-cent pieces, quarters, dimes, nickels, and even pennies are now purchased in huge quantities in the hope of a quick price rise.

The very interesting difference between this bubble and others that have preceded it is that practically all the participants in the coin craze are quite aware of the potential possible collapse, but each feels that the bubble will not burst for a year or two yet, and that they individually will get out before that day occurs. In the meanwhile these collectors have succeeded in making silver dollars completely disappear from circulation; 50-cent pieces are almost gone, and silver quarters are not far behind. The United States government has aggravated the situation by debasing the silver coinage, thus adding silver hoarders to the coin collectors in helping to make coins disappear. The hoarders realize that if silver reaches a price of $1.38 an ounce, it becomes profitable to melt down the coins and sell the silver.

This gives the coin bubble its one chance of not bursting, for silver has already jumped from 90 cents to $1.29 because of increasing consumption. The U.S. government will probably be unable to hold the price at this level even by selling its entire stockpile, and within a few years silver could easily move to $2.00 an ounce. In this case coin hoarders will of course make money, but it should be remembered that they would do best if they bought coins at face value, regardless of condition. Those who are paying a premium for common coins in uncirculated condition must ultimately show a loss on their investment."

Today I am quite proud of the preceding words, for the U.S. was unable to hold silver at $1.29, and the price did go to $2, but despite this the phony market in silver coins collapsed and the hoarders all lost money. Today the same bags of coins that sold for $1,600 are offered at $1,100 with no buyers. The moral is, avoid like the plague any investment that depends on artificial scarcity.

The collecting of old coins is a different matter entirely. Thousands of persons have earned much pleasure (and profit) from the collection of ancient coins. Here the scarcity is not artificial, for with time most coins are lost, worn, or melted down. I heartily endorse the collecting of old U.S. or Canadian coins or even better, the coins of early England or ancient Greece. It is a most exciting feeling to hold in your hand a coin minted by the emperor Vespasian or by the ancient Greeks during their revolt against the Romans, or perhaps a coin used during the lifetime of Christ. These coins are usually inexpensive and despite their antiquity can often be purchased for only a few dollars — although the rarer gold examples are much more expensive.

This type of coin collecting can bring great pleasure and although you won't get rich you should not lose any of your investment and probably will see a small but steady increase in the value of your collection.

STAMPS   Stamp collecting, on the other hand, fortunately has not slipped from the hands of the collector to that of the speculator. It still remains the most popular hobby in the world and has brought pleasure to millions of children and adults throughout the years. As an investment U.S. and Canadian stamps have treated their purchasers very well, increasing in value yearly by a modest percentage. Although collectors have not tended to get rich from this hobby, its peculiar distracting and time-consuming pleasures have paid large dividends in fun and satisfaction, and in addition it has been a rarity to lose money in this investment.

WINE   Today the very best investment in the non-securities field is — wine.

For over 100 years, wine collecting has been common in Europe but the collecting and laying down of fine wines is relatively new to North America. The beauty of wine collecting is that with only a modicum of care one literally cannot lose, for good wines automatically become scarcer and increase in value.

There are two risks in wine collecting, but both are controllable. The more serious is the ever-present temptation to share the investment with your friends by drinking it; the second is the danger of spoilage, but this risk is very small.

Just as the stock market investor does not buy just any old stock, the wine collector does not collect just any old wine. Unfortunately the vast majority of wines, delightful as they may be to drink, are not a very good investment, either because they spoil and turn to vinegar within a few years or alternatively because they are like modern automobiles, serviceable but terribly common.

A cardinal rule is that you should never buy a North American wine for investment. Most U.S. and Canadian wines are pasteurized which means that they cannot improve in the bottle — what is put in today comes out the same whether it be tomorrow or 10 years hence. Secondly, the soil in which our grapes grow does not have the special richness found in France, and the variant French weather explains why French wines have good and bad years while Canadian and American wines are the same year in and year out. Finally, most Canadian and U.S. wines are blends of different years' grapes. This produces a constant uniformity which is fine for ordinary drinking purposes but precludes the possibility of finding something great and unusual in one year's product.

Therefore, for investment purposes you must restrict your purchases to French wines, but you must be very choosy for most French wine is meant for immediate consumption and is actually not as good as California or Niagara wines.

The best wines for "laying down" are the top Chateau bottled wines of the Bordeaux region. It is best to restrict yourself to the top wines because even if you happen to pick a bad year the scarcity and demand for this type of wine almost automatically ensures a price rise — and in addition the best wines will last for many decades. In fact there is a restaurant in Paris, La Tour D'Argent, which today still serves wines bottled in Napoleon's time. My own experience has been that the best of these wines will improve during their first 20 years in the bottle and will remain delicious for anywhere from 50 to 75 years after that.

As an investment, one can purchase fine French wines from any year, but one should purchase the most recent vintage that is available because it is the most plentiful, the cheapest, and the one on which the most rapid and largest profits will be made.

(It is easy to buy a case of wine fermented 30 or 40 years ago, and what a magnificent gift it is to give someone wine bottled in the year they were born — but that is not investing.)

For the novice, the simplest way to begin a wine investment programme is to deal through a wine merchant, and in areas like New York State this can be quite easily done. In many areas (alas, including my own) this method is so expensive as to prevent profitable investing. I was shocked when I first learned that the price of a case of wine in Toronto purchased from a wine merchant is three times its price as quoted in Bordeaux.

It is best to deal directly with one of the French shippers or alternatively you can buy your wines through that wonderful auction firm of Christie Manson and Woods. This London auction firm runs monthly sales of fine wines at which prices are near the wholesale level. Their bulletin "Buying Wine at Christie's" explains the operation of the auctions. Furthermore, before every sale the firm sends out a wryly humorous description of the contents of the sale which is an excellent guide to value. I reproduce a recent sales memorandum which speaks for itself.

Reproduced by permission of Christie, Manson & Woods

NEWS FROM CHRISTIE'S
WINE DEPARTMENT

SALE MEMORANDUM SEASON VI No. 7
Fine Wines mainly from Private Cellars—Thursday, February 24th, 1972

The wine market

After a dreary start, 1971 turned out be a good year for the English wine trade as a whole, and even in recession-bound America the one product unaffected seems to have been wine, virtually all wine producers and importers achieving record business. Dollar devaluation seems to have made no difference and the import surcharge made hardly a dent in the soaring demand for wine.

Indeed this universal demand for fine wine is responsible for one of three spectres on the wine front which 1972 wine auction buyers ought to be aware of. Spectre one is the high demand resulting in a strong seller's market. The growers in Bordeaux and Burgundy in particular seem to be taking unwholesome advantage of the situation. Spectre two is cost inflation which is hitting *all* the producers and overseas shippers. Spectre three, V.A.T., doesn't seem to have registered yet, as it merely appears to be a glint in the Chancellor's 1973 eye. Although there is a large degree of uncertainty over the level and detailed application of the proposed value added tax, in our opinion V.A.T., in conjunction with stricter enforcement of wine names after we are fully in the Common Market, will *undoubtedly* push up the prices of middle quality and fine wines.

1972 may well be the year for *anyone* interested in wine to look at his future requirements and to buy whilst the going is good.

Contents of the current Fine Wine sale

A nice mix, if we may say so, but particularly strong in good mature burgundy, though claret, as always; forms the major part of the 'ist. Incidentally, when we say 'mainly from Private Cellars' we mean just that, although we include wines lying in merchants' cellars offered for sale ex-customers' paid reserves.

Mouton 1929: I think we all laughed incredulously or shrugged our shoulders when we heard of the American dealer (not in wine) who paid over £2000 for a large bottle of Mouton '29. Clearly he and the almost equally auction-dazed underbidder were under the — false — impression that this was the very last left in anyone's cellar. Of course Mouton '29 was, and still remains, a very fine wine, though we have put a rather more modest and realistic estimate on the magnum (lot 8) and the case of bottles (lot 12) in this particular sale.

Yquem 1921 (lots 61-64): Here is another opportunity to buy a great classic. It is lotted up in two's and three's *not* to extract the highest possible price but to give more people the chance to acquire some. In any case, a little sauternes tends to go a long way.

Chateau-Chalon (lot 138): This is one of the world's unsung rarities. It is not a chateau but the name of a village in the south Jura which gives its name to the locally grown and made Vin Jaune.

Warner Allen, somewhat obscurely, wrote that Chateau-Chalon 'may well have claim to the title of the first of all modern vintage wines' in reference to a venerable 1774 which had cropped up in bottle in the 1920's. Its acknowledged longevity is of less interest than the actual style of the wine and the way in which it is made.

It is a dry white wine made from Savagnin grapes (reputed to be of Hungarian origin) which are late-harvested. The juice is run into casks where it slowly ferments and is left slightly on ullage for a minimum of six years (hence the significance of the bottling date of the wine offered in this sale). During this unusually long period in cask 'flor', similar to that which grows on the surface of fine sherry in the bodegas of Jerez, forms a skin over the wine, preventing its oxidation and leaving the wine with a curious nutty bouquet and flavour. It is something of a cross between a dry old fino sherry and a good old Tokay Szamorodni (doubtless from the combination of 'flor' and the Hungarian type grape).

The wine is rarely seen outside the area of production. It is even hard to find there, and old vintages, certainly pre-war vintages, are virtually unobtainable.

Wines from a Paris restaurant cellar (lots 80-138): The Chateau-Chalon is just one of the excellent accumulation of old vintages brought over from a Paris restaurant cellar.

If one's instinctive reaction to restaurant stocks is to shudder at the thought of steaming kitchens, careless handling and possibly any-thing-but-ideal wine storage conditions, then let a word of re-assurance be written.

From a recent inspection of nearly 100 Paris restaurant wine lists (a rather interesting assignment) we conclude that the greatest concentration of old and fine wines in the world must be cellared below restaurants and hotels in the few square kilometres represented by the 'best' six or ten arrondissements. If the condition of the other 99 cellars is as perfect as the one we inspected and from which we removed *this* stock, Parisian drinkers, and their overseas counterparts, should have nothing to worry about.

Estimated sale prices

For the benefit of the many new subscribers we seem to have at this time of the year, we would like to draw attention to one or two features of our service.

An estimated price list is prepared for every wine sale. It is *not* automatically sent out with the catalogues as we have found that only a proportion of subscribers actually buy wine and of these, few if any buy at every sale.

To obtain estimates, telephone for individual lots or send a stamped and addressed envelope for a full list.

Commissions to bid

This is the most interesting type of sale to attend. But if you cannot come, *we* can bid on your behalf for any lot or lots, up to a maximum limit, and, if necessary, up to a total maximum expenditure. A great deal of our business (and practically all the overseas buying) is done in this way. We make no charge for this service, which includes postal notification after the sale.

Deliveries and splitting of lots

It is quite normal for delivery instructions to be left with us. We customarily arrange collections, deliveries within the U.K., and also shipments overseas.

Please note, however, that *lots cannot be split:* we will not accept more than one delivery address per lot, no matter how big the lot.

Two centuries ago, in Boston, Mass., and in London

American subscribers might like to be reminded that two centuries ago, almost to the day, the Boston Assembly threatened secession unless the rights of the colonies were maintained.

A week earlier, on Monday, February 17th, 1772, to be precise, and oblivious to impending revolts, James Christie sold the chattels and wine of a certain Captain O'Kelly, possibly one of the earlier Irish immigrants. The gallant captain left behind 12 dozen bottles of Madeira, sold in 4 dozen lots at 22/- per dozen, and 9 dozen 'champagne' (correctly spell't; normally it appeared as champaigne) in lots of 3 dozen which realised between 27/- and 30/- per dozen).

Forthcoming sales

After our customary slow New Year start, wine sales got up steam in March and April. We have seven scheduled for those months.

The current wine sales programme, 'Buying' and 'Selling Wine at Christie's' is available on request.

All enquiries to THE WINE DEPARTMENT:
CHRISTIE, MANSON & WOODS, 8 King Street, St. James's, London, SW1Y 6QT. Tel.: 01-839 9060. Telex: 916429. Telegrams: Christiart, London, S.W.1.

JMB/RW
24.1.72

After you have purchased the wine — of course it is not necessary to go to London, this is done by mail — the wine will be shipped to you either by boat or air. I strongly recommend sea shipment because it is so much cheaper.

Among Christie's other services is advice to the amateur as to which wines are good for laying away — and if you will attend their auctions, they will give you the extra pleasure of tasting the wines that are for sale.

In many jurisdictions you can end up with the wine in your cellar at a cost considerably less than it is priced at the local wine store. The reason is that auction prices tend to be close to those paid by the wine merchant himself and so you can eliminate his markup.

In addition, government boards of the various provinces mark up the wines which they import for sale by anywhere from 100% to 200%. If, however, you import the wine yourself (and in Ontario this must be done by having it sent to you c/o the Liquor Board), then some boards only charge you a flat dollar a bottle markup. Take care to check the wine and liquor regulations of your particular province or state.

During the years 1969 to 1972 when the prices of stocks were tumbling, when the value of real estate slipped, and when even the art market showed a drop in price, only one commodity moved steadily higher and that was wine.

The Chateau wines which I recommend for purchase for profit or pleasure are: Chateau Lafite Rothschild, Chateau Mouton Rothschild, Chateau Latour, Chateau Margaux and Chateau Haut-Brion.

There is one problem in resale for the purpose of realizing a profit. The resale must take place in the country where the wine lies in order to avoid paying of further customs duties. This is no problem for U.S. investors because now regular wine auctions are held in New York by Heublein and other companies. It is a serious problem, however, for Canadians because the market for wines in Canada is so very narrow. The only *immediate* answer for a Canadian buyer is to leave the wines on deposit in storage in England. I don't find this very satisfactory — I like to be able to see my wines and I recommend that Canadian buyers do take delivery of their wines in the expectation that in coming years the Canadian market will broaden and wine auctions will begin in Canada.

Because of the rigidity of Canadian wine price structures, an occasional fantastic buy develops. The Liquor Control Board of Ontario sets the price for each wine and the price does not vary until the lot is sold out. In spring 1972 the North American selling price for Chateau Lafite Rothschild 1967 had soared to $40 a bottle while in liquor stores in Ontario it was still available at $22. A number of speculators were busy buying it by the case in Toronto and driving to New York to double their money.

As an example of how wines increase in value, the U.S. buyer who originally purchased 1961 Chateau Lafite at $60 per case in 1964 can easily resell it at $400 per case today.

Cases that fetched $40 in 1969 brought $60 in 1970, $70 in 1971, and sell for $100 today! Wine collecting today is still relatively rare in the U.S.A. and if it catches on, today's prices will appear ridiculously low — but even if it does not, one thing is certain and that is that the value of these wines will not fall.

The 1959 Chateau Mouton Rothschild pictured above sold for $4 per bottle in Ontario. Today it will bring at least $38 per bottle and is almost impossible to find. The 1909 Chateau Lafite sold for $12 per bottle as recently as 1966. Today it would bring at least triple that price at an auction in New York City.

As an interesting offshoot to wine collecting we should consider collecting old brandy. At the end of every English and U.S. wine auction there now appears for sale anywhere from a few to as many as several hundred bottles of ancient brandy, dating back to the late 1700s. Unlike wine, brandy never deteriorates with age, and the finest brandy *ever* bottled was prepared in 1811.

This hobby is a completely new one and the prices are still ridiculously low. In fact the prices this past year for 100-year-old brandies at the Christie and Sotheby sales were *less* than the current Ontario retail prices for modern Courvoisier or Remy Martin.

The three bottles pictured were all purchased this year at Christie's sales. The 1811 Napoleon cost $158, the 1856 Berry $16 and the 1885 Girard cost only $11. I bought two cases of the latter and have been

using it for gifts and find that it is better received than would be an ordinary $50 to $100 present.

If ever I have found a ground floor investment, this is it. If you buy this year you too can participate in the inevitable boom which will follow.

Finally, if someday there should be a market collapse the holders of worthless stock may end up eating their shares — the wine or brandy collector will not be as unhappy if he is forced to consume his investment.

23

IN CONCLUSION

— THE IDEAL INVESTMENT

Some years ago a member of the New York Stock Exchange ran a series of ads warning that there was no ideal investment, but that they could assist the investor to success after he had made up his mind whether he was seeking safety, yield, or capital gains. As we have shown, the broker was wrong. There are ideal investments, carrying little if any risk, giving a good yield, often producing large capital gains and being liquid.

Unfortunately, the vast majority of the investments in which the public participates are far from ideal. In fact, most of them offer high risk, low yield, and little chance of capital gains. If investors and speculators will follow the advice given herein, if they will concentrate on high-grade convertible securities, their market results must improve spectacularly.

For those who wish to gamble, but with the odds in their favour, small participations in the commodity markets or in warrant purchases or in the if, as and when market can satisfy their gambling instincts and probably produce big profits as well.

Finally, the true secret of success in the investment and speculative world is not so much which good securities to buy, but rather which investments to avoid. In this book I have tried to point out the dangers and pitfalls in several investment fields.

And now the most important factor of all. In your investments and other activities, let us hope that you find — good luck!